Author's Statement

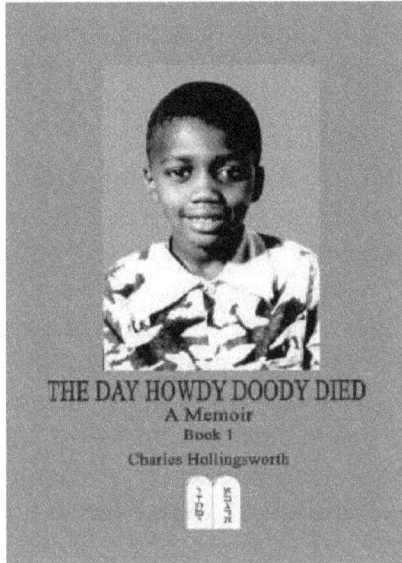

THE DAY HOWDY DOODY DIED
A Memoir
Book 1
Charles Hollingsworth

The above book cover is from my original
Book 1 Memoir, showing me at Beck Street
Elementary School in Columbus, Ohio in 1952

The striking new look of **TheDayHowdyDoody, A Memoir Book** is the *Time-Capsule Edition* with the word **"Stolen"** brazenly displayed on it, and a photo of my younger brother, Virgil also in 1952 at Beck Street Elementary School. Redesigning the cover, hopefully will help thwart off those big corporate crooks like 1st Book Press now AuthorHouse (or whatever name they're using these days) from pulling unsold stolen copies of my Memoir from their warehouses to sell. Even after subscribing and paying for my U.S. Copyright, these thieves were powerful enough to somehow invaded my paid Copyright subscription as well as the ISBN and place it in their name. In speaking with the Copyright Office at the Library of Congress, they say that they can't locate my Memoir's Copyright. I, unfortunately, had lost what I had during Hurricane

i

Katrina's devastation of my home, in 2005. However, I did pay for the subscription of my Memoir's Copyright, and one would think that my records and file number would be available at the source for Copyright in the U.S. As strange as that sounds, I was told that the Copyright Office would gladly research for my Memoir at a fee of $200.00 an hour. Since that conversation, I have all my copyrights processed in Canada. It's cheaper and less of a hassle and is validated worldwide same as the U.S.

My Memoir is as delicately subjective given the nature of my family's survival existence of living in American's historical racist system. I became terribly depressed after discovering that I and my family's history was hijacked and sold just like my ancestors. Please know as an African-American, and having my work stolen by thieves who profited greatly from me and my cherished family's lives has emotionally affected me. The ordeal caused me to compare seeing my ancestors standing naked on a slave auction podium while the arrogant, dominant-culture crooks took advantage of selling us. It angers me to a point of wanting to possess a tub of Vaseline ointment and a flame thrower to use as a medical instrument to relieve those crooks of their hemorrhoids and tonsils.

Reader, please forgive me for being so graphic. But the idea of corporate thieves stealing my life's story to makes themselves wealthy with criminal activities is about as repulsive as my above surgical ambition on them.

At any rate, since the theft of my Memoir, I now have my own home-based self-publishing company. And instead of using a flamethrower as its logo, my Guardian Angels advised me to chill-out. Thus, with their blessing, I named, it **"Written-n-Stone"** after miraculously receiving the Tablet Images on my computer one night while in the process of initially writing my unfinished Memoir prior to its theft. The image of the tablets, some would say, was either caused by a computer virus or that I'm a sleepwalker. But I give the credit to my Guardian Angels.

Having the Ten Commandments' stone tablets, which I use for my logo, seems rather fitting as a reference for deterring evil publishing thieves to respect God's Eighth Commandment: **"Thou**

Shall Not Steal." All authors and artists—or anyone who put their hard work, creative-time, and energy into crafting their skills, should be awarded for their work and not have it stolen from them by the evil greedy influences of wealthy rodents.

The reason for calling this version of my original Memoir, *Time-Capsule Edition* is because as you read the pages, most of the dialogue is still in the past when it was initially written back in 1997-2000/2004. Years after my Memoir was hijacked, some power source prohibited its sales globally. Whoever they are, I want to thank them. It, however, was only after I went berserk online and as the Memoir's author, I gave it a **One Star** rating in order to discourage further sales. Please Google search my original grey-cover *The DayHowdyDoody Died Memoir* and see for yourself.

The back cover of this Memoir is the same as the original back cover even the photo of me was taken back in 2000. **Book Two's** back cover, of *The DayHowdyDoody Died Memoir,* will of course, be current and please try not to compare my previous photos with the current one unless you're close to a toilet.

Charles H. Hollingsworth, PhD

Written-N-Stone
Springfield, Ohio
© 2020

Virgil

The photo on the front cover is that of my little brother Virgil, a year younger and one grade behind me. He was Mom and Charlie's (our dad) Christmas present in 1944. Thus, his name. The picture was taken the same day as mine back in 1952 at Beck Street Elementary School, Columbus, Ohio. Virgil was like a twin brother but smarter and more talented than me. He always made the honor roll, and I never did. He was also a good athlete in track and basketball. Plus, he could dance well, unlike me (there's a photo of him doing the "Twist" with our younger sister Sandy around pg. 112 or so.) However, since I was his older brother, I was the one who protected him from bullies and adult perverts when we shined shoes and sold newspapers in the Southside neighborhood and various neighborhood taverns.

He was the smartest one in the whole family and functional in just about everything he put his mind to do. Later on in life, he became, to my surprise, a minister whose sermons were quiet and intellectual. I have only been to one of his sermons to just to witness the experience. In his late 40's, he was diagnosed as having early stages of Alzheimer's. And sadly, he died miserably 20 years later.

Virgil and I were close, and I continue to "feel" his presence around me. Sometimes I'll call out his name unconsciously as if he's right next to me if I recognize someone that we both knew. In reality, whenever I write or become involved into anything needing a deep cerebral opinion, he's part of the conversational environment. We did this as kids when we worked in the evenings selling newspapers or shining shoes in various taverns and streets because we were vulnerable, but as his guardian, I didn't trust some of the men in the white taverns because of them rubbing our wooly heads for good luck our slapping our backs. If I found it a bit tasteless, e.g., slapping our butts, I would turn into a nine-year-old *Lone Ranger* or *Superman* and a few other in the tavern would intervene and help the two Black shoeshine/newspaper boys. As the older brother, I guess I was more sensitive. Virgil was sensitive in a different sense. He could "read" people and would non-verbally give me a sign if there would be trouble.

My little brother VIRGIL, although small, he was the altar piece of the family because we all looked up to him for his many great achievements in life physically, academically, and spiritually.

Contents

THE DAY HOWDY DOODY DIED

A Memoir

Book 1

Charles Hollingsworth

January Chariot

I viewed the world between beats of ice
Laden wiper blades and
A slush-streaked palette of
Road salt and ice crystals.
Each rhythmic swipe briefly cleared a
Kaleidoscope view of time and space
Swirling before me an overcast sky the
Color of forgotten tombstones.
I became intoxicated with the slow pace of
The moment,
The silent submission of motion,
The gentle seduction of the perpetual,
A letting go.
Looking through the glazed windshield,
Cars drifting by me;
And I, remembering of the past,
Disillusioned of the future,
Hovering a few feet above the road
Floating on a cushion of tears,
Journeying forward into a white
Whirling Universe

Charles Hollingsworth

The Past and How I Forgot the Future

Chapter One

(January 30, 1995 around 9:08 a.m.)

IT WAS A TYPICAL dense Ohio winter morning. The atmosphere hung like a dingy curtain over the city casting a foreboding gloom everywhere. The blur homes still adorned their Christmas ornaments blinked in vain, trying their best to retain a glimmer of the gaiety they had known only a few weeks ago.

I needed some sort of diversion to take my mind off the moment and the despondency of the drive. What I needed more than anything was a smoke (and I hate the smell of cigarettes.) The thought of having a menthol Kool, the so-called nigger cigarette, was what I craved. I remember a White Marine once called them that one day forty years ago. He forgot I was his passenger in the jeep as we headed for the rifle range.

Remembering Kool's logo with a little black and white penguin on the green and white packet, and the sweet smell of tobacco laced with menthol, and how I would place my large nostrils firmly on a freshly opened pack and inhale deeply.

And now, at this moment, I craved for that tangy tart taste to swirl around my tongue. But I quit smoking many years ago. I played mental gymnastics like these in my head as I drove trying to displace myself from the now and think back to the "once upon a time" of things, when as a boy I was full of curiosity and adventure and time seemed unhurried.

I clearly remember when I ate my first pizza during the summer of 1951. Columbus was extremely hot and air conditioning was not an option for most people. They had to be content with opened windows, cool drinks, and electric fans. Even at night, the inside of Dino's Pizza parlor was bathed in heat. Fans were positioned everywhere in an effort to circulate a cool breeze, but they only succeeded in bathing everyone with the hot air emitted from the large overworked ovens. Dino's was the place. Actually, "ate" is too subtle a word; "inhaled" would be more appropriate. I was eight and my younger brother, Virgil, seven. The pizza eating event was the reward for our hard work shining shoes in the White neighborhood's taverns on the Southside near our home. After placing our shoeshine box in one of Dino's booths, we strained to look up at the large menu pasted on the wall behind the cashier. A stocky Italian smiled down at us as we dug into our pockets producing two buffalo nickels for our Coca-Colas, and two quarters for the cheese pizza. We chose cheese simply because we did not know what pepperoni and anchovies were. These culinary delights were not part of our menu at home. The closest thing we had to Italian was the delicious meatball and spaghetti dinners Mom

2

prepared. Even though we never had pizza before, we were certain that it was good judging from the expressions on people's faces in the taverns as they stuffed their mouths by the handful and then washed it down with cold beer.

Pizza parlors were just becoming the in-thing in post war Columbus and throughout the nation. There were not many fast food enterprises except a couple of White Castle hamburger diners that served small burgers smothered in onions that had the tendency of making us fart a lot. So whenever we referred to White Castles, we appropriately dubbed them "fart-burgers." The general population, however, was unaware of low-density lipids or the high-hydrogenated fat and salt contents in the foods at that time. People usually ate and drank what they liked, and enjoyed a smoke at their leisure.

Unlike today, a vast part of Columbus was divided into various ethnic neighborhood restaurants serving the traditional food of their community. A great many of them did not allow Blacks to patronize them. For years Jung Mei, a Chinese restaurant, located on Broad Street near a Black section of town, did not allow Blacks inside to eat. They could, however, phone for take-out orders, but had to come to the rear of the building to pick up their food. Pizza parlors, on the other hand, were convenient and friendly.

When the cheese pizza we ordered arrived at our table, the Italian proprietor seemed to take pleasure in serving us, inviting us to enjoy our meal. The moment we bit into the gooey tomato sweetness, Virgil and I looked into each other's eyes. We had just discovered something wonderfully new. Now we knew what our patrons in the White taverns knew, and we wolfed it down, guzzling the Cokes afterwards. We ordered another, ate it, and took another one home.

A large glob of frozen slush hit the windshield from a passing car, shaking me out of my nostalgic reverie and back into the cold reality of the present. I glanced at my watch and noticed it was 10:14 a.m. I had yet again been lost in the matrix of my consciousness. And I remembered that less than an hour ago, I had not been looking at the smiling brown face of my little brother from across a table enjoying our pizza eons ago. No, on the opposite side

3

of me was the solemn face of a middle-aged man with moist eyes who gingerly assisted me as we lifted our sister's body from the black Cadillac hearse. I remembered my warm hands meeting the cold bronze handles of the casket, and I prayed that I would maintain my balance and not fall on the frozen slippery grass. A couple of other male family members helped lift Flo onto the green nylon webbing that would lower her into her final resting place.

The gravediggers with their hip boots, picks and shovels, shielded themselves behind the heavy canvas tarp from the icy wind separating them from the ceremony. They were huddled in a small group next to a backhoe, smoking, speaking softly, and blowing into their hands trying their best to keep warm. It was obvious that they wanted us to hurry and leave so that they could return to the warmth of the cemetery office for their ration of hot coffee and more cigarettes. Looking at them, I thought how odd seeing a backhoe at a gravesite. One lobe of my brain said that the awkward looking contraption was out of place. But my other lobe - the logical one - said it made perfectly good sense. The mechanical device saved time and energy, and to be honest, from where I was standing, I saw that it did carve a perfect rectangle into the frozen ground. I tried very hard to meditate on things like that to help distance my mind from what was taking place. I closed my eyes and imagined special moments when my sister Flo was alive and the good times we shared. Just a few weeks before, I had given her a wool-lined electric foot massager as a Christmas present. I could not think of a better gift because she always complained about her poor, aching feet.

As the chilly wind blew against my face everything seemed to move slow and surreal. Sounds and colors were muted in tones of grays, blues, and browns. The dominant sounds I heard were the wails and sniffles of mourners, and a ceaseless thumping sound beating rhythmically inside my chest. The only vivid colors I saw were the brilliant array of flowers and the red and black plaid wool jackets of the gravediggers. The setting reminded me of Courbet's painting, *The Burial at Ornans*. If only I could wake up from this dreadful dream and make a long distance call, asking Flo if she liked my Christmas present. This moment in time, however, was real, not

4

a dream, and as I stood there, motionless, the only thing I could hide was my own self behind the dark sunglasses that concealed my reddened eyes and frozen tears.

Flo

Chapter Two

FLO WAS SIXTY-TWO when her seventy-five-year-old husband, Malvern Johnson emptied the deadly contents of his pearl handled, nickel plated thirty-eight caliber special into my sister's soft, fleshy body. Malvern had never before appeared to be a violent person, simple, perhaps pathetic, but not violent. In actuality, he was a small, frail man, and if observed in a crowd, he would not be very distinguishable except for his Stephen Fetchit-like appearance. His body language conformed to a permanent stoop, a fixture much like his life. He was a country boy from a small town in Arkansas called Malvern from whence he got his name. Malvern lived in the past and loved to impart tales of his glory days as one of the last U.S. Army Calvary's Buffalo Soldiers to anyone who would listen. He talked with a special fondness of horses, while also expressing his deep dismay of a mechanized Army, especially tanks. Proud of being a Buffalo Soldier, he was equally proud of his weapons. He was to retire, however, as a lowly buck sergeant from the U. S. Air Force and now worked as a janitor to supplement his military pension. We learned just before the shooting that he had been diagnosed with Alzheimer's, as well as having prostate cancer.

My siblings, in sequential order are: Flo, Junior (Robert), Ronnie, Bunny (Gerald), Me, Virgil, Sandy, and Dottie. Although Flo was only ten years older than me, she seemed much older, and I had always envisioned her being so grown-up. Perhaps it is because when one is younger, time and space have a measure all their own. When we become adults, unfortunately they seem to compress and finally collapse along with a good part of our imagination. The old neighborhood streets where I grew up now seem much smaller and past experiences seem more colorful than the present-day ones. Only since Flo's death has time and space come into full perspective.

Flo's actual name was Florida, and she resented the fact that Mom named her after a state. Neither she nor my mother had ever been there nor, as far as I know, ever planned going. I often heard Flo ask Mom why in the world she gave a name like that to her first-born. And, if it *had* to be a state, why not Virginia or Georgia? But my mother was only fifteen when she gave birth to Flo, and as a young girl, she may have had some desire to visit Florida. As far as

I can recall, however, my mother never took any kind of vacation in her life. She was a full-time homemaker and a mother who immensely enjoyed children. She did, however, take weekend fishing excursions around central Ohio when she was married to Archie Armstrong, her last husband. I think Mom liked the way the name Florida sounded. Perhaps she enjoyed how the sound seemed musical to pronounce and the way the three syllables of Flo-ri-da seemed to roll off her tongue with Mom's breathy effervescence. I also believe Mom had a fuller understanding of aesthetics that Flo never quite developed.

The distinct hierarchical structure Flo conveyed to her siblings had the same enormity as a pyramid flow chart. She let all of us know who was in control of things since she was the eldest. Even when we were adults and had moved ahead educationally or in our various positions, she pulled rank. She would organize meetings to which only my brothers and sisters were invited. No in-laws were allowed. She called the shots, asked for suggestions, and would let us know who had the last word. She was the eldest–period. With all of her implacable ways, she was actually a paper tiger. When one of us achieved something, no matter what accomplishment it may have been, she expressed great appreciation. Besides a big smile and a warm embrace, she usually produced a token award. But it was her embrace that we came to recognize as Flo's priceless gift. And if there were a special occasion, a wedding or a birth of a baby or whatever, she would open her pillow-like arms and give a warm sincere hug. When her arms enveloped us, time stood still, and we felt like we were ascending. Flo emitted a radiance that told us we were truly loved. She was without question the glue that held my family together.

By the time she was almost twelve, Flo had given birth to her daughter Patricia (Patty), who was only a year younger than I. Mom said the event made *The Columbus Dispatch* with the caption blaring she had become a grandmother at the tender age of twenty-seven. To provide for her baby, Flo dropped out of school and worked some physically demanding jobs with her boyfriend, Ray, hauling and unloading refuse on his pickup truck. I only remember him as a short stocky man who always wore big apple caps or jitterbug caps, as we called them back then. He had to be in his late twenties, and although I must have been about three or four at the time, I could easily see that Flo was in love with him and he devoted to her.

When Ray died, I don't recall how, Flo had a nervous breakdown and had to be admitted into a mental home. I have no recollection how long she was gone; all I can recall was that there was an empty void in my preschool life. Upon her release, she worked in various restaurants helping out in the kitchen or serving customers as a waitress. She also pressed and washed clothes in hot steamy laundries. Flo spent most of her life working as a domestic in White people's homes in the swank districts of Columbus like Bexley or Upper Arlington, where she was paid humble wages and, if lucky, bus fare home.

After Flo was killed, I was the one selected to go to her house and clean up the mess. It seemed logical that the task would fall on me. I had been a medic during the Vietnam War era and had taken gross anatomy courses at Ohio State University. My brothers and sisters were right, I was the one best suited for the job ahead and had the stomach for it. But the truth of the matter be told, I did not want any of them to do something that would undoubtedly cause psychological distress afterwards. Uncle Sam and Ohio State University did a good job conditioning me the task ahead. Taking a plastic pail, rubber gloves, sponges, rags, plastic garbage bags, and a bottle of Pinesol cleaning solution, I drove to Flo's house. Her small wooden framed home was located on one of the narrow streets on the near west side of Columbus in a typical working-class neighborhood. It was similar to most of the houses in the neighborhood. They had been built close to one another and many with small porches. Flo's house had a chain link fence with a small gate that opened onto a narrow concrete pathway that brought you to the steps of the front door. The concrete pathway had dead grass poking out between the cracks and around the edges. As I stepped onto the landing, I could see some mail in the mailbox. It contained last month's telephone and electric bills and a few assorted advertisements. I stuffed the mail into my shirt pocket and opened the low screeching aluminum storm door. I stood in the doorway for

8

a moment fumbling with the keys. Then I went in. Some imaginary force, however, seemed to impede my entrance, a slight hesitation that I imagine would be akin to entering another dimension of going from the known to the unknown. Once I shoved myself inside, I tried to shrug off the unfamiliar silence. I noticed for the first time, Flo's deep aquamarine painted walls, which took on a surreal aquatic ambiance.

As I slowly waded in, encumbered with my pail of sponges, it seemed that my impediment was an invisible lifeline that tugged at me from above, restricting my every move. And, I, in a deep-sea diver's mental landscape, trudged along on an oceanic floor, hearing my own breathing within the confines of a bronze diver's helmet, seeing a liquid world through round portholes. I expected schools of fish to swim by at any moment. And I wistfully wanted Flo to float from one of the rooms with her arms wide open to greet me in her usual loving fashion. But all traces of aquatic visions quickly vanished when, just outside the bathroom floor, I saw a large black glob of Flo's congealed blood.

I stood motionless looking at the thing for a long time. In certain religions, it is believed the soul is contained within the confines of one's blood. Looking at this black congealed object, I doubted that Flo's soul was reduced and trapped inside this two-day-old heap of Jell-O lying on the floor. Soon after I put the pail down, the reality of my task lay on the floor before me. I was about to put on my rubber gloves when I heard a rustling noise coming from the kitchen's door leading to the back porch. I went to investigate. Chained to the porch were Flo's two large dogs. They probably had not been fed or watered since the incident. It is odd how, when a tragedy happens, people lose their sense of rhythm of day-to-day activities. Time stands still and the normal landscape becomes a blur of running images. The immediate event of a tragedy takes precedence as one desperately tries to find some sense of order, while forgetting some essentials of life. It is like packing to go on a trip but forgetting your credit card or medicine. Flo's dogs had been forgotten in a similar fashion. In our grief, no one had bothered or remembered to see about their provisions.

When I went to the back porch, the two dogs seemed to sense something was wrong. They did not bark, but only looked at me with a strange animal suspicion. Without hesitation, I gingerly back stepped to the safety of the kitchen and closed the door. Finding dog food, I prepared an oversized portion, placing its contents in their large containers and filled a bucket with water. Finding a broom, I used it and carefully slid the food and water on the porch. Returning to the safety of the living room, I found the Christmas present, the wool-lined electric foot massager, I had given Flo only six weeks earlier. It was still unused in its box. I also noticed that above the couch hung the familiar picture of Jesus looking skyward. I had never paid much attention to that picture before, but for some reason, it now seemed alien. Perhaps Jesus' glaring Whiteness seemed to be a stark contrast to the gloom and disparity of the room. But Flo never thought in terms of White or Black. I can honestly say that she never, as far as I can recall, ever said a racist thing in her life. Flo wasn't like that. She didn't see the outside superficialities of a person; she saw the inside contents of an individual.

I tied a handkerchief around my face and put on rubber gloves to begin the grisly chore ahead. I felt like a surgeon preparing to perform a major operation. Bent on my hands and knees, I scrubbed, scraped, gathered tissue, and cut blood-soaked sections of carpet surprising myself how mechanical my movements had become. Just like a surgeon, I detached myself emotionally from the scene. Witnessing the event, I tried not to let my emotions overrule the activity that was now taking place. The automatic mechanical motion of cleaning up my sister's two-day-old blood left me numb. I thought about the past. I especially felt loved by Flo. But she had a way of making everyone she knew feel special.

Flo struggled with her weight much in her life. As I look back, she appeared pleasingly plump rather than fat, and she carried it well with an enthralling Oprah Winfrey grace. She certainly had no problems finding boyfriends. I suppose her feminine fleshiness would have been very appealing to Rembrandt or Rubens, but in my boyhood youth, I constantly teased her--all in fun, of course. I would say things like, fat funky Flo, ho, ho, ho, and was always prepared to run like a jackrabbit hoping she wouldn't catch me. When she did, she would just hug me in her loaves of arms smothering me with kisses, telling me how much she loved me. She really enjoyed recounting the story about how, when I was a baby, she chewed food to a soft gooey paste and then placed small portions into my tiny infant mouth. She would imitate, with great animation, my infant chewing motions and then say how much I relished eating after her. I envisioned myself looking like a baby falcon snugly nestled in the comfort of a nest eating the regurgitated food from his elders. I cringed every time I heard the story, even as an adult. Flo was good-natured and always forgiving. One of the first visions I had of Flo was of her at Buckeye Lake's Amusement Park located about thirty miles due east of Columbus. I must have been no more than four when Flo and Ray took Mom and me to the amusement park one hot summer's night. I vividly recall Flo saying that she wanted to ride the Red Devil, a newly installed roller coaster. She urged Ray to take her on it but he seemed too preoccupied trying to win some stuffed toys at a shooting gallery. Finally, Flo had her way and Mom and I stood outside the small metal gate leading to the ride. Mom held my hand as I wrapped myself around her leg waiting for Flo to return. I watched them get on the ride as it slowly moved up one of the steep climbs and then disappeared in the night's darkness. Suddenly, there was a roar and then screams. I could hear Flo's screams above all the others. When their car came back into view, it shot past me and all I could see was Flo's eyes and mouth wide opened. She sounded much like a fire engine's siren. The image of it all horrified me. She passed us several more times and I clung tightly onto Mom's legs, fearing for Flo's life. I had never seen anything so frightening. When Flo and Ray got off the Red Devil heading toward us, the evening's crowd of spectators began laughing and pointing in the direction of Flo. As I eased around Mom's legs, I could see the basis of their laughter. I saw a large dark circle on Flo's gray skirt. In her excitement or fear (or both) she had peed on herself. The sight of Flo's "accident" left an indelible mark on my life for years to come. Every time I see an amusement park's roller coaster rides, I remember The Red Devil and Flo's inextinguishable experience. Today, you can't pay me to go on one of those damned things. I have never been on one and have no plans ever doing so in this life.

****

When I became a young adult, Flo took great pleasure in pointing her finger and telling me (in an amicable way) to change my sinful ways. I wanted no part of it. I would reply saying, "Quit banging me on the head with your Bible, Flo. I'm just doing what you did when you were me at my age."

Sometimes I would jump up and mock her gestures by pointing my finger at her. Then I would do my Black preacher impression. I would do this by over-exaggerating and mimicking preachers like old Reverend Stevens' gyrations at the Galilee Baptist Church. I would strut, shout, wave a handkerchief, and perform something exceedingly close to a James Brown performance, all the while proclaiming hell's damnation and the wickedness of too much partying. While I was doing this routine, I made very sure that nothing blocked my way to the nearest exit.

Flo eventually became an ordained minister at the Greater Ebenezer Apostolic Church. Unfortunately, I never got a chance to see her preach. The few times I did attend the church, I would always see Flo sitting at the very front of the congregation. I asked her one time why she didn't sit with the other ministers in their big throne cushioned chairs behind the pulpit? She looked at me woefully and said, "Because I am a woman." Although she said it with dismay in her voice, there was neither hostility nor envy in her reply. Rather, she stated it with accepted resignation. It seemed such a pity. Here were these men, many less educated and perhaps even less spiritual, sitting pompously on their thrones of sanctification, while my sister, on the other hand, sat as part of their congregation simply because she was a woman. Since then, the only times I attended that church have been for the many funeral services that have occurred in my family.

Almost more than going to church, Flo loved to read. She gave us the key to learning by teaching us how to read and taking us on excursions to the world of free books at the Columbus Public Library. She would read to my brothers, sisters, and me, every night until we were fast asleep. The stories she read took us far away to magical places. Not yet fully introduced to the public, television would not replace radio in our community for almost half a decade. As a result, Flo's readings gave us clear pictures and stimulated our youthful imaginations.

But Flo had a peculiar habit of sucking her thumb while reading to herself or when she was intensely interested in something. Of course, this habit added fuel to further the teasing. At six or seven years of age, I would park myself next to her as she read and suck my thumb just waiting for her to take notice. One of two things usually would occur: she would either ignore me or else she would suddenly grab me and begin hugging and kissing me while I was trying to run away. We kept this routine up until our adult years, my impersonations and her loving and affectionate response.

When I came back to the reality of wiping up visceral remnants and globs of Flo's congealed blood, I began feeling guilty for being so mechanical and indifferent. Why was I not feeling anything? During the Vietnam War, my attentions were not to become too wrapped-up in my emotions. I held men in my arms knowing perfectly well that they were going to die. I conditioned myself to become detached, but that was war. Southeast Asia had existed some twenty years ago and in a strange place far away. This was home where life was supposedly safer. Incredibly, I felt the same old detached feeling and I realized that it was unresolved after all those years and that it had never left. But this was my sister who used to say how beautiful life is. Where was the beauty here?

Although, I didn't want to, I found myself, while cleaning up, reconstructing the incident in my mind of Flo's final moments. There were bullet holes low on the wall outside the bathroom. Did she fall down after the first bullet struck? Were these burned bullet holes on the lower wall and floor the result of Malvern pumping the remaining rounds into her as she laid crumpled and bleeding on the floor? Is that why she had wounds on her arms? Was she lifting them, trying in vain to protect herself from the hot lead? I still felt nothing. There was just silence, the sanitized scent of Pinesol, and that rosy-cheeked picture of Jesus. Before leaving the house, I stood by Jesus feeling a strong urge to rip that picture off the wall, but it

13

was Flo's, and she obviously treasured it since it hung well lit in the living room above her sofa. So, I surrendered and calmly began to pray. Flo would have wanted me to. I needed to. There were no struts, shouts, or James Brown gyrations, just a solemn prayer asking Jesus to open his arms and welcome my sister. I then caved in. Tears ran down my face in torrents, and I crumpled on her couch under Jesus' picture and wept.

Later, I heard voices outside the house. I peeked out the window and saw two uniformed dogcatchers, one male and the other female, cautiously approached Flo's chained dogs with a long pole with a rope noose at the end. Each managed to loop a noose around a dog's neck and quickly led the reluctant pair to a van and departed. The whole thing took about three minutes. The fate of the animals was obvious, and it had occurred to me that I had perhaps given them their last meal.

I then gathered the cleaning solution, plastic pail, scrub brush, and rags. I took off the rubber gloves and put everything in a Hefty bag and placed it in the trash container outside. I looked at Flo's house for the last time, locked the door and left.

Chapter Three

ONE OF MY EARLIEST memories as a toddler was my fondness for warm milk mixed with Karo syrup. Karo syrup comes in two colors, clear and caramel. I preferred the caramel colored syrup, but in reality, they both tasted great. Baby bottles back then were not like the ones today. (No plastic designer screw-on caps or bottles bent at a 45-degree angle.) The rubber nipples were small enough to slip snugly over most soda-pop bottles, and most of the time, Mom simply prepared the mixture in them since they were readily available and cheap. I remember the various colorful *Pepsi, RC Cola*, and *Canada Dry Ginger Ale* labels on them and how milk took on a greenish hue due to the thickness of the bottles' glass. Mom sterilized the bottles and nipples then poured warm milk and syrup into them. If the nipples were brand new, she would jab the amber colored rubber heads with a sterile sewing needle. She would test a few drops of milk on the inside of her wrist to ensure the correct temperature before handing it to me. This snack-treat continued until I went into the second grade at the age of seven. Karo syrup sandwiches were also part of the menu. The sandwich called for pouring Karo syrup and spreading chunky peanut butter between two slices of white bread. It catapulted me into seventh heaven.

When my brothers were asleep or outside playing, I felt especially lucky because this was when Mom would pay special attention to me. She would pick me up and snuggle me in her arms while I fed on the Karo syrup and milk concoction. I would listen to the rhythm of her heartbeat as she rubbed my head while she sang Puccini, *Oh, Mio Babbino Caro*, or *Indian Love Call* in her soft soprano voice. The mixture heightened my five senses and created a hypnotic effect so relaxing that the only thing I could do was to sleep. I can recall those moments vividly - the taste, the sweetness of the milk and the sound of my mother singing as she rocked me in her arms.

I also hold fond memories of Bubbles, our Scott-Irish Appalachian babysitter. Bubbles lived across the street with her parents in a tidy gray-framed house on Parsons Avenue. Her mother and Mom were about the same age, and both enjoyed smoking filtered *Pall Malls* cigarettes and drinking *Coca-Cola* in the kitchen while listening to the blare of swing music on the radio as I snuggled contentedly in my mother's lap. But it was Bubbles' beauty that captivated me even at this preschool stage. Her dark brown eyes and black hair were the epitome of what I later considered attractive. For years, I would measure a girl's beauty by Bubbles' good looks. Perhaps it was because she was so nice to me that I thought her beautiful. A child's conception of someone who is kind to him surely exemplifies an attraction of some sort. At any rate, following my Mom's directions, Bubbles mixed the same milk and Karo concoction when she babysat us.

I remember how excited we'd get when we discovered that Mom had made arrangements for Bubbles to babysit us. After Mom and Charlie left, she waited a while before her transformation. After doing some babysitting chores Mom had prescribed, Bubbles produced cigarettes from out of nowhere and started smoking them while heading for Mom's RCA Victoria record player. She would shuffle through some 78 records and, when she found the ones she liked, she'd launch into a Jitterbug throwing Bunny and me around the floor. Virgil, still in diapers, wouldn't join in the festivities until a year later (1947) when he would be three. Bubbles told us about the wonderful world of junior high school and what it was like being thirteen while she was swinging us around the floor. Exhausted afterward, we rested while she prepared our Karo concoction. An unforgettably intense look came on her face when she gave us our Karo concoction because it signaled playtime. Bubbles made us feel special because she was the first person who taught us the mystery of secrets and our responsibility to keep them. We kept them for decades. (But the words "our secret" became magical, and we promised never to reveal what she did to anyone. My parents never did know what went on when Bubbles baby-sat.) If we told a secret, she said, it would make her angry, and she'd never see us again. We dreaded the thought of losing a junior high school friend who told us wonderful stories, danced, and did magical things with us. She was our friend and told us so. And to lose a friend by snitching (another new word she taught us) would be too much of a loss for us to handle.

What Bubbles did was to fondle us. Not only did she fondle, but she also stood us on the kitchen table sucking and nibbling on us one at a time as we stood side by side drinking our Karo concoction from the bottle. The first time I noticed my circumcision was at this time. My brothers had foreskins, and she found it interesting to

fondle and examine them. However, she favored fondling Bunny's more because he was the biggest, which he received special treatment. We had no idea why she enjoyed this, but it seemed to make her feel good. She would hand us each our bottle of the *Karo* milk concoction, and as we trumpeted them, she would work on each of us one at a time. The effect of feeling a warm bottle on my hands and having the sweet, warm brew flowing into my stomach while her warm lips worked us over was our first sexual experience.
I had no idea what was going on except that the milk tasted good and that we made Bubbles very happy. We could see it in her eyes. To us, she was a figure of authority, and we simply wanted to make her happy.

As she became older, her babysitting activities were less frequent. At age 16 (1949) she became pregnant, married her boyfriend, and we never saw her again.

"Shhh," I still remember her saying. "This is our secret. Don't tell anyone or I will never come back to play again." And we didn't.

South Lane Street

Chapter Four

ONG BEFORE the Civil War, Ohio Blacks had already been a significant component of the Mid-Western landscape's developments. But it was the *Great Migration Movement,* during the First World War, that daily transported hoards of Blacks leaving southern farms to work in the bowels of the northern cities' (the promise land) factories escaping the horrific conditions of the Jim Crow South. As the flow continued to grow during the Great Depression, and during much of World War Two, the Black community of South Lane Street comprised many from all parts of the South.

The area where I grew up in German Village is a piece of real estate situated on the Village's far southeastern fringes. The narrow red brick street of South Lane that at one time supported horse and buggy traffic, runs east and west. South Lane runs parallel to busy Livingston Avenue (a block away) and runs perpendicular into Parsons Avenue's traffic, which runs north and south. Paralleling South Lane Street is Beck Street, one block south that also runs into Parsons Avenue. The total length of the narrow South Lane Street stretches only about an eighth of a mile and cars pull over to allow the other to pass. During my childhood, Livingston and Parsons Avenues both bustled with businesses, traffic, and the clang and clamor of trolley cars that crisscrossed Columbus. The clattering trolleys are now gone as are the two large flamboyant Victorian three-story framed homes on Parsons Avenue where the trolley cars used to stop. Living in those two ornate homes where the White families of the Courtwrights in one, and the other, the Slousers. The two homes were showcases of the residential shotgun community of South Lane Street.

Inhabitants on South Lane Street all lived in neat little two-story double shotgun bungalows. Instead of having a front and rear doors aligned on either end of the rectangle typical shotgun style house, the doors on South Lane were designed with the entrance were located on the broad side of the homes. These houses sprung up during the Reconstruction Era and around the Spanish American War. Some homes even had chickens in their yards and others had large vegetable gardens. Each home included the comfort of shade from a variety of large trees in their yards making it ideal for mounting tire and rope for swinging or for building tree houses. All the homes had an assortment of wooden fences dividing the backyards of each home. The fences concealed the few homes that still had outhouses from public view.

South Lane Street's Black community could be defined as a culture within a culture, an ambiguous complex involution within an involution. The community had two distinct Black cultures: The Black Southerners and the Black Appalachians each proud of their own perspective heritage. Each, however, was paradoxically entrenched in the community and into each other. My family comprised both heritages. South Lane's Southern Black families came with distinct traditions of rural agricultural traditions like a few of the families that came from the sea islands of South Carolina and were called "Geechies." Other Black Southerners came from places like Virginia, Georgia, Mississippi, and Alabama. The Appalachian Blacks, on the other hand, came from West Virginia, eastern Kentucky, and Tennessee and had a different way of life. They essentially were rigorous Blacks who came in various monochromatic hues (usually light skinned) having lineage of Black, White and Indian blood and are termed "WINS," meaning White, Indian, and Negro.

Other South Lane residents were ex-GIs who, after being discharged, decided to leave their Southern roots and venture north for a better life like Mr. Ware who brought his family from rural Mississippi. Many families having been brought up on the land now had to adjust to an urban industrial environment. They were all willing to scrape a meager living for their families by working at whatever job they could find until a better opportunity came along. Most, if not all, of the residents on South Lane were lower income families who worked as laborers in both skilled and unskilled trades. Some landed prestigious positions as porters on the railroad. They crisscrossed the country with tales of adventure and seeing faraway places, while others spent their days as perfunctory smiling elevator operators. Others worked for the city as garbage collectors. Most, if not all, of the residents on South Lane were lower income families who worked as laborers in both skilled and unskilled trades.

Some shined shoes downtown or at the train or bus stations and janitors could be found at any office building and hospital. The higher paying workers labored arduously in the sweaty, cramped factories like Federal Glass, Buckeye Steel, or Timken Roller Bearing. These factory jobs could be suffocating, demanding and dangerous. Nevertheless, it meant food on the table and shoes on their children's feet. They worked hard having to compromise with the ruthlessness of industrial labor and the biases of White employers. These factory jobs, however, were the ones that gave distinction because of the pay and various unions. In spite of the fact that most unions limited their officers to White only, it was the lesser of two evils and the unions did provide some limited opportunities compared to the companies' white-collar personnel who always were White.

Essentially, the residents on South Lane were socially active, hard working, caring individuals who shared good conversation but kept mostly to themselves. Most of them were Black except for a few German families who lived at the far west end of the street, and the polite a middle-aged German man, his wife and sister-in-law who kept quietly to themselves in their small framed neat bungalow. They drove an impeccably clean gray 1946 Chevrolet sedan. South Lane seemed enormous and very much alive with interesting individuals who lived there. Anything beyond its boundaries was an adventure into alien territory to me.

****

There was a phenomenon in those days called the iceman. He wore a tank top and a thick rubber apron wrapped around his massive bulk. In the hot summer afternoons, the iceman made his rounds in his old black truck with its thick canvas tarp covering the cold ice and the kids followed it hoping to retrieve a few ice chips. We all admired the strength of the iceman as he carried enormous blocks of ice over his huge shoulders all supported by ice thongs and watched him place the ice wearily, but gingerly into the upper compartment of our icebox that seemed to contain a smell all its own.

We would roar down the neighborhood streets with our homemade scooters made from a wooden milk or pop crate, a two by four, and a pair of metal street skates nailed at both ends of the two by four. Summer time was full of promise and adventure.

****

Being a skilled carpenter, Eddie Courtwright's wardrobe consisted of faded bibbed overalls, tee shirts, and a blue and white ribbed denim railroad cap that he wore on his tall thick frame. His potbelly protruded through his bibbed coveralls, and I remember distinctly the thin red hairs on multi-freckled forearms, and wrinkled red skin of his sunburned neck. His house was one of the two three story framed houses on Parsons near my home that rested on the corner of Beck across the Street from Ziegler's Drug Store. Mr. Courtwright and his wife had two grown children and a teenage son living with them. The teenager, Shorty Courtwright, loved Mom's cooking and was a regular fixture at our dinner table. He wore his jeans low on his butt and did odd jobs around the neighborhood. Netty, his older sister, was one of Mom's friends married to an Army veteran fresh from the European war.

Netty had just given birth to a baby girl, and I remember watching the baby's blue eyes widen when she began feeding. I watched with fascination the way the baby gulped the nipple attacking Netty's swollen freckled breasts. I had never seen freckled breast before, but it was common seeing women breast-feeding babies in public. Soon after gulping enough milk, the baby would close her eyes and fall to sleep. Mom and Netty would eat lunch together, talk about babies and general housewife gossip, each telling the other guarded secrets. Mom would change and feed the baby when Netty was too tired. Netty would stare out the window toward her father's house while breast-feeding. Sometimes she just stared at nothing in particular. Mom treated Netty like a sister. The two of them simply enjoyed each other's company. They were inseparable. I seemed to be always nearby quietly observing them.

I vividly recall Netty's husband, who recently had been discharged from the Army, wearing olive drab Army "Ike" jackets (with colorful patches on the sleeves) and chain-smoked Lucky Strike cigarettes. I don't believe he got along with Mr. Courtwright because one day Netty and her husband and their baby moved in with us. Mom's concern for them was genuine, and Charlie did not mind them living with us either because he would have done anything for Mom. Charlie and Netty's husband had conversations about the possibility of getting work with Charlie at the Federal Glass Company. One day, however, Netty, her baby, and her husband, suddenly were gone. It resulted when the two men were drinking beer at the kitchen table, and Netty's husband started telling stories about the war. The way Charlie told me the story many times and many years later, always had the same effect on him. He would retell the story often and each time he told it, his normal calm composure took on another form. His transformation started with his chewing the inside of his lower lip and then his face twitched followed by his stammering, cursing, and finally rage. Charlie would end the conversation abruptly, excused himself, and walked away. The event still was unsettling to him.

"Charlie, you are not like the other niggers I've come across. You're a good nigger." Now that was more than enough reason for Charlie to have kicked his ass. However, Charlie was a very patient man and words didn't mean much to him when a person had been drinking. Besides, Netty's husband was a veteran, something Charlie highly respected since the Army rejected him because of his flat feet. (The Army, however, did draft his older brother, Phoebe, who was a cook with the rank of tech sergeant, and Charlie was extremely proud of him.)

"Charlie, when we were in Europe, we didn't like the way some of them Black boys acted over there. We'd see those White girls throw themselves on them and how those boys seemed to forget who they were. So me and a couple of my buddies would go 'coon' huntin'. We'd wait and ambush some nigger troops and get away with it. We shot a lot of them and no one knew the difference 'cause the Nazis got the blame."

Immediately after that, Netty and her family were gone. I remember Mom's sadness, but she remained in contact with Netty until they moved to Wyoming taking Shorty with them and I never heard from them again.

****

In the other large home on Parsons Avenue lived the Sloushers, a newly arrived Jewish family who came from a strange place in Europe I had never heard of before. They lived next door to the Courtwrights. The three children of the family were, Viktor, his younger sister Mary, and baby Jay. They became an important part of my childhood neighborhood. I enjoyed playing stickball, tag, hide-n-go-seek, and tag football in my neighborhood, and Viktor was a pretty good athlete. And there were other new Black arrivals on South Lane, one in particular who had a house full of kids who came from South Carolina. I christened them the "pygmies" after watching a *Tarzan* movie and because there were so many of them. However, they all were a welcomed addition to our stickball team. Mary Slouser, whose long blond curly locks made her look very much like Shirley Temple, bonded with Dottie, who both were the same age. Mrs. Slouser became a good friend to Mom after Netty left.

Mrs. Slouser was very attractive with thick black hair that she wore down to her shoulders similar to Mom's style. She confided in Mom and they would talk for hours sharing her black and white photos of her family and large European villa (that included several maids) prior to the war. They obviously came from a wealthy family somewhere in Germany and she, like Mom, had been previously married but lost all her family (husband, mother, father, sisters and brothers) in concentration camps. The Nazis also confiscated her lovely home and fine automobiles. Her husband Herman was a huge man from Poland. Her marriage to him came from the result of a promise that they would marry if he helped her escape the Nazis. They somehow escaped and subsequently arrived in America. Herman, however, seemed always in a world of his own. His English was not as refined as his wife's. He did not speak very much except in deep grunts of a foreign tongue that I learned from Viktor to be Yiddish. Their large house was situated next to the Courtwrights' on Parsons Avenue. Herman was as massive as the neighborhood iceman. Like Mr. Courtwright he also had red hair, enormous freckled arms, but with a huge barrel chest giving him the appearance of a circus strongman. As a matter-of-fact, he was a circus strongman before the war. Herman, however, was very gentle and showed it through his great affection for Viktor, Mary and baby Jay. Viktor's pride in his father's strength was obvious. Viktor claimed his father could break chains. When all the neighborhood boys coaxed Viktor to have his father give a demonstration, we were stunned when he grasped a chain in the palms of his hands, made a few grunts and "pop," the chain burst and the links scattered to the ground. We were extremely impressed and Viktor beamed.

Viktor's baby brother Jay had been born shortly after they settled in their new home. He was a huge baby taking after his father, but he did not walk even though he was going on three. He also spoke in a grunt vocabulary and crawled everywhere, especially in our backyard. I later learned that Jay was mentally challenged. His small and bulky body did not encumber him from our back yard where our big black boxer, named Buddy was chained.

Buddy had been given to Willie from a salesman who worked for Bobb Chevrolet across the street. Buddy had been trained by the Army to go to Korea but was a reject because he fought and killed several other Army dogs. He was shiny black with a white apron, very muscular, ugly as hell, and mean except with us kids. I have never since seen another black boxer. He broke so many chains that we had to go to the hardware store and buy special ones just for him, and in due course he broke them too. When we took him for a walk, people walking their dogs detoured or gathered their dogs in their arms backing away while Virgil, Bunny and I all held Buddy's chain until they were out of sight. Buddy loved fighting other dogs. If another dog attempted to bark furiously or wanted to first draw blood, they always ended up bloody and running with their tails between their legs or lay on their backs as a sign of giving up. We did not encourage him to fight, but either the Army did something to make him vicious or it was just in his blood. However, he displayed gentleness to us and I grew very proud of him especially whenever we went to Shiller Park. The bigger White guys there would not threaten us. And, whenever Jay escaped from his back yard and crawled into ours, Buddy was very tolerant with him, even when he pulled and pinched Buddy's balls. Buddy would merely glance at Jay in resigned disgust and trot off as far as his chain would allow and lie down while Jay slowly crawled to Buddy and continued the ball-pinching process again.

****

Next door to Ms. Bessie lived "Big Chief" also called "Buck" by adults, a half Creek Indian and half Black with his wife Lucy. Their house sat on the corner of Parson Avenue and South Lane Street; the only thing separating their property from ours was a huge sycamore tree, for there were no fences. Big Chief enjoyed hunting immensely and had an assortment of shotguns, pistols, and

26

rifles in his house. In the autumn and winter months, it wasn't unusual seeing him bring in slain animals from a hunt. It was strange for me to see dead animals other than rats, which I despised, but to see dead rabbits, ducks, and deer, which I associated with Disney's characters, was another thing. I'm almost sure that when he hunted, he had been drinking. He had a weakness for alcohol.

He drank so much that when the city garbage men came to collect the trash once a week, they would gather around his large trash containers and marvel at the quantity of the empty whiskey bottles inside them.

Besides his passion for drinking, Big Chief loved baseball. He loved listening to a baseball game on the radio and told Virgil and me baseball stories about the Negro League. He claimed he had pitched for a Negro League in Georgia, and indeed I was impressed how he could accurately quote baseball records of his heroes, Jackie Robinson, Satchel Paige and even many White major league players. In the yard he would show us how he used to throw for his team. It was interesting seeing him so animated. He'd stand with a ball in his hand and sneak a glance to first base, and then at second, talking all during the wind-up until his release. He was good. It was poetry watching him relive his past. His favorite team was the Brooklyn Dodgers because on that team Jackie Robison played second base.

He had a patriarchal fondness for Virgil whom he called "Red" because of Virgil's red hair and his light complexion. While I watched in envy, he showed him how to hold a bat, how to pitch a fastball, curve ball, and a spitball. Sometimes he took Virgil to ballgames or to Isley's Ice Cream Parlor on Livingston and Parsons. Big Chief said that I was too dark and wasn't as smart as Virgil. So I was excluded from many of their baseball activities. Since Big Chief and Lucy didn't have children of their own, I think Virgil was the son that he wished he had. I just didn't fit what he envisioned in a son. But Big Chief wasn't a terrible person. I still enjoyed listening to him talk about the old Indian ways and *poontang*, which he said was what women had that men wanted and that we'd find out [about] later in life. And sometimes I was invited for ice cream, baseball and ballgames at the Red Bird stadium to watch The Columbus Red Birds or some Negro League exhibition. He instructed the kids in the neighborhood, including Viktor and Mary, to holler out his name whenever we saw or passed him on the street. Afterwards, he would lead us all up the street to Isley's for double dips of vanilla ice cream cones. He would not allow us to order chocolate ice cream--it had to be vanilla for some strange reason.

Everyone on South Lane Street respected each other's space and secrets. Every family had them. Some were greater than others, some lesser. Big Chief's secret, which everyone in the neighborhood knew (because when he drank, he'd give slurring long narratives of his escape from a Georgia lynch mob after killing a White man who had discovered an affair between the man's wife.) He would impart his adventures after a couple of swigs of one of his favorite libations of Old Grand Dad, Jim Beam, or bootleg corn liquor he purchased somewhere in the neighborhood. Old Grand Dad had preference because I remember seeing its orange labels on the many amber color bottles in his trashcan. Although some may have thought that Big Chief's exploits were a bit exaggerated, they became believers when one night he actually shot and killed a man in front of our house. Big Chief had just been hired as a plain-clothes security guard for Bobb Chevrolet automobile dealership across from our house. He noticed a parked car on the lot with two occupants in it. A man and his girlfriend were in the car, apparently making-out. When he asked them to leave, the guy got out of his car and became belligerent. Unfortunately for the young man, he made the fatal mistake of calling Big Chief a "nigger." The newspapers stated that he was while casually reaching in his pockets (probably for a pack of cigarettes) when Big Chief shot him once in the chest. The guy stumbled a few steps backward and died on the street in front of our house. Big Chief claimed it was self-defense because he didn't know what the man had in his pockets. I remember looking out my upstair's window and staring below at a Yahoo (policeman) drawing a chalk outline of the man's body on the street where he had died. I was surprised how young he was and at the amount of blood that ran on the street. The Yahoos took Big Chief downtown for a statement, but he wasn't arrested. A few days later he lost his job. The neighbors now didn't dismiss anything he would later say whenever he was in the mood to talk, which meant when he was drinking.

Frequently, Big Chief's nephew, Archie Armstrong, visited when he came home on leave from the Army. He became the father of my sister Sandy while Mom was still married to Charlie. Archie, many years later, became her last husband. She was 55 and he 35 when they married in the early '60s when I had left home to join the Marines.

Big Chief was certainly a colorful figure in our neighborhood, and whatever his faults may have been, I would be the last to judge him. He was a brave, brawny and bronze hero of my Black American youth--the true grit, Technicolor version of John Wayne. Certainly, his presence allowed me to develop a powerful imagination. Although he has been dead for quite some time, when I often think of him, I recall the grand metaphors of my childhood. The result of his influence, imagery inspires me even today. He gave me the opportunity to see beyond the superficiality of the mundane, and to embrace the passion for life. Indeed, we as children delighted in calling his name as loudly as we could, "Big Chief!" His reply would be a throaty, "Well, all right!"

****

Another neighborhood celebrity was Miss Rosy Woodson. This elderly white-haired lady periodically put on exhibitionist performances on South Lane Street for the busy traffic on Parsons Avenue by hoisting up her dress, exposing her drawers--if she felt like wearing that particular day--and dance some sort of shuffle while holding on tightly to her whiskey bottle. The charade ended after she pissed on the curb in full view of the world and eventually staggered back home, fortunately not too far away. People knew better than interrupt her performance because if disturbed, she fought like a Marine and used a few choice words that would make a sailor blush. When she was sober, however, Rosy Woodson was forgiving, passively polite and had a dazzling angelic smile. She was an incredible different person when sober.

****

One of the garbage men, who marveled at the weekly collection of whiskey bottles strewn in Big Chief's trash, lived in a small rooming house above a neighborhood grocery store on Parsons and Fulton Avenue, up the street from Harry's Bar and Grill. He had the same short stature and humble mannerisms as my father. Both men were hard workers and lived alone in their meager one room world. They were also avid readers. The garbage man, whose name I've forgotten, purchased the Journal Nightgreen from me nightly, either at Harry's Bar and Grill or somewhere on my paper route near his home. He always seemed eager to read the newspaper. One evening he opened his second story window and hollered down asking if I could bring him up a paper. I climbed the two flights of stairs and entered his room. It was the first time I had been there. His living space reminded me very much of Charlie's cramped quarters, and there was the same heavy sorrowfulness that emanated from his room. He handed me a quarter and told me to keep the change and immediately began reading the paper. Some old sepia photographs of Black soldiers on horseback were displayed on his dresser, and he caught me looking at them. He told me that they were pictures of him when he was a cavalry soldier. I didn't believe him at first because the pictures didn't look at all like him. And besides, I thought, he was only a garbage man. It was as if he read my thoughts because he suddenly laughed and said that he was much younger when the photos were taken, and that life has funny way of dealing cards to you. I examined all the photos closely, and I could see that, indeed, it *was* in the pictures. Wearing a khaki uniform, riding boots and a Smokey Bear hat, he was a striking figure setting on top of a dark horse. He appeared taller and much younger. My eyes grew wider because I knew I was in the presence of a real hero. In his room, he showed me souvenirs, ribbons and medals from various campaigns. He told me that he was under General "Black Jack" Pershing's command and served with him in the Philippines Insurrection, and the Mexican Expedition, chasing the elusive Poncho Villa around Texas and eventually inside Mexico. He said that Poncho Villa was a bandit, but the Mexican people considered him a hero. They never captured him. Among his souvenirs was a wicked looking knife angled at 45 degrees, with notches on the blade that the Philippines native rebels used to cut the throats of cavalry soldiers as they rode through the bush. The rebels swung down from trees and attacked without warning.

Here was this American hero in my presence, who told me about the infamous Buffalo Soldiers, but there was nothing in the history books at Mohawk that even mentioned anything about these brave Black men. It was the first time I heard anything mentioned about them. Looking at my new hero now, I felt mixed emotions. How could such a brave man be relegated to such a lowly task of collecting garbage? After that, every time I'd see him either collecting garbage on his garbage route, drinking beer at Harry's Bar and Grill or walking along the street, my heart swelled but at the same time, I was angered and questioned what would be my future.

****

Layman Avenue, located just up the street from where I lived, projected perpendicular out of South Lane like a rich woman's outstretched arm laden with fine jewelry. Only two and a half blocks long, Layman's working class residents reigned superior to those on my street. The only thing we had common was the neatly lined red brick that made up both streets. I envied the families living in the homes on Layman, not because of their beautiful landscaped yards or the canopy of Maple and Elm trees that provided ample shade on their large porches with swings-chairs on them. Or their spacious back yards, which grew various fruit trees and grapevines that I used to climb and rob their sweet produce. Or the extravagance of their paved sidewalks with walkways lined with shrubs or picket fences leading up to a porch.

My envy had nothing to do with of the exterior of Layman's dollhouses; it was merely of them having the luxury of indoor plumbing that I envied because I never knew how it felt to stretch out in a bathtub with hot soapy water by just the turn of a handle. I was confined to the hard circular edge of a small, galvanized laundry tub whose supply of hot water came from a teapot.

31

At any rate, the residents on Layman were more racially segregated—or so I thought. Many White people living there were not actually White. Some were "passing" which was their way of escaping to the comforts of the good life. Their light skin allowed them the opportunity to live in better neighborhoods and work as supervisors in the factories. Many even married Whites, and by doing so, they dissociated themselves from their dark relatives. And there were plenty of them. Their light skin simply gave them an elevated position on the racial flow chart. The notion was that those with lighter hues were supposed to be less of a threat to White folk in order to feel more comfortable than the darker ones because of *near-to-White* association that existed since slavery times. Unfortunately, many Black folk bought in to that insipid concept for associating dark with being ignorant, lazy, dangerous, and dirty.

The elderly Mrs. Fox who "passed" for White, lived on the corner of South Lane and Layman bought into that notion and despised everything dark. She had a strong dislike for Black children, especially the darker ones, which made me her number one enemy. She was married to a quiet White man—or I believe he was White—and had little to do with the residence of South Lane Street. Old Mrs. Fox had all the makings of a witch. Whenever we played baseball, in the large field behind her back yard (separated by her wooden fence) we tried not to hit fly balls over it. If a ball did land in her yard, she would run outside and wave the thing at us calling us a variety of awful (racial) names that would ruin our game. Even the White guys we played with disliked her.

"You little Black niggers. Get the hell out that lot. And you (pointing to me) you're the one. You're the worst because you're the Blackest." She never returned our balls no matter how much pleading and begging we did. Since we were out of earshot of our parents, our frustrations got the best of us and we now had a chance to practice a few selected cuss words on her. I would turn my backside to her, pull down my pants, expose my narrow black butt and pat it a few times telling her to come and kiss it.

****

My mother's family came from an area around Logan, Ohio, which is located in the Southeastern part of the state. On that side of the family, the eldest living individual during my youth was my great-Aunt Viola, Mom's aunt, better known as Aunt Vi. Mom was named after Aunt Vi, a very spirited woman who enjoyed dancing and partying during much of her younger life. However, after the death of her sister, Mom's mother, she spent most of her adult life living across the Ohio River in Ashland, Kentucky where she quietly assimilated into a White world and "passed" to work as a bi-spectacled librarian. Though, whenever she visited relatives in Ohio, she would head directly to a record player, put on the latest record, ask what the latest steps were, and proceeded to kick up her heels and party. She did this well until her 90s. She enjoyed the company of dark skinned Negro men, but when angered, she would be very quick to assimilate to her White side. I wish I knew more about her, but I only know bits and pieces from family members. I have no idea where she's buried, but I think maybe her remains are in Kentucky.

****

When Mom washed clothes, she boiled water in a round galvanized tub heated on top of the kitchen stove; she would carry the heavy tub (sometimes one of my brothers would help) and the hot water poured inside her prized *Maytag* wringer washing machine. The source of all our hot water came from the top of the kitchen stove. We took baths in the round galvanized tub that conspicuously hung on the side of our house next to a washboard, but the homes in the neighborhood were all kept scrupulously clean. Poverty does not necessarily thwart sanitary conditions. Mom adhered to the biblical scripture and would constantly remind us that, "cleanliness is next to Godliness." It seemed like a mantra in our household, as well, I suppose to the rest of South Lane's community. Mom would often receive complimentary praises on the whiteness of her sheets when she hung them out to dry. They reminded me of pictures of Clipper sailing ships I saw in the *National Geographic*.

I recall many Monday mornings watching her labor over the *Maytag*, and I was fascinated by the mechanical sound of its motor. The music made from the motor of the Maytag was melodic and I would dance to the rhythm of the washer in the kitchen. I would spend a lot of time just watching the washing arm as it whipped and churned clothes one way and then back the other in a cadence similar to the beat of Charlie's windshield wiper blades on his old pre-war Plymouth. And the wringer on the Maytag was another fascination. I was fixated watching the two rubber cylinders squeeze water from the soggy clothes and seeing them compressed flat on the opposite side, cascading gracefully into the galvanized tub on the kitchen floor. Mom was always warning us never to get our hands too close to the wringer because we could get our arms caught in it. Sometimes, however, when she wasn't looking, I would poke my finger and touch the rolling rubber spools being very careful not to get my fingers caught between the rollers.

Mom would sing or hum to herself as she washed clothes. Sometimes she sang along to a tune heard on our kitchen's small wooden radio, songs of Ella Fitzgerald, Diana Shore, Billie Holiday, The Dorsey Brothers, Benny Goodman or a litany of post-war soap commercials tunes advertising *Lava, Rinso Blue, or Lifebuoy*. When ironing, she listened to the radio broadcast production of *As the World Turns* or *The Guiding Light* way before it became a television series.

Other than playing outside in the yard, the kitchen was the main area where I spent most of my boyhood time. We ate our meals in the kitchen on a red and white checker oil tablecloth. The window's drapery had little red roosters printed on them and the wallpapered walls had an assorted array of floral designs. Colorful, bright patterns covered the linoleum floor that Charlie seemed to replace on a regular basis.

During mealtime, Mom would prepare scrumptious meals, which always included cornbread or homemade rolls for supper. The smells that came from our kitchen still linger with me. Of course, Sunday meals were prepared with special consideration that included greens or green beans, fried chicken, mashed potatoes and gravy, and cakes or sweet potato pies for dessert. At Thanksgiving,

Mom would spend all Wednesday cooking and getting things in the right order. When it came time to eat, she would have a gleam on her face knowing that all her efforts of what she had prepared were incomparable. If I waited long enough, while she was preparing a cake, my reward meant licking food remnants from the dessert bowls. Mom had a grace about herself in the kitchen, taking great care in her chores. She was happy being a housewife, and I enjoyed watching her perform. When Charlie came home from work, he was very content. We were a poor family replicating American family norms of the post war period.

****

I remember another one of South Lane Street's enigmas, Reverend Johnson who made his living as an independent junk dealer or "junkman" pushing a heavy laden wooden cart. He collected scraps of metal and other assorted discarded things within a walking radius allowable from one pushing a heavy cart. He did not have to answer to any biased union, or White employer; he was his own boss. Reverend Johnson always wore an inexpensive sweat-stained brown fedora, a clean white shirt, and a necktie underneath soiled bibbed denim coveralls. His wooden pushcart was hand built that prominently exhibited a "Pushcart License" plate (similar to an automobile license plate) nailed on its front that he renewed each year. There were two large wooden wagon wheels analogous to the ones used on the Conestoga wagons that hauled pioneers out West. There were two sturdy wooden legs attached to each end of the crossbar handle. The legs were about three feet high, which supported the cart when lowered. He wore large work gloves when he sorted through trash, picking metal scraps and other junk materials, examining each piece with great care before placing them in his pushcart.

Reverend Johnson spoke in a low venerable voice and carried himself in a dignified but humbled manner. Whenever he paused for a conversation, he took off his dirty gloves, mopped his brow with a clean white handkerchief, search for his pipe in his deep denim pockets, and lit it blowing out a huge plumb of sweet fragrance pipe tobacco smoke all done with an air of stateliness before he began to speak. For a preacher, he was a man of few words. His manner of speech was not a discourse, but an exchange of easy conversation. He listened more than he spoke. And no matter who you were, he made you feel relaxed and important. Even the few times when I spoke with him in my boyish stammer, he took his time and never talked down to me. I believe Reverend Johnson was a true empath. His eyes conveyed this--the acute awareness and sensitivity of his gaze as he absorbed one's sorrows through them making one feel refreshed after the conversation.

Although, he preached at various churches in the area, he was not associated with any particular one. Nor did he preach hell and damnation, even though, he probably could have earned a better living if he did. He could have effortlessly established his own church by pulling in a congregation of folk who felt a need to be "saved." Rather, his calling of piously pushing a junk cart had its effect by touching the needed few instead. He chose to live his hermit way of life remaining aloof, cloistered in the confines of his cluttered cottage, only being sociable when on his daily pushcart route. He, no doubt, was the antithesis of Big Chief and Rosy Woodson who lived just down the street. Even in their worst state of intoxication, when they saw Reverend Johnson coming down the street, they morphed themselves back to sobriety and greeted him cheerfully. No one said a negative thing about him. Then perhaps, that may have been because people came to him whenever they needed emergency money. It was rumored neighbors borrowed money from him for utility bills, money for medical needs, or funds for getting a loved one out of jail. It was also rumored that he had a large sum money stashed somewhere in the collection of his clutter. I don't know, I was just a kid and only heard rumors but I do know that Mom borrowed money from him whenever Willie (her third husband) drank up the grocery money. Reverend was highly respected indeed by everyone and I do know that everything he did was with sincerity and a quiet humility.

Reverend Johnson was one of the senior residents living on our small street. Not many people knew what part of the South came from or what he did before coming to the neighborhood. Some claimed he had been an ex-convict from a Southern prison, others said that he had been married but lost his wife and children in a tragic fire leaving him to become a vagrant, living a hobo's life before finally settling down on South Lane Street. The folks in the community respected his privacy letting him live alone among his collected junk of odd items dispersed throughout his yard as well as the artifacts in his house. I never went inside his home, but I often caught a glimpse when selling caramel popcorn for school. From what I could see, the interior was a maze network of collected items looking like a Salvation Army store. In the middle of his living room was a large black wrought iron bed and dangling over it suspended an electric cord hanged a dimly lit bare light bulb. One summer night, I passed his house (coming home from my nightly newspaper route, full of my Huckleberry Fin curiosity) crept to his fence, extend my neck, peeked past the old discarded appliance items in his yard, and observe his long slender body, still dressed in his white shirt and overalls, stretched on top of his bed fast asleep holding an opened Bible all in the glow of that dimly bare bulb. I can honestly say that I've never met anyone with such humility in all my years since. Looking at him that night through his opened window many years ago, I envision him as a reincarnate of Abe Lincoln, a tired and lonely Black Abe Lincoln.

****

The walk home from Beck Street Elementary School seemed like miles to my home on South Lane Street. Beck was a predominately White school located in the heart of German Village. I held the distinction of being the only Black male in my class at Beck. There was a very shy Black girl named "Sister"(Elizabeth Kimbrough). She lived with her five brothers and sisters in a duplex on Parsons Avenue. Sister's mother, Miss Idea, an attractive big-boned woman, had strong physical characteristics I have no clue why people called her "Miss Idea." I only know she was another good friend of my mother who periodically interjected an ear shattering, "Gal, hush yo' mouth!" in much of her conversation with Mom. It was Miss Idea's way of confirming my mother's sentiments, usually something about their husbands. Miss Idea's husband, a small delicate man, also worked in one of the nearby factories. They came from somewhere in Alabama, and I truly enjoyed hearing Miss Idea's joviality when she talked. She had a positive attitude about life in a time when both families had little to share but good conversation and friendship. Louvinia, Sister's younger sister, was in the same grade as Virgil. Flo teased Virgil and me saying that I would marry Sister and Virgil would marry Louvinia when we grew up.

****

On Parsons Avenue, Plank's Bar and Grill's bartender skillfully poured beer from the tap into large trumpet glasses. Plank's patrons were blue-collar factory workers and master tradesmen who were the grandsons of German, Irish, and Scotch-Irish immigrants. Emanating through the swirl of smoke, the neon lit room of beer advertisements, the jukebox spewed post war songs of Hank Williams, Frankie Lane, Teresa Brewer, Johnny Ray, Diana Shore, Doris Day, and Nat King Cole. *The Little White Cloud Who Cried* and *Nature Boy,* was favorites. The choice of cigarettes at Plank's were Camels or Lucky Strikes. Up the street on Livingston Avenue, the elegant but notorious *Stone's Bar and Grill* maintained its live weekend music, and an elite charade of working-middle class patrons. The mix of white-collar and factory workers frequented *Stones* under the same illusion--to get laid. The white collar came in the assumed pretense of authority. Sometimes they rendezvoused with a female worker from either the office or assembly line wanting precariously to mix pleasure after business. These ladies were used to work, and stood out from the bored housewives whose husbands were either working third shift, out of town on a road trip pulling an eighteen-wheel rig, or in Korea. However, most of the women simply seemed bored. The divorced ones--or soon to be--sipped round after round of mixed libations hopefully paid by an admiring adventuring soul. In the back in the dim lit area sat the girls who wore layers of powder, rouge, eyeliner, and bright inviting lipstick. They tried giving off impressions of something between a Jane

38

Russell or Jane Mansfield cleavage look. In actuality, they were students from St. Mary's or South high schools out on the town with fake I.D. cards trying dangerously to prove their fledgling femininity testing the limits of their push-up bras.

There were the usual car and insurance salesmen relaxing from a day's theater of their workplace. Now they could unwind and become themselves with a few rounds under their belts. On the same street only a few steps away, and across Parson's Avenue next to *Harry's Grocery*, was *Harry's Bar and Grill* operated by a Jewish immigrant. I do not know if the owner of the grocery store was the same person who owned and operated *Harry's Bar*, even though both were Jewish and both had the same name. In contrast to *Stone's, Harry's* was smaller and his customers were Black factory workers, janitors, and garbage men who drank Pabts, Schlitz beer from brown bottles. They enjoyed watching Sugar Ray Robinson or Jersey Joe Walcott beating the hell out of any White opponents on a black and white television set through the haze of eye burning cigarette smoke. Except for Fridays and Saturday evenings, very few women ventured into *Harry's*. On Fridays, they came to drag their husbands away from barflies before the hard-earned money ended up wasted away on booze, gambling, or in pockets of other women. These taverns served as a convenient way station between work and home. For many it was an escape from both. There they watched television, shot pool, drank and smoked their choice of cigarettes: *Lucky Strikes, Camels or Kools*. The world of the Black working-class at Harry's Bar and Grill was a smoke-filled, blue universe conveying the sounds of Muddy Waters, Bill Doggett, Joe Tuner, and B.B. King. It was a smoky façade world of sovereignty where people looked elegant in their work clothes. And, it was a world where visible signs of lonesomeness were just one glass away from the next.

****

The pizzas Virgil and I ate soon grew into pepperoni and other luxury toppings from the money we earned after we expanded our shoe shining business to include selling The *Columbus Evening Journal Nightgreen* newspaper. Besides the many taverns and bars we visited, we would walk our routes until late at night in German Village screaming from the top of our lungs the day's headlines. We devised a clever sing-song style concluding with, "Joournaal-Nightgreeeen, Joournaall!" Porch lights would come on and we ran to the houses, opened small wrought iron gates, and leaped up porch stairs with the paper in hand. It was always interesting looking at the impressions on our customer's faces as they read the news. At that young age, we felt we were providing a needed service--news.

The shoe shinning and paper selling business forced us to venture into the unknown territory, mostly a world of working class White adults at leisure. We did not want to stand out as anything special; we tried to manage to become a blur passing through the night selling headlines or dispensing coatings of polish on brogans or winged tipped shoes to our patrons. And business was good. We were very preoccupied with the business of making money because it just seemed so easy to do and it helped with provisions for our family. We felt responsible at the ages of eight and nine.

On the streets, we were urchins enjoying a sense of freedom and a small portion of our earnings went on pizzas, Bazooka bubble gum, and comic books. The rest we turned over to Mom. We learned to replenish the cans of Kiwi shoe polish and developed elaborate ways of making the rag "pop" for an extra quarter. We learned a lot about a person by the type of shoes he wore and how well he took care of them. If a person wearing factory brogans wanted his shoes shined, he usually did it merely to give us business and he was usually generous with his tips. Those who wore suits usually were car or insurance salesmen tipped to show-off. We dreaded shining their wing tipped shoes because it was time consuming, which involved digging out the polish from each hole with a toothpick or a wooden matchstick, and the occupants of those shoes sometimes proved to be lousy tippers. At times, we felt more like adults than the drunken men whose shoes we shined or bought our papers. Each tavern had its own character and ethnic clientele, and in those crowded places, we learned and valued the priceless gift of observation. Our sense of intuition developed and grew with each paper we sold and every shoe we shined. We observed human nature and at times, braved the racial insults in the White taverns where sometimes we braved derogatory names such as "Sunshine," "Snowball," or Snowflake." We seldom heard the word nigger in the taverns we visited perhaps because people respected two hard working Black kids trying to make a buck. Verbal territory in those bars at that at time was respected, to trespass it by using racist words meant one was a low-life. Actually, being called Snowball or Snowflake was, in fact, rare. Those who made the remark were often rebuked. Any outlandish behavior from drunks was usually quailed merely by the glances from a few patrons and bartenders. Apologizes were given and just as quickly as it had begun, all was forgiven and people continued drinking, played table shuffleboard, shot pool, or threw darts. Virgil and I eased our way quietly out the door with our pockets loaded with "apology" money.

Although Virgil may not have known it, I always kept an eye on him making sure he was safe. He was my kid brother and I felt obligated to see about his safety, but I didn't want him to know that I was doing it because he would have been disgusted. Bunny never worked with us, and I often wished he had because some street men terrified me. Sometimes they followed us, and I would pick up a heavy brick and place it in my canvas paperboy's bags making the weight even heavier. Sometimes these men looked quite normal. They would call me over to their parked car giving the impression of wanting to buy an evening newspaper. Once at the side of the car, however, they would make propositions saying they would buy all the papers in exchange of having them giving me a blowjob or vice versa in their cars. Others would ask if I knew where any little colored girls played at that time of night. It was sick and I wanted to be transformed, somehow, into an adult just for five minutes. However, I would be polite and back away to a safe distance in a lighted area holding on to the brick inside my canvas bag. I was always frightened and worried about the safety of Virgil first. In addition, there were the never-ending German Village narrow alleys that by day ran behind enchanting backyards of neat Village cottages. But at night, the alleys loomed mysteriously malevolent in the darkness. Horrible stray dogs would surprise you, but at least they gave you a warning with their growls. Trees possessed eerie forms where perverted predators hid whispering,

"Pssst, hey kid. Com'ere. Give ya' five dollars for all them paper if you let me... ."

Fear gripped me around the knees. It seemed to rise up from there and settle in the pit of my stomach drying out my mouth. We would pick up our pace looking over our shoulders as our hearts pounded. Holding onto our bricks, we prayed The Lord's Prayer and prepared to run like hell out of the alley into the safety of streetlights. I looked desperately for our Guardian Angel and sometime he would unexpectedly drive slowly by in the alley. Every time we ventured out into the alleys during winter nights, I was afraid. It got to the point that I dreaded its short days. Only the light of the long summers seemed to provide a blanket of protection.

The Guardian Angel watching over us may have been a figment of my imagination, but to me he was the soft-spoken stranger with many faces who wore laborer's work clothes and a knitted gray big-apple cap. He would sit alone idly drinking beer in the Taverns and his racial composition changed with the ethnic clientele of each tavern. He wasn't tall, but strong and stout like a prizefighter. At Planks, he was German looking. In Stones Grill, he was Irish and at Harry's he was the stout Black man. He always tipped us well when he bought a paper and gave us a kind look of sincere admiration. The Angel appeared in many ways similar to my father Charlie. Because this guy seemed to regularly appear in the various taverns, I imagined him with us in those dark spooky alleys watching over Virgil and me. He, however, was nowhere to be found at home after Mom divorced Charlie and married Willie. And given the choice of staying at home with Willie or going out in the wintry cold selling papers in the dark German Village alleys, I would opt for the alley.

Chapter Five

F LO'S MURDER would be the second killing by a handgun
in my family within two years. Both family members were
generations apart and killed by someone they knew. William
"Wee-Wee" Hollingsworth had just turned fifteen and had not even

started to shave when he was murdered. When Dottie, my baby sister, called me in mid-February 1994 to come home to yet another tragedy, I was angry at the waste of potential.

Wee-Wee's assailant, like Flo's husband, took a momentary swan dive into insanity that forever changed the course of events in the lives of my family. I had warned Wee-Wee only a few weeks before his pathetic death that he would have to change his ways. Dealing drugs is a dangerous business, and the streets are meaner than they were when I was growing up. His response was something between a laugh and a smirk. To him, I represented a generation light years away from his world and I am afraid he was right. What takes place in America's streets in this generation are nine-year-old girls starting their menstrual cycles and kids who can articulate with exact detail the nomenclature of a 9mm Beretta, its firepower, and how many rounds can fit in its magazine. Yet, few know much about American history, world literature, or geography. Advertisers, meanwhile, promote competition in brand names targeted at children's egos. Kids believe they will not be accepted unless there is an emblem or brand name clearly stamped on the products they wear and use. A pair of tennis shoes now costs more than my first used car. In addition, Hollywood constantly cranks out imagery of violence and ludicrous plots. And television (especially talk shows) produces images of violence and hatred merely to gain celebrity status or high ratings. Indeed, there is little respect for life. Life is just an illusion played on video games where weapons of mass destruction are in the hands of seven-year olds. War is also an illusion on television showing bombs blasting away sections of Middle-Eastern cities just like video games. Today's kids would take The Howdy Doody Show as a joke. In order for Howdy to be successful, he would have to throw away the cowboy image and wear a baseball cap slung backwards on his head, sport a Tommy Hilfiger or FUBU shirt, a pair of baggy Calvin Klein jeans hanging low on his ass, and a pair of $150.00 Michael Jordan tennis shoes. And instead of singing, *Its Howdy Doody Time*, the song would be something insipid and fowled-mouth.

Like his mother (Pudding), Wee-Wee was a very bright, easygoing kid. He easily made the honor roll when he did attend school and had all the makings of success--a bright mind, a caring family, and the school principal who adored him. Many people admired him. He was a charmer: mild-mannered and smooth talking, just like his grandfather Bunny. He even had a Big Brother associate. A successful attorney named Greg had for years taken Wee-Wee on weekly excursions, camping, football games, and so on. He bought Wee-Wee clothes, games, and involved him in his family life. When Greg married, he bought Wee-Wee a boys size tuxedo and included him as an essential part of the wedding ceremony. Greg cared for him like a son and by any standard, Wee-Wee had it made. When Greg purchased a house in the Short North area of Columbus, he regularly invited Wee-Wee there. Greg even wanted to adopt him, but Mom could not bring herself to allow that. It was not the fact that Greg was White that she rejected his offer; it was, I believe, that Mom's love for Wee-Wee was a substitute for Bunny who was incarcerated. And Wee-Wee was a lot like his grandfather in many ways causing Mom to lavish excess affection on him. She spoiled him with money that she couldn't afford and dressed him with the latest styles in clothes. If it were not for the fast money made from hustling drugs, Wee-Wee would have had a future. He was killed watching TV at one of his friend's house. I'll never forget the grief-stricken looks on the faces of Mom, Pudding, and Greg's at Wee-Wee's funeral.

****

After waiting outside alone in the cold, Pudding had gained enough courage to come inside the church. The funeral service had already begun when she nervously entered aware of everyone's eyes fixed on her. The realization that her first born, her only son was now dead, had hit her like a hard slap to the face. Upon seeing the white, flower-strewn casket, she made the most remarkable sound I've ever heard. I will never forget it. It was one prolonged primordial wail--the universal sound of hurt--an exhalation that animals make when gripped by the jaws of death. If the soul was a blackboard, her wail was one long fingernail scratch on it. Everyone in the congregation paused momentarily, shaken, teary eyed, trying to gather themselves the best they could. As she approached the

45

casket, her knees buckled when she came into view of Wee-Wee's small frame lying still. He looked peaceful and reposed and even now she must have noticed the crooked smile on his smooth baby face. Again her knees buckled and she stumbled and bent low almost falling. I approached and gathered her in my arms willing myself not to show any emotion. I *had* to be strong for her. I held her throughout the service, patting her on the shoulder, blotting her tears with my handkerchief, whispering to her that the person in the casket was not really Wee-Wee, but just a shell of who he had been. I meditated throughout the service pushing back tears, thinking of Wee-Wee's chuckle and intelligence and the time when Pudding was a little girl herself. Indeed, the problem about coming from a large family is that sooner or later there will be many funerals to attend.

****

The affinity for nicknames runs deep in my family. Perhaps it's a Black Appalachian obsession, I just don't know. I lived in a family of nicknames. Mine, of all things, is "Sugar Pie," an endearing name reserved exclusively for family and dear friends. There have been times, however, when the name caused me a lot of consternation and embarrassment--especially as an adult.

Soon after I was born my brother Bunny, who is one-and-a-half years older than I am, told my mother that I looked like a "Sweetie Pie." Hell, he was just learning to talk himself when he pinned it on me. Eventually, Sweetie Pie somehow became Sugar Pie and I have dragged it around ever since. Charlie bestowed the name "Bunny" on him associating his brewing mischievousness with the infamous cartoon character, Bugs Bunny. My father's wish was that everyone referred to him as Charlie. Thus, those today who remember him utter his name with loving reverence.

Then there is my oldest (half) brother's nickname, "Junior" (Robert Simons). He was born a year after Flo by Mom's first husband, Robert Simons, Sr. I am sure that Junior's nickname had caused him much consternation too.

Pudding (Viola) is Bunny's oldest daughter whom he named after Mom. Even she had a nickname that all my uncles and aunts called her: "Doodle." But Mom is the guilty party for most of the nicknaming my siblings, nephews, and nieces. She bestowed Pudding's nickname on her as well as Pudding's son William, a.k.a. "Wee-Wee." He lived with Mom, his great-grandmother, who furnished him his nickname when he was an infant. Although we all tried to discourage her from calling him that, as he grew older, it was useless. William was her Wee-Wee, and that was that. Mom nurtured several generations of children and took her duties seriously. They gave her an immense sense of purpose and happiness. She simply loved children--the younger the better. For some reason, however, she had a very special fondness of Wee-Wee.

My mother raised both Pudding and Wee-Wee in two distinct generations, and each generation seemed to spawn a genre of turmoil. It was Wee-Wee's death, however, that caused her to suffer a series of (five) strokes that ultimately led to her blindness, dementia and demise. Her last stroke was the worst, which required round the clock nursing care. Mom's doctor urged us to place her permanently in a nursing home. That proved to be a very difficult decision for the family as Flo was not around to advise us. Because of this, we had to rely solely on the doctor's suggestion. So, with deep regret we placed Mom in a convalescent center one that had received high recommendations from friends and members of Mom's church where she was regarded along with Flo, as a Saint.

****

My mother's family came from the Southeastern Ohio region where some of her relatives opt to pass for White. Along with Mom's Black heritage, there is a diverse racial cocktail mix in her blood: Cherokee and German-Jewish with the family name of Zimmerman. Historically, racial mixing is not too uncommon in many parts of Ohio and throughout Appalachia. Black Appalachians come in various monochromatic hues (usually light skinned) and are referred to as "WINS". Many towns and small villages are so intermingled that it is hard to differentiate the Whites from the Blacks. Ohio towns such as London, Chillicothe,

47

Zanesville, Jackson, Logan, and other areas in the southeast of the state have amalgamated for generations, so that it is virtually impossible to discern one's racial origins.

In 1927, when Mom first married (at the age of fifteen), it was not considered unusual to marry young. This was especially true in central Ohio's Appalachian culture. Her first husband, Robert Simons, was the father of Flo, Junior and Ronnie. Robert senior gambled and was physically abusive to Mom according to what my uncle Earl said about him. Uncle Earl, Mom's younger brother is an ex-boxer, who did construction work most of his life. He is short, strong, and built like a fire hydrant, the type of person you don't mess with. He'd recently told me about Mom's first husband:

"Look Sugar Pie, that nigga' your Mom first married, was one mean sonnafabitch. Do you hear me? I mean I had to go over to your Mom's house and whoop that nigga's ass on more than one occasion. I told him not to be hitting my sister. Oh, buddy, he was something else. He was one mean bastard who loved hitting on your mother. Your Mom was just too young at the time. Those were times when niggas out here would kill you if you looked at them the wrong way. It was during the start of Depression when people were out of work. It was just hard times there. Yeah, buddy they were some hard times. I stopped over to see your mother and noticed her with a black eye. He was sitting down fumbling with a deck of cards. I looked at your mother and then back at him, and grabbed an iron skillet she was cooking with and commenced beating that nigga upside his head all the way down the fire escape steps. I mean I beat his ass with that skillet and told him if he ever laid a hand on her again, I'd kill him."

Mom was a widow when she met Charlie that was not due to any of Uncle Earl's activities to her first husband, but because he died a Stagger Lee type death simply because of the type of man he was. He died not long after Mom gave birth to Ronnie.

Charlie is the father of my older brother Bunny, Virgil, and me. He worked as a laborer for 47 years at the Federal Glass Factory and worked all through the Great Depression. He also held a part time job as an usher at the Royal Theater to earn extra income.

In 1946, when I was three, Mom gave birth to Sandy. I still remember the occasion. When a significant event occurs at a young age, they say that we have a tendency to recall it in minute detail. Sandy's birth was significant enough on its own merit, but it is what Bunny did that textured the event.

Mom gave birth to all her children at home, except Dottie, her last child, in 1951 at Grant Hospital. It was Doctor Lynch who delivered all of us at home in the confines of her small bedroom. He made house calls when one of us became ill, and I still remember the black leather medical bag he carried around and that he never complained about the time of day he was called. He seemed to fit right in at our modest home with no sense of arrogance or pretentiousness and he seemed genuinely concerned for our health. The night of Sandy's birth, for instance, he told Charlie and Flo to assist him. Flow was to boil some water and bring in some clean towels. I remember there was an air of excitement in the house. Mom was in her bedroom with the doctor and Flo. Charlie told Bunny, Virgil, and me to keep out of the way by staying in the kitchen with Junior and Ronnie who had come with Flo. Charlie paced around, nervously excited. He opened a box of cigars and handed a few to Junior and Ronnie. I wanted to see what was going on, but Bunny had prevented me from entering the bedroom. He had posted himself as sentinel at the closed bedroom door. I still, however, remember him peeping in a few times. The sound of Sandy's cry was the apex of the evening. Charlie gave a cigar to Dr. Lynch and lit one for himself. People were celebrating, toasting, smoking, and congratulating Charlie. Flo remained in the bedroom with Mom and Bunny smiled at me. It was one of those smiles that meant there was something behind it.

Bunny handed me a bottle of Vernor's Ginger Ale, my favorite soda pop. This act of his sharing something with me was unusual, and I should have been on guard. But everyone was celebrating, adults smoking cigars and toasting the gin Charlie opened. The bottle of Vernor's was unusually warm for it to be soda pop, but I was only three and Bunny was my big brother whom

I trusted, so I took a swig of the amber colored drink and immediately gagged, spitting out its contents. He set me up big time. Bunny had peed in the bottle and passed it off as Vernor's Ginger Ale. The liquid was the same color as Vernor's and in a Vernors bottle. He rolled over, laughing. I wanted to tell Mom, but the other adults guarded her, and obviously, she had other things to deal with. When I mentioned the incident to Charlie, he just laughed and went on with the business of receiving his congratulatory reception. The whole thing was beginning to frustrate me, and I especially didn't like being ignored and laughed at. It angered me so much that it triggered a permanent imprint of the whole incident in my consciousness.

The joyous occasion of Sandy's arrival in the world was celebrated by cigar smoke, adult laughter, and the salty-bitter taste of Bunny's piss. And to this day, every time I see a bottle of Vernor's Ginger Ale, I recall the incident.

With all of Charlie's celebration, it didn't seem to matter to him that Sandy did not look like any of us. She was fair skinned with straight hair and an uncanny resemblance to Archie Armstrong, the teenage soldier who occasionally visited next door at Big Chief's house. I think Charlie knew--he *had* to--it was too obvious. However, he treated her as if she was his own flesh and blood and considered her *his* daughter until the day he died. In fact, I think sometimes he treated her better because she also had a strong resemblance to Mom. Sandy today refers to Charlie as daddy with fond affection.

Around 1949, Mom divorced Charlie and married Willie Howard in 1950. She gave birth to my baby sister, Dottie in June 1951, her last child. Although, there are half brothers and sisters in our family, we never refer to each other as half anything--we are family, no more, no less. Archie and Charlie were dwarfish compared to Willie's six foot six inch frame. And for some reason or another, Mom married Willie twice. Their final divorce was in 1956-7. She married Jasper "Jack" Lovingood soon after and divorced him in 1962. When Archie finally married Mom, she was fifty-three and he thirty-four. It may seem strange to some that my mother married six times, but knowing her first husband died and that she married Willie twice helps qualify her reasons.

Precipice

Chapter Six

I N THE EARLY 1950s, radio was at its ebb, fast being replaced by television. I listened to radio programs like *Gang Busters, The Shadow, The Fat Man, The Lone Ranger, Straight Arrow, Amos n' Andy* and a host of others. I would huddle around the radio listening intently with Bunny, Virgil, and Sandy. Our imaginations did the rest. I think kids today are really missing what the imaginary experience radio drama provided back then. We have simply lost the fine art of storytelling and listening. That may be one of the reasons why many Americans today cannot read. There are no similes and metaphors in today's visual media. TVs, VCRs, and DVDs have replaced the boundless imagination of a child. But early television, new and exciting then, had a certain wonder and fascination for me and I wondered how a visual image could come through a box.

Our first TV started a neighborhood sensation. Neighbors would drop by indiscriminately and were just as enthralled with the TV set as we were. They enjoyed themselves with us during the hot summer nights watching boxing, a sit-com, or a movie while drinking Kool-Aid. Soon afterwards, everyone in the neighborhood had a TV set. The staged scenery of *Captain Video and The Video Rangers*, one of the first programs I enjoyed watching, seemed too artificial for my taste. When the camera panned the interior of the space ship, the gadgets looked too familiar for something supposedly to be in the future. Only the ray guns held my interest. Their futuristic shapes and sound effects came more realistically from my own imagination than anything they produced. The television's version of the Lone Ranger, for instance, did not do as much for my imagination. I much preferred the radio's version of the Lone Ranger. Even I could see the mistakes in many of early television productions. Television's Lone Ranger, for example, looked a little overweight for my taste, and unlike the one produced in my mind's eye from the radio. Tonto, the Lone Ranger's faithful Indian companion, on the other hand, made more sense to me. Many years later, I discovered that Tonto was a real Native American Indian and an accomplished collegiate Canadian athlete. A man of few words, Tonto had a mystical, stoic character that made his physical presence stronger than his counterpart. Why wasn't the Lone Ranger Tonto's sidekick? I longed to see people-of-color playing a hero's role--someone I could relate to. In sports, Jackie Robinson and Joe Lewis had been around and other Black athletes had proven themselves, but Hollywood did not have any serious actors until Sydney Poitier, Dorothy Dandridge, Harry Belafonte, and a few others that came on the scene. Black heroes like Paul Roberson, for their part, were systemically ostracized and relegated to lesser roles. I was living in the dark McCarthy era and too young to know what was going on. The only person close to breaking the heroic color bearer for me was The Cisco Kid (Duncan Renaldo.) His ethnicity was the only reason his television series held such a fascination for me. The fact that he came from a minority and was able to maintain his Mexican heritage held my attention weekly. Renaldo, a Hispanic doing heroic deeds, challenged the nation's consciousness weekly in a way the buffoonery of *Amos n' Andy* or themes of subservient characters, such as Jack Benny's Rochester or Beulah, the Black maid, had not. The Cisco Kid's television series evoked a sense of pride for my brothers and me. Even though we had never seen a Hispanic or Mexican, we could still relate to him as he rode "Diablo," his beautiful Pinto horse. Cisco wore a large ornate sombrero that never fell off his head when fighting or chasing bad hombres. Sometimes, near the end of the thirty-minute show, The Cisco Kid would kiss a White heroine (my brothers and I would shut our eyes, turn our heads and cry out, Oh mush!)

Pancho (Leo Carrillo), Cisco's funny sidekick, rode "Loco," his strikingly handsome Palomino. Both actors were athletic and their horses had to be strong and nimble, because both men were obsessed with sprinting and jumping on their horses' backs. At the end of the program, they would look at the camera and say, "See you next time, amigos." And with that, they laughed, slapped their horses' rumps, and raced-off into the sunset.

William Boyd, who performed Hopalong Cassidy on radio, the movies, and television, seemed to me the coolest of all cowboys. Hoppy, along with the Cisco Kid, were probably the most aesthetic-minded of all the cowboys. Hoppy wore black cowboy attire and a black hat that contrasted with his silver colored hair and his white

53

horse, "Topper." He was one very smart horse. Hoppy, an older cowboy had to be at least forty-something, but he stood his ground in a fistfight and rode better than the younger cowboys. Mom often mentioned that Hoppy was a handsome White man who originally came from Cambridge, Ohio not far from Columbus and somewhere out West. Of course, I refused to believe her. Hoppy, a cowboy's cowboy, had to have been born and raised somewhere like Texas or Montana. Montana would have been more to my liking.

"Gabby" Hayes was Hoppy's much older sidekick whose derelict appearance included wearing tattered Western clothing, an old dilapidated hat, and sported a scraggly beard that he rubbed and scratched when deep in thought. When he spoke, however, words of wisdom came out on the right side of his toothless mouth. Oddly, he was Roy Roger's sidekick too. Roy claimed the royal title as "King of the Cowboys" and his popularity was in part due to Trigger, his beautiful tan Palomino horse. Trigger's IQ seemed higher than Gabby's and had to have been in the genius range for horses. He was beyond smart. He would do things that were almost human and when Roy rode him, it was pure poetry in motion. When Roy fought, his hat never came off and his handkerchief always remained neatly tied around his neck--sure sign of a "good" guy. My father said that Roy was born in Cincinnati, Ohio, and that his house was located where second base was at the old Crosby Field home of the Cincinnati Red's baseball team. I had my doubts about another cowboy being born in Ohio. It didn't make sense. Cowboys come from out West, period. In my mind's eye, Roy Rogers probably came from Wyoming or Arizona--not Ohio. Roy wore an expression of trust on his face and he seemed sincere and trustworthy much like a father. Indeed, I equated him with my father.

When one thinks of Roy Rogers, one has to include Gene Audrey who also rode a fine-looking Palomino named Champion with an extraordinary resemblance to Trigger. We would say that the two horses were brothers. Gene, however, did not exactly fit the bill for my kind of cowboy because he had a double chin and was more than slightly overweight. Gene Audrey simply had a big butt, and it was evident when you saw him ride Champion.

I remember vividly Mom saying that Hopalong Cassidy made other movies besides cowboy ones and that he even kissed women.

"Whoa, hold on," I said, "You probably have gotten your people mixed up. Hopalong Cassidy doesn't kiss girls. No way!"

This was also about the time when I caught Bunny putting a nickel under Virgil's pillow while he was fast asleep after Mom pulled one of his baby teeth. Mom gave Bunny the coin and I remember him putting his index finger to his lips and told me to go back to sleep. That did it for the Tooth Fairy. After that, I even questioned him about the existence of Santa Claus, and he shattered my world with his answer. How was I then to believe Mom's story about my favorite cowboy kissing girls?

One day Mom led me to the front of the television set and I sat down on the floor. I saw a man resembling Hoppy on the screen wearing a double-breasted pinstriped suit and a necktie. As I watched in awe, the man resembling Hoppy did the most unforgivable thing--he kissed a woman! I could not believe my eyes. I just sat there stunned. And sure enough, the credits at the end of the movie stated, that it was William Boyd--my cowboy hero, Hopalong Cassidy. I was torn-up over that. Mom laughed as I went back outside, wiped my lips with the back of my hands, and spat on the ground. I eventually got over it, but the picture re-played in my mind for a long time. Hoppy, kissing a woman? How disgusting, ughhh!

****

Early television had many problems and watching it during those early days could be frustrating. Often the TV would go blank just at the most interesting point of a program, and an announcer would say: "The program you are watching is experiencing technical difficulties, please stay tuned." I never heard the word "technical" until television. Many of the television programs produced came from the heart and broadcasted live. It seemed that viewing them implied a sense of honesty, integrity and innocence. During the 1950s, Mom enjoyed Lucille Ball's antics in the *I Love Lucy Show*.

Her all time favorite television program had to be, *I Remember Mama*, staring Peggy Wood. Its Christmas production, shown every Christmas, touched Mom. She would have tears in her eyes watching the Christmas miracles on the program. And during the day, she would watch and sometimes cry for the participants on the *Queen for a Day Show*. Three destitute looking women requested items like a washing machine so that, for example, their kids could have clean clothes for school or a new crib so a child could have a place other than an apple crate to sleep in. The audience would clap for the contestants they thought most deserving, but even as a kid, I considered, with humility, about the two contestants who lost. It seemed very unfair how the poor were exploited and put on display just to sell soap for the big sponsors like Lever Brothers or Procter and Gamble. Sometimes I imagined my mother being on *Queen for A Day* and wondered what she would say would be her needs.

****

Saturday mornings were our day--the kids' day for watching *Andy's Gang* and munching on ginger snack cookies and drinking chocolate milk. *Andy's Gang* was an amazing program with limited special effects. The original program started out as *The Smilin' Ed Gang*, a kid's radio show in the 1940s that eventually came to television in the summer of 1950. In 1955, after Smilin' Ed's death, graveled voice of Andy Divine became the show's new host and was renamed, *Andy's Gang*. Of course, Bunny, Virgil, Sandy, and me, would do a ritual of clapping and singing. We knew all the commercial songs, theme songs and corrected each other if one of us got the lyrics wrong. The commercials were very entertaining and raised many questions for us as we tried to figure out who exactly this kid Buster Brown was? Why did he dress in a broad brim 19th Century sailor's hat and shorts reminiscent of the characters in *Our Gang* movies? At the end of the program, the kid would hold up his little dog and say, "My name is Buster Brown, I live in a shoe [the dog would bark]. This is my dog Tide, he lives in there too." The camera would fade out into a cartoon character of Buster Brown and Tide, which would be located inside the heel of a kid's shoe. We had no idea why a kid and his dog wanted to live in some kid's stinking shoe. It soon dawned on us that the kid was in the business of selling shoes because every boy and girl wanted a pair of them.

One of the main attractions was Midnight, a black cat puppet. There was also a weird and playful gremlin (also a hand puppet) named Froggy. Andy Divine would say to the gremlin, *plunk your magic twanger Froggy,* and there would be a twang sound and Midnight would do amazing tricks like running up a nearby grandfather clock that bonged. Andy's program also showed episodes of old movies. Our favorite one involved an exotic East Indian elephant boy named Sabu, an indigenous Eastern Indian adolescent who fought tigers with his famed dagger, talked to jungle animals, and road around on the backs of elephants. He symbolized a real jungle hero because he was in his own element and not some White character that the media made into a muscle-bound godlike icon beating up on Black people with the help of a chimpanzee, a White boy and a White woman. Sabu did not have massive muscles and his youthful character made him vulnerable and a bit naïve. For me, this made his appeal true to life.

****

After working our paper routes, Saturday evenings ended with the viewing of Jackie Gleason's *The Honey Mooners, Gun Smoke,* and *Paladin.* Sunday evenings ended watching Ed Sullivan's *Toast of the Town.* I remember seeing Elvis Presley for the first time on television. It was a big sensation, and the girls in the audience went crazy. Although Elvis looked young and sultry, he seemed a bit nervous but when he started singing, it reminded me of Black rhythm and blues singers, and I knew he would become a huge success.

The Howdy Doody Show was telecast in the afternoons immediately after school from Doodyville. We'd race from school to our house and become a part of the program. Howdy Doody and Buffalo Bob performed in front of the "Peanut Gallery's" audience made up of visiting children to NBC's television studio in New York City. There were all sorts of Howdy Doody paraphernalia in those

57

days: Howdy Doody coloring books, Howdy Doody comic books, Howdy Doody lunch boxes, Howdy Doody T-shirts, and so on. His cast included Buffalo Bob, the host and originator, a native American Indian maiden named "Princess Winter Fall Summer Spring" who would sing and dance; Flubadub who was a cross between a seal, giraffe, duck, and a couple of other assorted animals; Dilly Dally; Mr. Bluster; and, of course, Clarabelle, the mute clown who communicated by gesturing and honking a couple of horns attached to a box he carried around his waist. Clarabelle also had a rambunctious habit of squirting people with seltzer water from his seltzer bottle, and was up to all type of antics on Buffalo Bob. (The very first Clarabelle was actor Robert James Keeshan who, in 1955, would later start his own kid's morning program, and becoming the person known as Captain Kangaroo.)

Howdy Doody's freckled face--one for each state--had a warm perpetual smile. Actually, he was a marionette dressed like a cowboy and we could easily see his strings. It made no difference to us because he gave an illusion of things good in the Cold War era. He was a real kid to us whose positive attitude toward life gave us a lot of joy.

As I matured, television motivated my young curiosity about the adult world, and I had many questions. I used the media as an educational tool to learn what the world was like both past and present. Most of all, I wanted to know what people were like in other parts of the world.

On Sunday afternoons, I enjoyed watching, with great interest, Alistair B. Cooke's *Omnibus* program. *Omnibus* had an entirely different approach to television. It was not only educational, but it dramatized history in very compelling way. Commercials seemed less intrusive and there was no hype and promotion of products, although the program did have sponsors. Alistair B. Cooke, the English-American journalist, who spoke with decorum of an English gentleman, hosted the weekly program. Every year around Lincoln's birthday, he presented an awe-inspiring performance and narrative about the life and times of Abraham Lincoln. And I vividly recall Alistair B. Cooke reading *Chicago* by the poet, Carl Sandburg. And I envisioned the city with *big shoulders* and was awestruck. The weekly series of *Omnibus* thoroughly hooked me on my awareness of thing outside my life on South Lane Street.

****

When Walt Disney introduced Annette Funicello of The Mickey Mouse Club to the eyes of the public in 1955, it was love at first sight for most pubescent males. From her first appearance as a Musketeer, she oozed stardom. It wasn't just her bright eyes and glistening smile that made her so attractive. It was also her budding womanhood, concealed beneath the white sweaters she wore, that drew the affections of every adolescent boy's dream. Every boy wished that he had Superman's X-ray vision so he could see through the sweaters she wore. As Annette's body matured on the set, all the wrappings and clothing adjustments that Walt Disney attempted to hide only increased America's pre-teen males' growing sexual awareness. Simply put, she was hot, and I would watch her with utter fascination.

Dick Clark's *American Bandstand* made its debut on national television in 1952 and visually introduced rock and roll into the living rooms of America. During its heyday around 1955, it produced doo-wop hits for the teenage public. Broadcasting from Philadelphia after school every day, it replaced Howdy Doody in our home as we grew into our early teens. On Saturday evenings when Dick Clark aired his *American Bandstand* program, we anxiously waited for the countdown of America's weekly top ten Rock n' Roll hits. The *American Bandstand* was a precursor to today's *MTV, VH1,* and *Soul Train*. What Dick Clark did for Rock n' Roll, he also did for pimples--the teenage plague. Pimple pharmaceutical products that sponsored the program made millions from the marketing of Rock n' Roll.

Dick Clark's Philadelphia-based production made a remarkably positive impression on America's White parents, who weren't threatened by his clean-cut grin. He looked like a high school teacher. Telecast in the city of "brotherly love," where high school kids danced after school, *American Bandstand* seemed harmless enough to most parents around the country. Clark hosted live Rock n' Roll singers like Chubby Checkers, Jackie Wilson, Little Richard, Deon and the Belmonts, Shep and the Limelights, Fabian, Bo Didley, Little Anthony and the Imperials, and a host of doo-whoppers and rockabillies. The introduction of new dances and Rock n' Roll songs caused a whole new generation of American kids who rocked to the beat of the music. It was, however, obvious to anyone looking at the program that whenever Black kids were dancing, the camera would immediately jerk away and focus on the White kids dancing. Once I saw a Black guy dancing with a White girl when the screen suddenly became blurred as the camera jerked away and to the floor, only to return abruptly to a group of White dancers. This was no accident and it happened too often. Although, Black guest artists could sing and dance on the show as entertainers, Philadelphia's Black teenagers were not shown enjoying life like their White counter-parts.

I became disenchanted and bewildered with Mr. Clark's show, like other Black teenagers across the country. Philadelphia, which boasted of being the city of "brotherly love," seemed at odds with itself and made me very suspicious of that city as well as Mr. Clark himself. Obviously he enjoyed Black music and profited from the image of the music's origins. But he ran a program that blatantly promoted bigotry to millions of viewers across America. Oh, one could argue that it wasn't his fault It, however, was wrong, pure and simple. A generation of minority youths felt short-changed and unwanted on one of the most popular televised programs in America. In a few years, those minorities would grow up having to fight (and die) in an immoral war. The show's name symbolized the irony and hypocrisy much like the "flesh colored" pimple products peddled on the program. In essence, Mr. Clark, with the aid of Rock n' Roll minstrels, promoted a very effective 20th century medicine show.

*Charlie, my dad's smug-looking face is like that because of his love of cigar smoking and restless habit of sucking on his upper front teeth. However, if you visualize no cigar, and look into his eyes, you'll see a gentle, kindhearted, diminutive, hardworking former farmer turned swing-shift factory worker of 47 years. I've only seen him wear a shirt and tie twice: When he pulled out a pistol on Willie, my stepfather for abusing me and my two brothers; and at his own funeral. I painted this portrait of him proudly displaying his **Federal Glass** employee badge and work clothes.*

From Farm to Factory
Chapter Seven

M y father, for some strange reason, insisted everyone, including his children, call him by the familiarity of his first name, "Charlie." He and his older brother Phoebe grew up on a small pig farm in Madison County, Ohio, between Dayton and Columbus with their father, Poppy. In 1926, at the age of twenty, Charlie pilfered one of Poppy's pigs, purchased a Model T Ford, and headed east for Columbus. There he found work at The Federal Glass Factory located in the industrial Southside of the city where he met a young coworker named Burke Clark who introduced Charlie to his attractive young widowed sister, Viola. A few years later they were married and three sons were born only a year apart from each other. I was the middle son and was christened with Charlie's name. It would be fifteen years after Charlie left the pig farm that Poppy was diagnosed with cancer and moved in our house where Mom looked after him.

I have few memories of my grandfather, Poppy, who died in one of the two upstairs' bedrooms in our small house when I was about three. The memories that I do have, however, are golden. Poppy was tall with a smooth coffee complexion under his gray stubble beard, and he was a gifted musician. His gentle eyes looked down at me from his sick bed, and he smelled of tobacco and earth. I was told that he was dying of stomach cancer, but I had no clue about death or cancer. I only knew that it was fun being around him, and I enjoyed playing with his stubble face as he slept—or pretended to sleep.

On many occasions, Charlie indicated to me how gifted and resourceful Poppy used to be. He made his earning from various manual labor jobs, singing, and playing the Blues on his acoustic guitar in the various Southern and Appalachian Black juke joints. His auspicious winnings from his compulsive crap and poker habit enabled him to leave Norfolk, Virginia, and purchase the small farm in Madison County, Ohio. Although dying in his sick bed, he continued to sing and play his prized acoustic guitar, which he strummed in the upstairs' bedroom. His songs were earthy and imbued a timeless quality of color and smells defining a bygone era.

Tall, lanky, and musically gifted, Poppy was a direct

contrast to Charlie who was short, squatty and couldn't carry a tune in a bucket if his life depended on it. And when it came to high stakes gambling, Charlie merely played the daily numbers game. When Ohio decided to legalize the numbers in the form of the lottery, my father played regularly, hitting a few times from the advice of one of his proverbial illustrated dream (numbers) books.

In one of the two bedrooms upstairs, Poppy rested and Mom brought food and nursed him. I loved it when he sang and played just for me. The guitar lay either with him on his bed or underneath where he could reach for it with little effort. I enjoyed going to his room, running my little fingers over the strings, and was intrigued by the low resonating sounds that came from this peculiar toy box. Awakened by my commotion, he would lean over the bed; look down at me and with smiling eyes that gleamed through a gray stubble beard. Sometimes Mom would chase me away, telling me to let Poppy rest. He didn't seem to mind though. At times, he even tried to teach me a few chords. His large hands guided mine over the thin metal strings, strumming low sounds with an ambiance of Henry O. Turner's, *The Banjo Lesson*. He would play and sing, I would imitate his sounds and hand movements. Brushing back time, I vividly recall those tender moments etched permanently in my mind of Poppy and me playing and singing. Little did I know that I would be his last audience.

Charlie worked at the scorching Federal Glass factory, and like his peers, took pride in his work. One day during one of Poppy's long naps, and being bored, I discovered that the thin wood veneer covering his guitar was easy to peel off. I started striping off some of the wood and then I began disassembling the strings. When my father came in the room and saw the damage I had done, he became very angry and I received my first and only spanking by him. I now know what perpetrated his feelings--the guitar, a symbol of his father, and lay in shreds next to the tangled strings. The commotion of my spanking awakened Poppy who was able to quickly quell my father's anger. Poppy then took me in his arms and held me, saying it didn't matter and it was just an old worthless guitar. A few days later I saw Charlie and my Uncle Phoebe descending the narrow stairs carrying Poppy's long stiff body

63

draped in the green wool Army blanket that he slept on. Both Charlie and Uncle Phoebe, I recall, wore long overcoats and wide brimmed fedoras. I stood in the kitchen holding Mom's hand watching them walk quickly past us to an awaiting hearse outside. I felt a deep, dreadful sensation and noticed tears on my mother's cheeks. She gathered my two brothers and me together and wrapped her arms tightly around us. It was my first experience of mourning.

****

Probably the first time I ever heard Jesus Christ's name came from the lips of Charlie. When he became frustrated, irritated, or angry, he would call out Jesus' name in vain. Charlie's exasperation was usually due to my mother's spending habits in which my father sometimes provided Jesus with a middle initial "H" to emphasize his aggravation.

"Jesus H. Christ, Viola, you think money grows on trees?" he would say, to which Mom would reply, "You shouldn't use the Lord's name in vain like that."

"Goddamit woman, you spend money faster than I make it. Christ Almighty!"

Charlie had genuine respect for Jesus, but His name was a good part of my father's Federal Glass factory vocabulary. I would often observe my mother and father's verbal tennis match moving my young head from left to right. Although Charlie seemed upset, the confrontations never became physical. I believe he enjoyed a good passionate argument with Mom. He could never win and he knew it. For the most part, it was simply a slapstick tongue-in-cheek venting act. Sometimes he would catch himself in the heat of a quarrel and suddenly burst out laughing. But if for some reason he didn't find the situation funny, he'd stomp outside and dig into his sweat stained Federal Glass work shirt pocket and pull out a bag of Red Man or Mail Pouch chewing tobacco. He'd stuff his mouth with the shredded stuff, chew, mumble a few more cuss words to himself, and spit perfect brown arches in the air that landed onto the black dirt yard that surrounded our house.

Mom never allowed her children to use the Lord's name like Charlie. We'd get slapped upside the head and then listen to her sermonize the prospect of burning up in hell. No, that was one thing we were not permitted to do. The Lord's name was sacred and not to be played with, but we got used to Charlie's cussing as Mom went about doing her house chores shaking her head in disgust and repeatedly telling him not to say such things like that in front of the kids.

****

Charlie and Mom divorced between my first and second grade school years. Shortly after Charlie left, Mom married Willie Howard, a tall enigmatic stranger I had seen a few times around the neighborhood. From the moment I first set eyes on him, I had a dread suspicion about him. Children can sometimes detect evil better than adults.

When we were old enough to ride the bus, one of the bi-monthly tasks Virgil and I had to do, was to visit Charlie to collect the alimony and child support money mandated by Judge Rose's divorce court. Charlie now lived deep in the Southside of Columbus near where the Parsons Avenue bus line terminated. He resided at various places in that part of town and always close to the Federal Glass factory where he could easily walk to work. From the bus stop on Parsons Avenue near our house, it took about twenty minutes to ride to his place. I had strong apprehensions about these bi-monthly visits and deeply dreaded my task. This went on for years, but it was also a relief getting away from Mom's new husband, Willie. Charlie's eyes sparkled when he saw us, but he knew the purpose of our mission. I also understood my responsibility given by Mom, yet those were the rare occasions that I despised her influence over me. I resented the bill collector assignment, but I rejoiced at having the chance to be in my father's presence.

"Here," he would say thrusting the money in my hands, "give this to your mother, and tell Viola if she died today, I would not go to her funeral."

Each time he said that, it was like having a knife stabbed deep into my chest. Of course, I knew he didn't mean it; I was becoming old enough now to realize that the words he spewed came from hurt and loss. After uttering those words, he would lie down on his soiled bed, with his oily, sweat stained work clothes, face the wall and close his eyes. I would sit next to him and hold one of his hands and try to make small talk--usually about school. I could not bear his suffering much longer, so on my eleventh birthday, I prayed that God would allow him to outlive me. His life seemed so unfair. Charlie's only relief seemed to be his job, drinking cheap beer, and playing the numbers as The Federal Glass Company became his world.

Charlie lived in various squalid rooming houses above bars or used furniture stores around Parsons Avenue. It was depressing seeing his paltry living conditions, and I can clearly remember the music that drifted through the smoke, laughter, and chatter from the Moon Glow Bar and Grill. And during the long winter nights, the Black juke joint's large neon lights blinked a scarlet glow into the lonely interior of Charlie's room. His rooms, as a rule, were small, dark, sultry, and smelled of sweat, factory oil, and cigar or pipe smoke. His life now rotated around his job. It was a revolving door where he went to work, came home, slept, and went back to work again. When he wasn't working, he lived in a state of depression, dragging sorrow around with him like a ball and chain. Seeing the contrast of his life when he had lived with us on South Lane, to the pathetic life of his current conditions, deeply affected me. From the once jovial father of South Lane Street to the brooding shell of a man who lived in small rooming houses above the various bars on Parsons Avenue, his pain was three-dimensional. One could see and feel it from all angles. He wore pain like a heavy overcoat, and it was devastating for me to see him so hurt. Besides being depressed, he was very lonely. The divorce from Mom seemed to have extracted all the life from him. All that remained was a heap of human pulp. He was shattered, and I felt rotten taking his hard-earned money.

The initiation of Charlie's alimony and child support came from a bizarre domestic courtroom ruling by the infamous Judge Rose who sanctioned the divorce in favor of Mom as he did for all women who had the fortune of coming before his bench whenever he presided over the Franklin County Common Pleas Court of Domestic Relations. Men, on the other hand, had reasons to fear Judge Rose, simply because he wielded his verdicts, more often than

66

not, in favor of women no matter how reckless a woman may have been in matrimony. Indeed, Judge Rose was a woman's true champion. When presiding over a domestic ruling in court, he had a peculiar habit of proclaiming all females in the possessive tense by referring to them as *his* women. I can just envision my father standing in front of Judge Rose wearing the only attire I had known him to wear--factory workmen's clothes. Maybe he wore a clean pair of green working trousers and a matching green shirt with the red and black Federal Glass logo above his left breast pocket. (I had only seen my father three times wearing a suit and tie. The first time, I was two or three when he and Uncle Phoebe carried my grandfather Poppy out of the house onto a hearse. The second was when he drew a pistol on Willie, and the third was many years later as he lay in his casket.)

I can envision Mom's Appalachian innocence at the divorce proceedings wearing the calf-length lavender dress with large beige orchards printed on it she often wore when dressing up. And I can also imagine the chagrin of Charlie's lawyer seeing her in it in Judge Rose's courtroom. Her shoulder length hair would have been pulled into a fashionable post-war pompadour and her appearance must have been absolutely stunning.

****

Charlie had previously been married before he met my mother. His first marriage to Mammie resulted in their only child, a daughter they named Christine. I have no idea how long their marriage lasted, but Mammie, a short, plump, coffee-brown woman worked as a maid at the Neil House Hotel in the heart of Columbus. Her roundness was not obesity; she was a solid woman in excellent shape from years of walking in front of the Neil House wearing a placard saying, "On Strike." The union's grievances with the Neil House led to ten or more years of pacing back and forth in front of Neil House in the rain, snow, and heat of summer. Mammie became an amicable downtown fixture who took her position earnestly. For some reason, she was the only person in the union--as far as I know--who walked the Neil House Hotel post braving the elements and stares. She walked her post so long that people became accustomed to her downtown presence. She stood out from the business-suited patrons who respected her ownership of the piece of real estate she paced. If it were in the wintertime, she would be bundled up, wearing earmuffs, scarves, gloves, and rubber galoshes. During the warmer seasons she would wear light colored clothing and an enormous straw hat befitting of a Southern field worker. The truth of the matter is that she looked out of place in any season. However, those downtown business patrons who got to know her didn't judge her for the character of her clothes, but for the person who wore them. It got to a point that they ignored the position of the union's grievance and conversed with her as a woman with a strong conviction and sincere ideology. Mammie was an angel in many respects.

The weather was always a fitting topic of conversation before Mammie questioned me about the well-being of my brothers, sisters, and Mom whenever she snared me in her amicable web. Whenever I went downtown to the Palace Theater, I would often cross her path. When I was growing in my formative years, I felt embarrassed by her one-person picketing campaign and I tried to avoid running into her if possible. I didn't want her wearing a protest placard in the heart of the city to stop and talk with me. Being a typical pre-teen, it was easy for me to feel embarrassed talking with a woman wearing funny garb and a picket sign. If I unexpectedly saw Mammie in a distance, I would quickly seek an escape by redirecting my route or nonchalantly trying to slip pass her hoping she would not recognize me, but she had keen eyes and she would spot me out yards away.

"Sugar Pie, is that you?" I would cringe as usual whenever hearing my nickname in public—and this was in the heart of Columbus where I felt God and everyone heard her. If I were with friends who didn't know my nickname, the same scenario always occurred: they would look at me with high arched eyebrows and try their best to compress a gut-busting laugh. Later my nickname would be mocked merciless by them saying, "Sugar Pie. Oh, Sugar Pie."

Mammie would amble over with a big smile and introduce herself to my friends and afterwards give me a warm hug. During those downtown conversations, she would ask me when the last time I saw my father. Although I saw Charlie bi-weekly on my alimony collecting assignments, I would never mention my mission. And, I found it odd how she cared about Mom's welfare without a sign of malevolence.

I genuinely liked Mammie. Years came and went and as I grew older, I became less inhibited about the downtown crowd's impression of me talking with her. She was, without question, a humble human being--much like Charlie. She and Charlie even resembled each other in looks and also in character: they both worked hard, held the same doggedly work ethic and enjoyed what little they had. Both complemented each other's alter ego with their integrity and demeanor to the point it could easily be consider them as one personality. Perhaps a better term would be *soul-mates*, and I often wondered why they divorced. I can only imagine how she must have felt when they divorced and Charlie married my mother.

Speaking with Mammie there, out in the open, in the heart of bustling downtown Columbus rain or shine dutifully wearing her union-picketing placard, I could tell she did not harbor any resentment or hard feelings for my mother or Charlie. She would take off her wool knitted gloves and dig down into her pocket and pull out some money and handed it to me for treats at the movies. I would protest telling her no thanks, but she would thrust the money in my hands and gently closing her hands over mind. Then give me a hug and a smile, and abruptly, turn away and continue walking her circle in front of the Neil House Hotel. In 1980, when the Neil House unexpectedly closed, did Mammie discontinued picketing.

****

After Mom divorced Charlie, he remained single until I was a grown man. Mary, a neighborhood alcoholic, opened Charlie's window one late autumn night, climbed in and slept on his kitchen floor. When my father went to his kitchen the next morning, he was surprised to discover a strange woman lying comfortably passed-out under the opened window. She came into his life when he was lonely and growing old. He took Mary in, cleaned her up, and

69

married her much to the chagrin of everyone--even Mom. But Charlie claimed that at his age he needed company. It took me years to understand what he meant by that. Mary did, however, provide him a semblance of home. She offered him some much-needed affection as well as someone to come home to after work. Just before he retired, he did something unusual, with his new bride; he purchased a small cottage away from the familiar Federal Glass proximity of the deep Southside. His new home was not far from our old Street neighborhood and close to Mom's new house. Charlie's new home was also walking distance to Mammie's home. She had retired and essentially became a cheerful recluse in her home. I don't believe that she ever remarried. Mom lived only seven blocks away from Charlie's new place, but it may as well have been seven hundred miles. She had made a good transaction with the Bonded Oil Company and sold the old house and moved the family into a beautiful big two-story brick house in a neighborhood near Livingston Avenue Park. With the new house, she, like Charlie, decided to remarry. Archie (my sister Sandy's father) would be Mom's last husband. I was in the Marines stationed in Camp Pendleton, California, when all this occurred.

The small-framed cottage that Charlie bought was a joy to him and he took pride in once again having a real home with a wife. He planted a garden in the backyard and pruned the Cherry and Plum trees that grew there. It was such a cheerful contrast from the dingy claustrophobic rooming houses that he previously lived in. Even Mary took pride in helping him with the chores and decoration, especially during the Christmas season. This brought stability into Charlie's life and home. He allowed her total freedom and offered help when he could. During Easter, there were Easter eggs, chocolate bunnies, and jellybeans all over the place, but it was Christmas that Mary relished. One Christmas, she lavishly decorated a tree and set it in the front window for the entire world to see. (The multicolored lights, shiny thin strips of foil, colored bulbs, the whole works.) It looked splendid and I was impressed. The Christmas tree, however, remained lit and decorated in the front window all year long including two Easters. In the muggy summer evenings, during the time of the fireflies and crickets serenading, people passed the house to marvel or giggle at the display. And, if they listened closely, they could hear emanating from a hi-fi in the living room Christmas music and Mary's inebriated singing voice.

****

One day, out of the blue, Mary brought home a pet monkey. Charlie, having been raised on a farm, loved animals and grew very fond of the monkey. Charlie now newly retired from The Federal Glass Company, had plenty of time on his hands, and the monkey proved to be a thing of joy for both of them. I have to admit, I was impressed. My initial reaction to the monkey was shock when I visited the house, not knowing anything about their new houseguest. I was freshly back from the war in Southeast Asia and my reflexes were still quite effective as they was tested when I entered their home. I usually knocked, hollered, "It's only me," and walked in. This time, however, after knocking and entering, I noticed a dark blur on my left peripheral vision causing me to suddenly duck to see an incoming monkey heading straight for my head. The damned thing shot past my face and landed gracefully on the living room curtains.

"Holy shit!" I yelled and noticed Charlie and Mary gleefully laughing. They had set me up knowing my procedure of entering their home. Still somewhat in shock, and having almost pissed in my pants, I couldn't help but seeing them together, laughing that produced a mental snapshot of the happiness my father deserved. Their laughter became infectious and I too joined them as the butt of their amusement. Then they proudly proclaimed that the monkey had just returned from Cuba after the plane it was on had been hijacked en route to Columbus from Miami. This was during the 1970's when there was a lot of skyjacking occurring around the world.

Charlie and Mary named the monkey *Castro* since it had been to Havana. And Castro soon became a popular sensation around my father's new blue-collar working-class neighborhood. Castro was kept inside the house and would scamper around the place jumping from lamps to curtains and on top of the refrigerator

71

scaring the hell out of people not expecting a flying monkey in my father's house. Besides feeding him bananas and other assorted fruits, Charlie also fed him fried bacon strips. Actually, Castro became addicted to fried bacon, which was news to me because I thought monkeys were vegetarians. His thin furry hands were very human-like, and it was odd looking at Castro directly in his eyes. He had a furlong look that revealed human-like sensitivity and stared at you as if he understood what was going on. They would walk down the street with Castro perched on Charlie's head or draped around Mary's shoulders, which for me was very evocative to a modern day, *A Sunday Afternoon on the Island of La Grande Jatte* painting by George Seurat.

Whenever someone came over, the doors were never opened very wide for fear the monkey would escape through the smallest crack. It eventually did escape one day when the door was opened a little too wide and Castro flew out seeking his freedom. He scampered up the backyard Cherry tree, then the Sycamore tree, and finally leaped onto a telephone pole swinging freely. Castro swung effortlessly up and down the back alley trees and telephone poles that lined alleys and backyards of the neighborhood. For days, Charlie tried coaxing Castro back waving bacon strips and bananas but it was useless. Once Castro had his freedom, he was no longer interested in returning home for bacon or anything else. And it was sad watching my father trying to cajole Castro to come home. We all watched with utter amazement as he leaped around the neighborhood obviously enjoying his freedom and totally oblivious to my father's beckoning. It soon became a backyard event for the neighbors. They stopped cutting their backyard grass, or glanced up from grilling their burgers and hotdogs as kids ran down the alley shouting at Castro with barking dogs in pursuit. It was a Norman Rockwell American moment, a summertime sensation when neighbors who never spoke to one another, now pointed up to the trees and carried on conversations. They brought out their lawn chair and tables, invited other over for a better view to watch Castro perform his talents. Hell, Castro was "Mr. Entertainment!" He was show business. The only thing he lacked was a top hat, cane, and a pair of spats. Even my father was impressed after giving up on capturing him. Like the rest of the backyard neighborhood, he and Mary sat down in their backyard, sipped their beers, and watched the show. Eventually Castro disappeared. I think he was caught by one of the street-wise alley cats that lived in the neighborhood.

****

Not soon after the loss of Castro, Mary bought a black French Toy Poodle puppy. Charlie fell in love with it too and named it *Beauty*. Beauty yapped too much as far as I was concerned. It got on my nerves and I remember asking my father what in the hell did he see in French Poodles? I told him that they seemed like sissy dogs. I mean why not a *real* dog like a Labrador Retriever or a Boxer? He merely looked at me, picked Beauty up, and kissed her. *Lord,* I thought, *he's flipped out.*

Mary and Charlie would go for walks with Beauty and later mated her with a male poodle and there were puppy poodles all over the place. The puppies were left in Charlie's care most of the time because Mary would be off on one of her many extended excursions, usually to California. The puppies were all over the house, on his bed, under the kitchen table, under the sofa, yapping and scampering all over the place. Eventually, people came by to purchase the puppies and Charlie sold all of them except Beauty. Beauty soon became the sole poodle and a comfort to Charlie. He let her coat grow and gave her freedom to run around the back yard.

A few years later when I attended graduate school in Cincinnati, I drove home to visit my father. Mary was out of town again. When I entered the house, I found Charlie lying in bed with his clothes on. He looked at me sadly and said that Beauty had been hit by a car and killed a week ago. He got up only to sit on a chair in the kitchen. Folding his arms on the kitchen table, he sank his head heavily to his chest and began to cry. I looked at his moist, unshaven cheeks, and I witnessed Charlie, my father, for the first time in my life, crying. He was crushed. I felt miserable.

****

Years before he met Mary, Charlie had been living in a first floor rooming house off Parsons Avenue, walking distance to his job at the Federal Glass Company, and befriended a White Appalachian couple from West Virginia, Raymond and his wife Peggy. Raymond was a retired railroad worker who drew a pension after hurting his back somehow, and his Peggy worked odd cashiering jobs in local neighborhood stores. They were chain smokers and they were a laid-back, easygoing couple probably in their early forties. They had an old emaciated apple tree in their back yard that produced emaciated apples. For some reason, they gave Charlie a bushel of half rotten apples that were full of worms. Charlie said that they were perfect for making wine. He made the brew in an old galvanized tub, which he washed his clothes and soaked his feet in. The vat was kept inside his room for a couple of months. In the hot summer, he lugged it outside in the heat, covered it with cheesecloth where it frothed, foamed, and drew fruit flies. The cruddy concoction had in it apple bits, apple worms, flies, and other assorted objects floating on it. When ready, he'd siphon the mixture into empty glass Clorox bleach jars, and between fillings; he'd dip a mug into the vat, wipe off whatever was floating on it, and drink. All his friends swore by it saying it was even better than *Thunderbird.* When offered a sample, I only had to remember what had been floating in the vat and politely declined.

Sometimes when I visited, I'd find Charlie in the backyard of the rooming house under a tree with six or seven of his old neighborhood cronies who came to taste his wine. Some lived in the same rooming house and others lived near. No one, for some reason, drove a car. Outside under the shade of a lone Elm tree, they swatted flies, and told lies, while listening to the Cleveland Indians, Pittsburgh Pirates or Cincinnati Reds baseball games blaring from an old Westinghouse radio with a coat hanger attached to it that served as an antennae. They argued who was the best team or player. They were split, however, between the Pittsburgh Pirates and Cincinnati Reds and loud arguments ensued whenever the two teams played each other. My father was an avid Cincinnati Reds fan but, whenever they happened to play against the Pittsburgh Pirates, he'd root for Roberto Clementé. They were all honest workingmen who became more animated with each inning as Charlie's apple wine circulated throughout their blood system. By the seventh inning, they were totally smashed. Usually, Raymond would be the last one left, passing out on a chair. Later, in their friendship, he visited Charlie almost every day staying late hours until his wife would have to come and drag him home. Raymond told me that my father's wine was the best he'd ever tasted causing Charlie to feel obliged to keep the vat full for their social libations. Unfortunately, Raymond became addicted to my father's apple wine, and he died within a year. He may have died from another ailment, but Charlie blamed himself for his friend's demise and curtailed his own drinking. He threw out the remainder of the batch and swore never to make any more wine. He only started drinking again with the arrival of Mary.

****

Throughout their marriage, I constantly rebelled against Mary's drinking and her influence on Charlie's increasing consumption of alcohol. He drank more than I had ever seen him drink before. There were times when I visited and found him sitting at the kitchen table grinning at an empty bottle of Old Granddad, drunk to high heavens with a grin stretched across his face of pure content. It was difficult to watch him become so attached to Mary's drinking ways. My noble father had now succumbed to this. I had seen what alcohol did to Willie and later Archie, Mom's last husband. Willie drank to hide from himself, and his demons made him brutal, but seeing Charlie drink in excess was bizarre, because years before he met Mary, he felt guilty for the death of Raymond. Mary now controlled my father with alcohol, and he drank to appease her. I think he was afraid of being alone. He would have done almost anything for her to make her feel appreciated and wanted. But Mary had alternate plans. She had an agenda that was manipulative and self-serving. She would get Charlie drunk, take his money, and go away for months at a time. On several occasions, she went to California only to return home broke and famished. She even had plastic surgery with silicone injected into her thin calves, scrawny hips and God knows where else. But Charlie's love for her was unconditional, all forgiving, and he vigorously defended her faults and troubled ways.

****

There were rare times when I found Mary sober. During these brief moments, I could easily see why the former heavyweight boxer Ezzard Charles dated her. Mary had a mannequin-like figure, and she could not have weighed more than 100 pounds if that. Although she tried covering-up her emaciated frame by wearing expensive clothes, the years of alcohol abuse had diminished much of her body, and her clothes hung on her like Spanish moss. And her thin lips conversed in intoxicated ranges of high-pitched whines to low moan syllable slurs. Perhaps it was from the plastic surgery, but she didn't have a wrinkle anywhere. Mary's smooth face appeared to be tight as though someone had pulled her skin and tied it behind the nape of her neck.

In a faded sepia colored picture, taken many years ago (that she loved showing to guests), was an elegant, beautiful woman sitting gracefully cross-legged on a piano whose bare shoulders were draped with a fox stole and obviously was quite the center of attention of the smiling faces of the heavyweight boxer, Ezzard Charles and famous jazz musician, Count Basie.

One couldn't help but notice her long tapered fingers holding a lengthy cigarette holder in one hand and a champagne glass in the other, smiling solicitously at the camera. Time, hard times, had now caused her long tapered fingers to habitually choke a filtered cigarette butt in one hand, and cuddle a half-empty bottle of *Old Granddad* with the other. The faded images she possessed of earlier times of the beautiful young woman, cavorting with Black musicians and boxers, at the various places she had lived from coast to coast, were quite a contrast to the person she would become: lost in an embryonic womb and suspended in an amniotic elixir of booze. I imagine those long-ago nightclub images and big-band melodies continued living in her head until her last breath. Mary promenaded through life, in a Scott Fitzgerald-*ish* world as if at any moment she would receive a standing ovation.

****

Actually, though, Mary did restore Charlie's love for animals and the soil. It seemed so natural for him to return to the soil from the factory. The son of a farmer, and an avid gardener, Charlie took care of Mary the way one takes care of a garden. He tended to her needs and tried weeding out her problems. But Mary took too many lengthy trips away from my father. By the time she returned from her last California excursion, she could not persuade him to take her back, even after having a facelift procedure done while she was in California. It was also purported from her that she was involved with a California motorcycle gang, in a drug scheme that had gone bad. Charlie was totally clueless about her alternate life until he found out from one of Mary's California relatives during a telephone conversation. He definitely did not want any part of any illegal activity. Eventually, she moved into a small apartment above a nearby used furniture store with the help of some of Charlie's meager financial support. There she entertained and continued drinking and whatever else. A year after their separation, Mary was found dead in her apartment. She was 76, and had been dead for two weeks or more.

****

Whenever I arrived in town, I would visit and tell Charlie about my progress in graduate school and discuss the scenery of central Pennsylvania. He would listen, chew on his lower lip (that was a habit), smoke his cigars, and talk about the lottery that he had just missed by a few numbers. And in the springtime he would show me his turnip, collard greens, okra, and tomatoes growing in the back yard. I'd drink beer with him and offer to take him to the store to purchase a newspaper and lottery tickets. I noticed how slow he was beginning to move, and when he noticed me, he'd do an animated jump-dance movement. Except for a few beers, his drinking had completely stopped after Mary left. Although he displayed a fiercely independent manner, I knew he was once again lonely. He seemed, however, resolved and at peace with his situation of growing old and being alone.

Sometimes we went to visit Bunny in one of the small towns where he was incarcerated. The drive to London, Lucasville,

Marion, Chillicothe or other places where my brother had been imprisoned always posed a solemn time with my father as I drove. He'd look out the window at the scenery and maybe reflect on the weather—the snowy hills of winter, the rolling autumn farm fields, or the sticky heat of summer. These moments seemed to be a chance for him to see his beloved Ohio. It was a chance to see Bunny also, his eldest son. We sometimes talked about those small communities where the penal colonies are located and how it seems such a direct contrast to the surroundings of beautiful stretches of farms that suddenly erupted into an infusion of red brick institutional buildings surrounded by high fences and shiny barbed wire. All the penal colonies looked the same. And many of the correctional guards come from those rural areas, which seemed such a cautious contrast to those who were imprisoned--mostly urban, street-wise, and predominately young Black males—a bizarre paradox. Our comments on the drive back to Columbus would be calm except for the drone of the radio. Once he blurted out, "If I could, I'd do anything to get Bunny out... no one belongs in a cage."

****

With Mary gone and no animals to care for, Charlie began to make nightly phone calls to Mom, but he never visited. I think he wanted to visit her, but was inhibited. Maybe he wanted to avoid being hurt. The four marriages Mom had after leaving him must have tormented him. Each time she went down the aisle, he made devious remarks like was she trying to break Liz Taylor's record. As they aged, however, Charlie's remarks about Mom became ambivalent and less severe.

Chapter Eight

THE ONLY PLEASURE *my brothers and I had in getting even with Willie was when he ordered me to make him coffee. He seemed to like my way of preparing him the instant brew that he so much loved to drink. This provided me, Bunny and Virgil the opportunity to express our creativeness. We would hurry in our bedroom where we each peed small amounts of urine in the coffee mug. Since Bunny and Virgil were not circumcised, they had an endless supply of "cottage cheese" under their foreskins to "cream" his coffee. We then spat globs of sputum in the mug and I mixed the remaining contents of instant coffee, hot water, cream and sugar. When I handed Willie his mug of coffee, he would say,*

"Nigger, you can't do anything right, but you sure can make a damn good cup of coffee."   He never complemented me on anything else. Grinning obsequiously, I would say, "Just let me know when you need a refill."

****

During the late summer of 1950, when I impatiently anticipated going into Mrs. Katz's second grade classroom at Beck Street Elementary School, Mom's divorce to Charlie and her subsequent marriage to Willie Howard, hit me hard. I had no idea why they divorced. Even worse, I had no idea why she married Willie. One day Charlie was gone and a week or so later, Willie entered our home and our lives. There were no formal wedding ceremony preparations, no family planning or discussion--just the presence of a very tall, grim-faced stranger who moved into our home. We soon realized that his living under the same roof caused great trepidation and a substantial amount of emotional trauma that continued well into our adult lives. Within three years, his presence would drive Virgil and me to work late into the evenings six nights a week. We felt it was better to take our chances in the streets selling papers and shining shoes than to be at home with him. And Willie seemed to take pleasure in our being away from home working. Little did Mom know that we simply wanted to stay away from her new husband. Our home life was not the same after Willie's arrival.

People called Willie, "Big Six" because of his six foot six inch tall frame.   He was lean and mean with long sinewy arms. Virgil said that his arms looked liked swinging pendulums. The description fitted him perfectly and he swung his long arms with an unforgiving malice. I also remember his large pink lower lip that contrasted the rest of his dark pigmentation. His larger lower lip protruded as though he was sipping a mug of hot coffee. Hanging from the pink bulbous flab, a cigarette usually dangled. It danced when he talked. He immediately began bellowing orders in our home, and we found ourselves jumping to fulfill them. The first command we were given was to call him "sir" and Mom, "ma'am." It was strange calling Mom ma'am and if we forgot to address him or Mom correctly, he would "backhand" us. Being slapped was a new experience. This new person in our lives and his method of discipline seemed strange and harsh. Mom appeared to be possessed. She grew indifferent to us and attached herself to him in a most peculiar way. I noticed that she had not related to Charlie the way she did Willie. She even started cooking differently by catering to his Southern appetite. We began to eat black-eyed peas, lima beans, Navy beans, and cornbread more than usual. Then Mom started cooking chitterlings and other weird pig things that were an affront to all the food she used to prepare for us. The smell of her cleaning and cooking those horrendous smelly things made it impossible for us to eat. Willie, on the other hand, would say that if we did not want to eat them, then we could starve. So we just ate cornbread and coleslaw, the compliments that came with those meals, and stayed hungry. The most revealing thing I can remember about Willie was the first time I saw him drunk. This was new to me because no one had ever been drunk in our house before. The only drunks we saw on the streets were our next-door neighbors Miss Rosy Woodson or Big Chief. Although Virgil too received severe beatings from Willie, he was smart enough to know how to avoid Willie's wrath by using Big Chief as his advocate. He would take Virgil to baseball games, buy him ice cream cones and invite him over to listen to a baseball game on the radio--especially the Brooklyn Dodgers where Jackie Robinson played second base. But I was often ostracized from their activities and Big Chief would say things like I was too dark or not as smart as Virgil. I became a little jealous of my younger brother especially when Big Chief took Virgil to ball games and not me.

We soon discovered that Mom had married a cruel monster who became more malicious by the minute when he drank. Willie, however, always seemed to have a bad attitude even when sober. He and Mom had only been married for about two weeks when I heard a loud crash in the kitchen. I jumped and ran inside the house to see Willie's huge fist crashing into the softness of Mom's face. Watching her crumpling to the floor proved the most terrible thing I had ever seen in my six and a half years of existence. Mom had been peeling potatoes in preparation for our dinner when he jumped her.

Bunny attempted to shield us from the event by pulling Virgil and me behind him. It was the first time I ever saw my older brother afraid. I was angry and shouted at Willie to leave my mother alone. Tearing myself away from Bunny, I started "selling wolf tickets" shouting as loud as I could in my little boy's voice for him to leave our mother alone. Surprised by my action, he paused with his fist raised for another blow to Mom's face. He glared down at me with jaundiced colored eyes, mumbled some vulgarity, and that's where I saw my chance. I noticed a toilet plunger on the floor near the sink and grabbed it. In my mind, the thing was a sword; I attacked Willie with the rubber end hitting his long legs with everything I had, wanting ever so much to inflict pain. I felt invincible. My rage surpassed all known fear as I hacked away at him with my sword, the toilet plunger. The next thing I knew, the ceiling became the floor and the floor the ceiling as I sailed across the room seemingly in slow motion. I picked myself up surprised that I was not at all hurt, started toward him again when he lurched out the kitchen door, slammed it, and staggered down South Lane Street cursing. I felt good and to my surprise, Bunny, Virgil and Mom remembered my bravery for many years afterwards.

A few days after my mother's beating, my father came and called Willie outside. We were glad to see him and wanted him to stay. He hugged us, patted me on the head and told us to go back inside. He remained in the yard looking intently at the house where he had once belonged and calmly called for Willie to come outside. I knew something was about to take place when I saw Willie languidly came out smoking a cigarette. He immediately started laughing and muttered something insulting about my father's short stature. Charlie stood around five feet four inches tall, if that--so different from Willie. Charlie wore a suit under his trench coat, and sported a brown fedora he looked a lot like James Cagney. He told Willie never to lay a hand on his kids again. Willie quickly interrupted him, retorting with some arrogant comment, and continued mocking my father. He stopped, however, when he was introduced to the business end of a snubbed nosed .38-caliber revolver that my father pulled from the pocket of his trench coat. Willie's hands instantly flew up into the air.

"Yyyes, sir. I'll be g ggood to dddem kids. Don't you worry about me doing aaanything like that again. I've been drinking a little... you know how it is, rrright? Sir, didn't know what I was doing half the time," he said.

I actually wanted my father to pull the goddamn trigger. It was amusing and without a doubt, a pleasure watching Willie becoming completely unglued and kowtowing to my father. Charlie's feathers had been ruffled a little more than he cared for. My father, a man who is the epitome of humbleness, surprised everyone that late afternoon. How did he know about the Gestapo treatments of Willie? Neighbors? I don't know. But I'm sure it bothered him seeing Mom's bruised face. It however, would be Charlie's first and last showdown with Willie. He never returned to our house again for many years. The following weekend after the incident, Willie forgot all his promises he made as the alcohol once again circulated in his blood system and he resumed his old turbulent self. That was the first time I wished I could be instantly transformed into an adult.

****

Wanting to exert more control over us, Willie made it mandatory that we attend *his* church, The Mount Galilee Baptist. Before he entered our lives, we had been going to The Church of God, Virgil's new friend, Maxwell Ware's, church. Mom did not attend, but granted Mrs. Ware permission to take us with them to their Sunday school and church services. The Wares lived a couple of houses down the street. Max's family had just recently come up from Mississippi. He would become Virgil's dearest and long-time friend. They were the same age, in the same grade, enjoyed the same interests. In a word, they were inseparable. Max had a younger brother named Dwight whose hair was much redder than Virgil's. I had a pre-adolescent, puppy love crush on their older sister, Marlene, which lasted for years. She had my heart and soul and I would have done almost anything just to hold her hand. Unfortunately, she hardly even noticed me. I think, to her, I was just an amusing little nappy-headed boy.

Mr. Ware was a World War Two veteran who had purchased a small plot of land on our street. I remember him taking string, cement blocks, and plotting out his homestead. His labor fascinated me. The neighbors were just as fascinated, as they watched him going about his business, digging, hauling, hammering, and sawing, without saying a word to anyone. He was a quiet man building his house all by himself until eventually a few neighbors pitched in and helped. When he moved his family in, I spotted Marlene immediately, and even at my young age, she had to have been one of the prettiest girls I have ever seen. Though she ignored me like the plague, I was smitten by her and fantasized that it would be me who saved her from villains and came to her rescue whenever she needed the services of a super hero. I would be her Superman and she my Lois Lane. Surely I would not reveal my true identity as a super hero who could fly and perform amazing physical feats. Like Clark Kent, I was bound to uphold my identity. But, unlike Clark Kent, my lot in life was compounded because I had to play the role of a poor stuttering little boy. Yet, I remember Marlene's diminutive, doll like ways when she wore white-laced gloves to church. I often tried to impress her when she came out on their small porch to watch us as we played stickball in the street. So, when Mrs. Ware asked my mother if we could attend Sunday school at their church, I was overjoyed. The minister was an intelligent Black woman with silver hair who spoke eloquently. To me, she was an elderly version of Marlene herself. Although my chief reason for attending church had to do with my feelings of love for Marlene, the service did captivate me and I actually understood things during the sermons. I took genuine pleasure in the Sunday school lessons and the regular adult services. I was just beginning to benefit from church when Willie yanked us out of Marlene's church, forcing us to attend *his* church, The Mount Galilee Baptist Church. There was no discussion, only Willie's decision and another ploy for him to exert his control over us. We were to go to *his* church and learn *their* Southern Baptist doctrine—period.

Like many storefront Negro churches in many inner-city communities throughout the United States, Mount Galilee Baptist Church had a humble exterior structure. Located on Mound Street, walking distance from our house, the music and sermons at Galilee Baptist were anything but humble. It came joyfully alive with the help of Reverend Stevens, his deacons, the choir and Sister Helen Lane's piano. Mount Galilee Baptist provided a striking contrast in style and services to the gentle experience of Marlene's church. I resented leaving her church feeling deeply torn from Marlene, but I could not display my real sentiments for fear of being whipped by Willie for being disrespectful. Now I had a negative feeling for religion because of being forced into something I had no choice of the matter. It was like taking castor oil. Willie's method of dispensing castor oil meant him holding a large cooking ladle full of the oil in one hand, and his thin belt in the other. We were to line up as he forced the large ladle in our small mouths, telling us to swallow, and if we gagged he'd thrash us.

Willie's hypocrisy on Sunday mornings was appalling. He put on a good front grinning to the church members, shaking their hands, going through the regular obsequious motions as a good, virtuous, hard working provider who married a woman who had all those kids. If they only knew what he did the previous night--or did they? And for the life of me, I never quite understood what Reverend Stevens or his deacons were saying half the time in the pulpit. It became boring watching the same sideshow every week, and I actually felt that I could have done better. Reverend Stevens began reading from the Bible intelligently, but halfway into the sermon, he would lose me. He began mumbling and grunting indistinguishable sounds causing the older congregation to become "happy." Mom even shouted along with the deacons saying, "Preach Reverend!" This was the cue for the overweight piano player, Sister Helen Lane, to bang out a few blustering chords, which caused Reverend Stevens' tall frame to gyrate and jump up and down waving his handkerchief in the air. This all seemed to further ignite the church. I would look around thinking, "This is crazy. Where is the message? Why can't I go to Marlene's church where things made sense?"

****

At nine-years-old, my spiritual escape from Mount Galilee Baptist Church, and Willie was found on television. I felt that I was in tune with the wonders of God and had a serious emotional and intellectual connection when I viewed Bishop Sheen's broadcast. Watching him, I entered into another state of consciousness where things made sense. For years I enjoyed his mannerisms and how he drew me into his spiritual realm. His eyes were hypnotic and the way he spoke intrigued and lured me in front of the television as I listened to every word he said. Smiling as he usually did, I once remembered him startling the audience by saying: "God is nobody." A strange hush arose from the audience and for a brief moment, I was dumbfounded. How could a man of the cloth say such a thing? Then he repeated very slowly saying, "God...is...no...Body." Then it hit me and I thought how can God be a body when he is a Spiritual being? I got it! I felt smart and in tune because I understood. I really understood and at that moment felt connected with this Catholic Bishop. I instantly considered the priesthood after that, even though I and no one in my family was Catholic. I sincerely wanted to be Catholic because anything seemed better than the clamor and cacophony going on at Mount Galilee Baptist. During those moments, I compared Bishop Sheen's delivery to Reverend Stevenson's. I then imagined myself wearing a Roman collar, saying Mass and giving Communion, speaking audibly in a devout manner, and making sure everyone understood exactly what was being said. Although girls and sex would be introduced far in the future, the idea of being a celibate priest the rest of my life perplexed me. And as I grew older, I felt haunted about my doomed destiny of becoming a priest. Yet, I still enjoyed the idea. I am sure that if I were Catholic, I probably would have become one.

In some way, we endured Willie's church even when we were forced to sing in Sister Helen Lane's junior choir as well as performing in other church related activities. I didn't enjoy Mount Galilee Baptist Church, but I actually did take pleasure in singing and getting to know other kids my age. More than anything, however, I missed Marlene and her church. The chance of sitting next to Marlene, seeing her with those white-laced gloves looking lovely and sedate, left an empty place in my heart knowing that while I was enduring the hectic pace of Mount Galilee, she was sitting quietly in her church looking beautiful. She wouldn't have fit in at Mount Galilee Baptist. I often lost myself day-dreaming about her on those Sunday mornings as I sat perfectly still surrounded by waves of swirling white handkerchiefs and Black hands fanning frantically on Black sweaty faces to the joyous beat and praises of Reverend Stevenson's gyrations and grunt pontifications.

****

Willie seemed to take great pleasure in whipping us as we danced in circles around him. After ordering us to pull down our pants, revealing all our boyhood nakedness, he grabbed us with one of his large hands, jerking us around as he whipped us across our buttocks, backs, legs and arms. The momentum forced us to go counter clockwise withering in pain from each lash as we skipped and dance to his beating. If it was a mass punishment, he made us wait in line while he whipped us one by one as we watched each other skip and hop in painful naked circles for the most minor infractions. We waited our turn in line, in terror. We watched each other in horror, withering in pain. He spared Dottie because she was his blood. Sandy got a few whippings, but Willie mostly concentrated on Bunny, Virgil, and me. (Bunny first, then Virgil, and then myself.) I usually was saved for last. I think he never got over the toilet plunger episode and the time when Charlie pulled a pistol on him. As a consequence, he took the greatest pleasure in whipping and insulting me. And my being named after my father seemed to fuel Willie's frenzy calling me insulting names like: "You Charlie lookin' nappy-headed nigga. You look just like that sawed-off bastard." And I would be slung around in circles like a minute hand on a clock. There was no escape. I had to dance the dance. Hop the hop and bear the pain. Being beaten with a thin leather belt or a stinkweed switch on bare skin really hurt and usually made welts form on our bodies. I grew to hate thin belts and cursed stinkweed trees. The welts on our scrawny arms came when we lifted them trying to protect ourselves from his blows. That would really piss him off and he beat us even harder. It was better to keep hopping and try to bear the blows the best you could without putting up a defense. If we stumbled and fell on the floor, that just gave him the advantage to striking a fallen target. The pain was so excruciating that I thought that if I could only get past the first lash I would be all right. But each blow seemed harder than the last--and each lash hurt. (Really hurt, leaving both physical and emotional scars that remained for decades.) After the whippings, we would huddle in our bedroom sobbing and attending to each other's welts. And my trusted guardian angel and Mom, for some reason, never came to our rescue.

I developed such a fear of Willie that I began to stutter. It was an uncontrollable stutter that never dissipated when I wanted it to. I would shake at anything that seemed like some kind of verbal challenge. It soon developed into an inferiority complex. When I wasn't being beaten, he humiliated me and continued spitting verbal insults at me so much that I began to not like myself. My fear of his punishments remained constant, as did his endless condemnation. It seemed that I could never do anything right. I could not do or be anything but negative. I started to believe that I really was ugly, too dark, and that my hair too nappy. His criticism about my deep chocolate complexion finally drove me to take a bath with chorine-bleach. I never turned lighter. The bleach just irritated my skin. I then resorted to buying jars of skin bleaching cream from the money I kept back from my paper route. I saw the advertisements in *Ebony* magazine for skin bleach, but that too did not work. Having exhausted all my attempts at trying to look lighter, I gave up, resigning myself to the fact that my complexion would always be chocolate and that I'll just have to live with it. I did think it was peculiar, however, why Willie enjoyed calling me names referring to my skin hue when he was darker than me. Nonetheless, with all these psychological and physical beatings, it is surprising I didn't crack-up at pre-puberty. I would often close my eyes and pray silently for God to enable me to become a strong adult for just five minutes. It didn't seem fair growing up this way, wishing to become an adult powerful enough to defend myself and my brothers from an adult tyrant. I wanted to inflict the same pain on him as he was inflicting on us.

It got to the point that whenever Willie called me I trembled. I couldn't help myself. There was a mixture of anger and fear boiling up inside me that surely must have confused my neurons and the only thing I could do was shake and stutter when I talked. Soon, however, he found a most devastating way of humiliating me further; he mocked my stuttering and laughed at me afterwards. I felt even more debased. This stranger who slept in my mother's bed made me feel lost and violated in my own house.

My stuttering affected my school and personal life. I began to be afraid of reading out loud. I'd cringe and break out into a cold sweat when it was my turn to read or present in front of the class. I endured the snickering shame I caused myself. And being next in line for anything provoked an uncontrollable stuttering act. This further fueled my severe inferiority complex. My phobias made me unpopular in school, and my stuttering continued until I was a grown man.

One night in the solitude of our bedroom after a beating, Bunny, Virgil, even little Sandy and I made plans to kill Willie. Rat poisoning his coffee, stabbing him with a butcher knife, and other bizarre thoughts entered our young minds, but we did not know how to go about killing anyone. And what about the possibility of our souls ending up in eternal hell? However, we had had enough. So we rigged a knife on the stairwell landing. The plan called for tying a knife from one of the banister rails just long enough so that it would poke him in the head when he climbed the stairs in a drunken stupor. We went to bed and waited for him to come up the stairs. The plan failed because we used a butter knife that only brushed across his head. He was livid, and we had to face the consequences.

For some fortunate reason, Willie did like the way I made his coffee.

****

When I was going on ten years old entering the fourth grade, Mom divorced Willie and I was happy. Happy? Hell, I was ecstatic. Finally the evil had left our once happy home. It was like I had to pee really bad but couldn't relieve myself until I found a toilet. A serious release came over the house and life was easy. I noticed that my stuttering had stopped and my overall mood felt light, especially when Charlie moved in. Although I do not recall the full circumstances of his arrangement with Mom about moving in, but it was Christmas everyday with him there. The strange thing about it, however, was that he didn't sleep in Mom's bedroom, but instead, he slept in ours. Of course, we loved the idea of Charlie being close to us. When he came home from work he was usually tired. His exhaustion came from working various stints of rotating swing shifts. This seemed to happen every week. He worked swing shifts from the day he started at Federal Glass until his retirement, forty-seven years later. But Charlie took it all in good spirits.

I looked in wonder at the day old rough stubble of graying beard on Charlie's face and took pleasure in watching him shave. After whipping the shaving brush from a mug, he would lather his face in foams of white mounds that contrasted his dark skin. He shaved with an old Gillette razor. The razor blades came in individually wrapped packets and were usually blue steel or copper colored. I would watch him pull the razor across his face, leaving behind smooth dark stripes of brown flesh, and more often than not, deep crimson spots of blood oozed and stained the white lather. I could not figure out how he could go through that ritual. When Charlie finished shaving, he looked like someone had taken an ice pick to his face. He would carefully drape each wound with tiny pieces of toilet paper to absorb his blood. They looked like little Polish flags streaming all over his broad brown face. Shaving was something I knew someday I had to do. The nicking and bleeding made me feel uneasy.

The sound that Charlie made when he slept was half between a snore and quiet exhalation. I used to observe him while he was sleeping and tried imitating his breathing rhythm. He often would pretend to snore by making exaggerated multi-leveled nasal sounds. We knew that he worked hard at the glass factory and could see the burnt scars on his hands and forearms that came from the hot glass. He always seemed to be exhausted but still found time to play with us or answer our childish questions. When he was asleep, I would look at him closely to see if he really was sleeping or not. Invariably, he would open one eye and catch me by surprise, then smile and go back to sleep. Those times with Charlie were blissful. The little things he did were meaningful. Even though Sandy was not from his seed, he protected her from Virgil, Bunny and me, because being boys, we often were rough when we played. Charlie gave Sandy the same love that he imparted on us. Dottie had not been born yet, so this must have been before 1951, which put me at the age of six or seven.

Charlie came home from work (usually at night) dragging himself up the flight of stairs completely exhausted. We would instantly become wide-awake, hearing the slow sounds of his fatigued motion and smelling his sweet pipe smoked clothing. The sound of him opening his black lunch box completed our revitalization, for we knew there would be treats waiting for us. He would fish out large sugar or oatmeal cookies that he purchased from the factory's cafeteria, and sometimes, he surprised us with miniature (animal) glass figurines he made at work. He then would sit heavily on the bed with a newspaper and begin reading to us. He read us the news, sports, and comic pages and even animated the sounds of the characters. We were in rapture with his presence. It is difficult to explain how wonderful we felt having him there with us, as we munched on sugar cookies, cuddling ourselves around him like Christmas tree ornaments as he read aloud, breaking only for a few seconds to puff on his pipe.

Though Charlie's thick glasses were held together with electrician tape, and his salt-and-pepper stubble face seemed to always need shaving, he glowed with love, gentleness, and compassion. He appeared to be unquestionably happy being with us once again. We certainly were. Then one night, after he had just begun reading to us, Mom surprised us by coming up the stairs with Willie! They were dressed up as if they had just come from church. Charlie put the paper down, laid his pipe aside, and looked just as puzzled as we were. Mom started to speak but couldn't. She said,

"I can't tell him, Willie, you tell him."

"Charlie," Willie said in a gruff voice, "You're going to have to pack your things and leave. Viola and I just remarried. When he uttered those words, I felt all the wind had been knocked out of me.

"No!" I screamed inside my head. "No, not this!"

I questioned how could it be that Mom betrayed us? And the look on Charlie's face was absolute pain. Pure and absolute. We all felt his hurt. The bedroom seemed to painfully revolve off its axis where just moments before, we were in a state of absolute bliss. Now, the room seemed like a living hell. Charlie did not say a word. He simply tapped the ash from his pipe into an ashtray, gathered the newspaper and scooted off the bed as we held on to him for dear life like a drowning man clings to a lifebuoy. He slipped on his work shoes, grabbed his few belongings and stuffed them into a small cardboard suitcase. He then took his lunch box, tucked it under his arm, all the time avoiding looking at us, and went out into the autumn night.

****

Those were terrible years. From my second grade to the time I was in grade eight, six years we had to put up with Willie's whippings, insults, and humiliations. Mom did not interfere and I resented her for not taking up for us. However, she too, I'm sure, was afraid of receiving the wrath of Willie's fury. Bunny began to stay away as he got older. He would sneak in at night when everyone was asleep and crawl quietly into bed. It was obvious why he stayed away, and I respected him for finding creative means of avoiding home. Virgil and I each had a paper route carrying *The Columbus Evening Dispatch* after school. Afterwards we came home to then sell the *Columbus Journal Nightgreen* until late in the evenings. When we came home around midnight, we were exhausted. On Saturday evenings, when we didn't sell the *Journal Nightgreen*, we shined shoes in White taverns in German Village. Willie and Mom kept our earnings and rationed 35 cents for our school lunch money. I didn't mind giving my money to Mom, but we were suspicious of Willie's handling of our earnings. Working, however, gave us the chance to avoid being at home as much as possible.

Those were the years that I daydreamed of running away to Kentucky and becoming a jockey. I sure was skinny enough, and the idea of working with horses fascinated me. I watched every movie Hollywood produced about horse racing and envisioned myself at the Kentucky Derby racing a swift horse to the finish line. And the money I would make would enable me to send for Virgil and Bunny to come live with me and maybe they too could become jockeys, taking care of horses, living in stables. Foolish boyhood dreams went in and out of my head just to escape my miserable home life. Unlike Charlie, Willie never had a gun. Thinking about it now, I believe he had a good reason not to have one in the house.

****

In seventh grade at Mohawk Junior High School, our English Teacher introduced us to the literature of James Thurber. It fascinated me that James Thurber had lived in the neighborhood of my *Dispatch* paper route. I read and enjoyed all of James Thurber's works. I would walk past his home and marvel at the wonder of his world in old Columbus. I imagined all the stories he wrote about the neighborhood and his house, family, and ghosts. During that time, his neighborhood would be considered upper middle-class, but now the large houses in the neighborhood were subdivided into apartments, funeral homes, or small business offices.

One Sunday evening, the only night I had off from my paper route, I was reading one of Thurber's books I got from the main Library and glanced up to notice Willie acting very restless. The whiskey must be starting to kick in. During those times we tried to keep out of his way. I'd start a house-cleaning project with Virgil or we'd find an excuse to leave. But it was getting late and leaving the house was out of the question. So reading provided a good excuse to be out of harm's way. Willie had been drinking heavily and I imagined he was waiting for Bunny to come home from his night of carousing. Bunny must have been thirteen, but he looked sixteen or older, and that made Willie more confrontational. Lately he had been provoking Bunny more than usual hoping he would react that would give him an excuse to fight Bunny like an adult. But Bunny's plan of offense was simple; he would remain non-aggressive. He told me he would not cry the next time Willie whipped him. He would just be passive. I put aside one of my Thurber books and had just turned out the lights when I heard Bunny entering the house. There was the usual bellowing from Willie's confrontational voice and I imagined Bunny at that moment. In his soft murmuring voice, he tried at best to explain his situation, but Willie constantly interjected in his whiskey-demented manner, telling Bunny to pull down his pants and underwear. Then there was the *whack, whack,* sound of Willie's belt beating Bunny's naked buttocks. Just like Bunny promised there were no screams. The whacks became louder and harder. Still, no cries. I heard Willie saying, "Nigger, so you think you're tough huh? Well, I'll show you." The crack of the belt was so loud that I started to shed tears for Bunny. I wanted to scream to Willie to let up. Finally, Bunny broke. He then did something very extraordinary-- he began screaming:

"Oh God! Oh Jesus! Sweet Jesus, please help me Lord, please deliver me!" It was pathetic.

Willie now pleasantly amused said, "So you think Jesus can help you. Ha, ha, I got your ass now Nigger. Not Jesus." Laughing in his drunken stupor, he frantically continued whipping Bunny. When Bunny came into the bedroom, he was too sore to lie down. He stood there shaking with welts all over his body. His eyes were in another world. Virgil and I got a cold washcloth and patted his swollen welts and helped him to his bed. Once again, I prayed to be an adult for just five minutes. The next day Willie had several of his drinking friends over from his job and I heard him saying to them, "I got something I want ya'll to hear. Bunny, get your Black ass in here!"

Bunny was outside working on the broken chain of my bicycle. Willie fabricated an excuse, accusing Bunny of some infraction. Bunny tried to explain himself, but this just provoked Willie further. He pushed Bunny upstairs as he snickered, pulling his thin belt from his trousers, winking at his drinking friends. When the beating began, Bunny immediately started crying for God and Jesus again for help. Hearing his cries ripped my soul to pieces. If there was a merciful God, why couldn't he just take a few seconds and stop this madness? I would have delighted in seeing a lightning bolt shoot from the sky and strike Willie during this moment of rage. Some of Willie's drunken guests started snickering, while others bent their heads saying that this was wrong. I just wanted a miracle, to instantaneously have access to a

94

handgun. Without hesitation I would have blown that son-of-a-bitch to hell.

Willie beat Bunny for entertainment and joked about it to his drunken cohorts, saying he helped him find the Lord. I will never forget the way Bunny screamed. It was like hearing a wounded animal. I compare it with Jesus being beaten. Did He cry out in pain? I can't recall Mom's reaction exactly because she remained quiet and reclusive. I developed a silent disdain for her. I had no way of understanding her emotionally trapped situation. I can now envision what she must have gone through seeing and hearing her favorite son being humiliated and beaten by the man she loved. Indeed, she had her share of Willie's wrath too. The whole ordeal lasted about two or three weeks until Bunny deliberately got into trouble and went to the juvenile detention center. It seemed a better place for him than home. At least he would be treated better there. Unfortunately, that was the beginning of Bunny's institutional, revolving door life. It eventually landed him in prison.

Bunny age 10, 1952

Me age 9, 1952

Virgil age 8, 1952

Sandy age 6, 1952

Me in the U.S Coast Guard Public Affairs Officer stationed at the 9th Coast Guard District Cleveland, Ohio, 1989.

1963, Virgil an Ohio State Freshman "Twisting" with Sandy

Bunny 1972/73, Age 30

My U.S. Marine Corps Photo
1962, Age 19

As an Air Force Medic, I volunteered to work in remote villages in Thailand. Here I'm giving inoculations to schoolchildren in 1968/69.

Chapter Nine

B Y 1952, MY AMBITION in life of becoming a cowboy had diminished. I was now going on nine and seriously considered becoming a doctor because of a Christmas present I received. I received a play doctor's kit for Christmas that included everything a doctor needed. It contained a play stethoscope, play thermometer, a few assorted bandages, and some hard candy drops for pills. I went around the house trying to make everyone well. I carefully inserted the play thermometer inside the mouths of those who would let me, vigilantly took pulses and dispensed the candy pills afterwards imparting sound eight-year-old medical advice.

Conveniently for me, Mom was covered with hives all over her body that spring due to an allergic condition. She rested on the sofa most of the time scratching and I could sense her discomfort even though she tried to give the impression that things were okay. There were welts and puffy patches on her smooth skin that sometimes bled. Wanting to soothe her misery, I put my hand on her forehead and told her she had a fever. My routine included checking her heart with my play stethoscope, taking her temperature with my play thermometer, and giving her some sound medical advice. Wanting to do more, I located some Vicks salve in the kitchen and rubbed her arms and face with it. It soothed her, and she liked the medical attention I was giving, saying that I'd make a good doctor someday. Miraculously, her hives went away within moments after the application. It was the Vicks Salve, I thought, and she was astounded and relieved.

That same year, I became fully conditioned to calling Willie, "sir," and Mom, "ma'am". Willie had thoroughly entrenched in us the use of these accolades with all adults. If we slipped, we simply were punished. Sometimes, he would tell us to go outside and find a stem from one of the many stinkweed trees. We had to strip off the leaves and present the thin flexible twig to him for his approval before he used that damned thing on us.

In the fall of 1951, I entered third grade. Virgil was in second, Sandy in Kindergarten, and Bunny in the fourth at Beck Street Elementary School. We were usually the only Blacks in our classrooms and obviously we stood out. This was even more so with Bunny because of his size. Miss Orf, his teacher, was a white haired post-menopausal woman who seemed to delight in humiliating Bunny for whatever minor infraction he allegedly committed. His punishment usually meant incarceration in the small confined space under her desk. Thus confined, he could only see the floor, three wooden walls of her desk, and the gapped legs of Miss Orf, which exposed, in full view, her droopy grandma drawers.

My impression of Miss Orf has always personified her image as a rosy-cheeked grandmother who looked a lot like a manifestation of Santa Claus' wife. Miss Orf wore her white hair in a grandmother's bun and walked on thick, square, granny heeled shoes laced snugly on her swollen ankles. She was the epitome of a spinster teacher. I was shocked that this woman did such a thing to my brother.

Virgil recently told me the story saying that Bunny, at first, began to play with her shoes out of boredom. Later, he was "encouraged" to roam other parts of her anatomy while she sat and taught the rest of the class. He was called to sit under her desk for the slightest schoolboy's infraction. He never mentioned this to anyone, perhaps because he had been conditioned, like myself by Bubbles to keep such secrets to himself. Miss Orf was one of the best teachers I had. As a teacher she was strict, thorough, and a hard worker who expected as much from her students. Fortunately for me, I did not have the same experience as Bunny.

I was in the sixth grade in 1955, when the movie *Blackboard Jungle*, with Sidney Poitier, featured Bill Hailey and the Comets' Rock n' Roll hit, *Rock Around the Clock* hit the charts. The years 1956 and 1957 were pivotal years for automobiles and music. Bernstein's *West Side Story*, Ahmed Jamal's piano jazz LP *Poinciana*, and the songs of a newcomer named Johnny Mathis left an indelible impression on my young life. Bunny always seemed to acquire the latest 33-rpm recordings, but it was the celebrated Rock n Roll 45-rpms he collected for his fledging teenage doo-whoop singing group that stirred me. We used to wake up to the blaring sound of Chuck Berry singing:

> *Up in the morning and out to school,*
> *The teacher is teaching the golden rule.*
> *American history and practical math...*
> *Studying hard trying to pass.*
> *Working my fingers down to the bone,*
> *The guy behind me won't leave me alone...*

My brothers and I climbed out of the warmth of our scratchy Army blankets and Army bunk beds (purchased from an Army/Navy Surplus store) and moved to the rhythms of Chuck Berry, Little

Richard, and Fats Domino. And as we brushed our teeth, washed our faces, and ate our breakfast cereal we moved in a rhythmic groove and bopped out into the frosty school morning headed for Mohawk Junior High. Rock n' Roll music was an integral part of our education and life experiences. Late at night, on clear evenings when the radio waves were most receptive, the Randy's Record Hour broadcast from Nashville played the latest Rhythm and Blues and Gospel hits. The whole neighborhood sounded like one huge stereo as the Black community tuned their dials to Randy's Record Hour. In Columbus, there was also Doctor Bop whose very popular radio program heralded in his famous bravado:

"This is Doctor Bop on the Sceeeene. With a stack of shellac and his record machine. Brought to you live and in living color." He played all the latest 45 rpm records, and it was the first time that I heard *Yakaty Yak* by the Coasters. It personified some of Bunny's teenage friends...

Just take your hoodlum friends outside,
You ain't got time to take a ride...
Yakaty yak
Don't talk back.

Bunny had style and wore clothes in a way that made him look mature and distinguished for his age. He wore silk socks, Stetson pointed toe shoes and was blessed with a handsome face and a good physique. He had a cleft chin that looked like a cross between Viktor Mature, Johnny Mathis, and Marvin Gaye. Not only was he handsome, he looked much older than his age, even though he was only one year older than I was. He had a sophisticated elegance that caused girls, Black and White, young and old, to throw themselves on him like white on rice. I remember once when a girl of around sixteen or seventeen years came to the door asking for Bunny. It upset Mom. She had always been leery about his preoccupation with older girls, but she could not repress his accelerating masculine development. She knew that he lied about his age all the time. This time, however, instead of putting the girl through a battery of questions and eventually telling her that he was

103

only twelve years old, Mom's plan was to show the girl Bunny's other preoccupation--shooting marbles. Bunny, Virgil, and I were in the back yard doing just that. Bunny seemed always to have the best cats-eyes and Bolgers (big ones) and his skill was impeccable. I loved to watch how he would twist his wrist with a marble between the tips of his index finger and the knuckle of his thumb and detonate a group of marbles inside the dirt ring. He always won. And I could never, as much as I tried, emulate his style of shooting. He had just shot and was beginning to pick up the marbles that he had blasted when Mom came in the back yard with this beautiful older girl. Mom was beaming, and the girl looked bewildered. Bunny stood up and brushed off the dust on his hands and slacks, and did the most incredible thing. He threw his prize bag of marbles on the ground, put his hands on his hips like someone of authority, and said,

"And that's how you boys should shoot marbles. Remember use your thumb knuckle to shoot with. Are there any more questions? Okay, I'll talk to you guys later. I have to go."

The girl's expression changed from confusion to admiration and Mom, knowing she had been outdone, hurled herself back inside the house in resignation.

Bunny's teenage hoodlum friends included Little Ronnie, Boochie, José Solis, Frog, Calfcart, Junior Craft, Big Bobby, Sam Cudgel, and a couple of others who were committed to girls, talking trash, and standing on the corner doo-whopped singing. They doo-whopped their hearts out to their favorite groups like the Moonglows, Frankie Lyman and the Teenagers, or the Platters. Actually, the guys in Bunny's gang were not bad. Women usually thought they were saints. They sang believing they had a chance to make a hit record. And they probably could have, if they had a manager who knew how to market them. They sang at high school sock hops, at private parties and special events. They all lied about their age and had plenty of girlfriends.

It was not just Bunny's good looks that made him popular in school. He also starred in basketball and track. In track, his specialty was the 100-yard and the 220-yard dash. Coaches from East, Central, and South high schools were interested in him with each vying for his attention. Even college coaches from Ohio State University and Dayton University expressed an interest when he was just in the ninth grade. Bunny also seemed always to have money. I didn't know where or how he got it, but girls competing for his time gave him expensive gifts, and more than likely, money. He knew a good thing when he saw it, and he capitalized on his charm and good looks. On the other hand, he was competent with various methods of hair styling, and his friends depended on him to "konk" their hair, which they rewarded with money, gifts, and favors.

Konkoline and Posner's Hair straightening cream reigned in popularity in the 1950s. For numerous Rock n' Roll, Rhythm and Blues singing groups, and Jazz musicians, "konk" or "processed" (the words were used interchangeably) hair was a chemically induced method for effectively straightening kinky hair. The chemical composition contained lye. It required huge amounts of hairgrease, like Dixie Peach, to be applied on the back of the neck, forehead, around the ears, and on the scalp. The problem was since Konkoline and Posner's Hair straightening cream contained lye as a chemical base, the mixture would leave second-degree ulcerated burns (or worse) on skin, if it was not protected with a substantial coating of hairgrease.

Nat King Cole's weekly appearance became the first African-American televised program, and his hairstyle was partly responsible for much of the celebrated Konk look. Many of the guys on the block processed their heads to mimic Nat Cole's finger-wave style. James Brown's pompadour with his slick sides and "duck-tail" in-the back was extremely popular too. There was also the Johnny Mathis look. He had just come on the scene with his harmonious voice. Bunny looked similar to Johnny Mathis, but he never tried to imitate his singing style because he preferred singing base. In addition, it was said that Johnny Mathis was a "queer," and the guys in Bunny's singing group were very macho. The term "gay" had not been used as a reference to homosexuals at that time. "Queer" was the preferred word of choice. To call someone a "queer" was worse than playing the "dirty-dozens" which meant talking about someone's mama in a vulgar manner. At Mohawk Junior High School, I witnessed more fights with fellows trying to protect the honor of their mothers' name as well as someone who was called a queer. Calling another a queer, at that age when hormones go amuck, meant to "throw down" or get into a serious altercation. Those were two things that guaranteed a fight. There were, however, many Johnny Mathis gay imitators singing in nightclubs who tried musically to imitate the popular singer.

Black people's notion of beauty comes in generational capsules. The mid 1950s had a very different appearance than the mid 1960s. Almost every Black woman in America had a hot iron straightening comb and curlers in her possession in both generations. Even though the Afro had been in, there were still many who preferred the straightened hair look. To achieve a straightened effect, one had to apply an ample amount of grease to the hair and use hot combs or curlers. The hair, in essence, was "fried."

Many Black Colleges and schools required girls to fry their hair or they were not admitted to class, but even this method of straightening had its hazards. It required the young women to sit perfectly still, as the hairstylers attempted not to burn areas of skin, such as the forehead, temple, ears, cheeks, and neck. Young Black girls were not too keen to sit still for long periods of time having their hair manipulated by someone about to brand them if they suddenly moved. As far as I am concerned, those young ladies were "she"-roes having braved the hot iron and hot curler routine weekly for church services or other social events. Black beauty shops and hair straightening products around the country profited greatly from the fashion of trying to achieve the "good" hair look just to mirror some White standard of beauty. In the Post war period, natural looking hair was considered uncultured. I lost my so-called good hair when I was about five. Older relatives would later say, "Sugar Pie, whatever happened to your *good* hair?" It made me feel guilty, as though I had done something wrong, just because my hair decided to defy gravity of its own accord.

Bunny's legend of processing hair grew throughout the community and he used a lot of Posners and Konkoline products. His creativity in processing hair (he specialized in a finger wave technique similar to Nat King Cole's, a patent leather look that gave him some neighborhood notoriety.) One day, however, Bunny ran out of Posners, and decided to produce his own konk chemical product, and experiment with it on Little Ronnie's head. Knowing that Posners and Konkoline were lye-based products, Bunny boiled some potatoes, mashed and mixed them with an unknown amount of Drano lye pellets. It looked like Posners. I even think he added some butter to get the creamy richness consistency like Posners. He prepared Little Ronnie's head with the required amount of Dixie Peach hair pomade and placed an enormous amount of steaming clumps of the concoction on Little Ronnie's head. Perhaps Bunny's mixture of Lye was too much because when he tried to style Little Ronnie's head, even the mass amounts of Dixie Peach grease did not prevent large patches of hair from coming off with each stroke of the comb. When the lye ate through the Dixie Peach grease, it continued to his scalp and that's when Little Ronnie started screaming for Bunny to rinse the damned stuff out of his inflamed scalp. Bunny rushed him to the kitchen sink and ran cold water, trying as fast as he could to rinse out the contents. Since we did not have hot running water, Bunny had to boil water in the teapot on the stove. The time lapse caused the stuff to play havoc with Little Ronnie's scalp as he danced and hopped around the kitchen like someone who had to pee really badly.

The highly skilled doctors, nurses, and staff at the Children's Hospital emergency room are trained to handle almost any child's emergency. I can just imagine the puzzled look on the young residents' faces when Little Ronnie came hopping and bopping in the emergency room as the staff tried to evaluate the complaint. The aftermath gave Little Ronnie's head the unusual appearance of a large pinecone with eyes. Needless to say, they never experimented with potatoes and Drano ever again. Little Ronnie, Bunny's lieutenant, remained devoted to him for years. I imagine that every time Little Ronnie spotted a can of Drano pellets, his hair went into shock. Nevertheless, they were inseparable in their love for doo-wop crooning and girls. There was a poem in our neighborhood that went like this:

> *Konkoline, Konkoline, rules the*
> *world. Not a kink, not a curl.*

On the top it looks like a mop,
Round the edges looks like hedges.

****

In the seventh grade, at the age of twelve, I still had a huge crush on Marlene Ware. It was more than a crush--it was love. I wanted to be the father of her kids, and take her away from South Lane Street and live happy-ever-after somewhere like California. Being two years and two grades ahead of me, made Marlene even more appealing. By today's standards, I would be classified as something between a geek and a nerd, but no one could tell me that my affections for her weren't real. I'd gauge the time she left her house in order for a chance to walk with her to school. I was thrilled just to be in her company and tried not to stutter when I talked, but I had competition, David Philips. He was in the same grade as Marlene and was in several classes with her, including music. David and Marlene were in the school band, where she played the flute. David played the trumpet. I too wanted to play a musical instrument, but Mom ignored the idea of allowing Virgil or me to do so. It actually bothered me why she didn't take my interest in music seriously. She did, however, allow my sisters Sandy and Dottie to take up the violin.

Bunny's class schedule was the same as Marlene's and David's, but he had a different group of friends and didn't associate with either of them. David admired Bunny's popularity and athleticism. He had serious academic plans after graduation, and his conversations and other senior talk with Marlene obviously excluded my seventh grade activities. I was jealous of David. My frustration and love for Marlene drove me to write on a billboard in huge lettering at the corner of Layman and Livingston: "Sugar Pie Loves Marlene." I wanted the world to see my love for her. As usual, she ignored all my affections and attempts to get her attention. She just placidly went about her business and disregarded my existence. As a consequence, I slowly began to feel humiliated about my junior high school puppy love affection and became depressed and pitifully withdrew into my shell. I needed a change--

and that came in the form of Chloe Jones, a new girl in my homeroom who sat next to me. I think I adored the name just as much as the girl, Chloe Jones. Her name seemed poetic. And she and her name evoked my innermost fantasies of her likeness and the femininity to Dorothy Dandridge in the musical movie *Carmen Jones*. Chloe even looked a bit like Dorothy Dandridge, but not at all like Carmen Jones. Chloe was sexy in a quiet, demure way. Her long frizzy hair and budding beauty had serious potential. However, in my adolescent awkwardness, she, like Marlene, merely looked at me with a sense of amusement. Like the rest of Mohawk's girls, her interest seemed to be in my older brother. It seemed my only good quality was being Bunny's brother.

I did try to devise ways that would make girls take notice of me. Since I proved to be horrible at playing sports (couldn't dribble a basketball and showed a lack of skill trying to catch a fly ball), people had a difficult time believing I was Bunny's brother. I resolved to gain the girl's attention by employing the use of my artistic talent, concentrate more on my academics, and pay more attention to my appearance. I owed much to the lyrics of Sam Cooke's song *What a Wonderful World It Could Be:*

Don't know much about history,
Don't know much biology,
Don't know much about the science book,
Don't know much about the French I took,
But I do know one and one is two,
And if this one could be with you,
What a wonderful world it would be.

Mom had taught all of us how to iron, and it came in handy. My faded jeans, khaki pants, and shirts were starched and pressed to a knife-edge crease. I shined my shoes, mended the holes in the heels of my socks, and even ironed them. By experimenting with various pimple medications, my skin cleared, but not with the help of Dick Clark's "flesh" colored pimple products he advertised on the television. Unfortunately, his advertisements did nothing for my complexion and only made me, and other Blacks, look like polka-dot handkerchiefs (I thought it very inconsiderate of paramedical and crayon companies to produce and promote "flesh" colored products. It seemed to show a lack of consideration and a flagrant exhibition of arrogance trivializing people-of-color everywhere).

All through Mohawk Junior-High School, Virgil and I kept our evening paper route jobs. However, we discontinued our shoe shining business. As we matured into adolescence, we found ourselves impatient with the demeaning racial attitudes of some White patrons. In order to make up for that loss, we both took on an additional paper route immediately after school, which enabled us the time to continue our evening jobs. In addition, perverts on our paper routes were less pervasive as we grew older.

At that point in time, Mom finally divorced Willie for the second time and life was wonderful. However, Mom didn't share our sentiments. The divorce left her in a state of depression, and she often confined herself for long periods in her bedroom. In the kitchen, I would sometimes catch her staring out of the window, as if expecting someone. Willie was out of our lives, and we definitely did not want her to marry again. One evening in our bedroom, Bunny, Virgil and I decided to take the financial matter into our own hands. We felt that if we could bring in a little extra income, she would not have to depend on a man to take care of us. The money we made would go directly into Mom's hands for household essentials. I was now thirteen, Virgil twelve, and Bunny fourteen (going on thirty-five.) Having grown taller, he had many girlfriends vying for his affection. He became a leader of a doo-wop street corner group of guys who crooned nightly. We each took on an additional paper route--a morning paper route, waking up around 4:30 a.m. and working until it was time to go to school. After school, we carried an evening route, and at nights, we continued selling *The Journal Night Green* newspapers until late in the evenings. We were determined to help with the finances. We developed strategies, carrying more papers by buying saddlebags for our bikes and new wagons with side rails for carrying heavy Sunday morning papers. Our unique enterprising efforts worked. Virgil and I both got a route on East Town Street delivering papers to large apartments. Virgil had one side of Town Street and I the other. It was ideal and we could stay together. We cut our delivery time in half and the new routes allowed us the pleasure of avoiding being chased by dogs, perverts, and hoodlums. We felt adult-like when we gave our money to Mom and paid the gas and electric bills.

Bunny, however, had other ideas. He gave up on the newspaper route his second week and started to hang around with his gang. He was still resourceful and got odd jobs with some of his hoodlum friends, like cutting lawns, washing cars or washing dishes in restaurant kitchens. He also found other innovative ways of coming up with cash. We began to grow at a fast rate now-- especially Bunny who had started shaving. He shaved with Magic Shave Powder. It smelled like farts or rotten eggs. But it did not cause razor bumps.

****

The jobs Bunny acquired usually did not last long. When he made enough money for what he wanted, he simply would just walk off. One summer job he had was having a Yummy Boy route. I tried every year to be a Yummy Boy but the White managers would look at me and just say that they had all the boys he needed. The job called for selling assorted frozen delicacies, such as fudge bars, various flavors of Popsicles, chocolate ice cream bars, orange, lime, or pineapple sherbet pushups, and my favorite, Drumstick ice cream cones dipped in chocolate and topped with nuts. Yummy Boys peddled a white tricycle cart containing its frozen contents. The carts were aerodynamically shaped, and the peddler sat high on a bicycle seat ringing a series of bells attached to a handlebar to steer the cart.

Yummy Boys were cool, and I would have given all of my comic books and marbles to be one for just a day. I was proud, and at the same time, a little envious of Bunny when he pulled up on South Lane Street with a Yummy cart. He had a cigarette dangling from the side of his mouth and summoned up all his little hoodlum friends, selling them his ice cream bars, Popsicles, Drumsticks, and other assorted goodies. With the cute teenage girls, he gave them free stuff if they gave him a kiss followed by some fondling and phone number. I got to look inside the cart and took out a small piece of hot-ice that kept the contents frozen. The hot-ice did not melt like regular ice. It just vaporized in a cloud of cold vapor. It also burned your fingers when you held it your hand too long. When the cart was empty, Bunny kept all the money and left the thing at Livingston Park to play basketball. The last time I saw the cart some members of his gang were taking turns riding it up and down Parsons and Livingston Avenues, ringing the roll of handlebar bells. Each year, it seemed, Bunny got another Yummy Boy route, if he so wanted.

****

The onset of winter called for a new coat to keep me warm on my paper route. Keeping warm is essential in the winter months of Columbus when you work outdoors. My feet, ears, and fingertips became numb because of the cold and I was afraid of being frost bitten. Virgil and I would have to find a place and sit down, take off our shoes, and stuff them with newspapers for insulation to keep our feet warm and dry. Carrying heavy papers stopped the blood circulation in our hands and numbed our fingertips to the point where they had no feeling. Leather gloves lined with rabbit fur were the warmest, but also expensive and impractical. You had to constantly take your hands out of your gloves to give change and sort the papers. We wore only one glove and stuck the other in our coat pocket. To combat the cold on our ears, earmuffs, or caps with earflaps were ideal. All this attire was okay for work, but made absolutely no impression in school. But practicality takes precedence over style when you work in the cold.

I decided to go Montgomery Wards, a downtown store, to buy a warm coat. I saw a blue and gray plaid one with a wool collar for $13.99. I tried it on and it fit. In addition, it had a belt fitted around the waist that made the coat snug and warm. It was a practical coat suited for outdoor work. But it surely would not attract the attention of Chloe Jones or Marlene Ware. A blond salesman, no doubt a college student, wearing a gray three-button suit and black horn-rimmed Clark Kent glasses, (fashionable in 1956) quickly waited on me. After he took my money, he placed the coat in a box, tied it with string and sent me on my way. He was efficient. (In those days, wrapping items in boxes and tying string around boxes was considered routine.) I felt a sense of accomplishment purchasing yet another item with my own hard-earned money. No adult had paid for this. I did it on my own and felt a sense of accomplishment. (I had the same feeling the previous year also when I bought a Davy Crockett coonskin cap, a Davy Crockett T shirt, and a pair of Davy Crockett moccasins. I felt so proud of my Davy Crockett gear that I began to feel like Phess Parker, the actor who played Davy Crockett.)

As I descended the steps of Montgomery Wards, I felt the chilly night air on my face and crossed the street, heading for home when I spotted it--a black hooded coat with wooden bottoms at Jack Clothing Outlet. Jack's clothes were cheaper, more fashionable and trendy, and their merchandise was poorer in quality as compared, of course, to Montgomery Wards. The jacket was not wool like the one I was carrying in the box, but it caught my attention and I would look stylish in it. The black cotton coat came with a thin liner. It clearly would not take Columbus' cold weather like the one I had just purchased, but it would be impressive. Indeed, the one I just purchased from Montgomery Wards, looked like the kind a mother would buy for her child. It was a *boy's* coat. The one in Jack's window would make me look more grown-up. I stood there, in the cold, looking at it for a long time, when I asked myself, *What would pretty Chloe Jones say to me if I came to school with this coat-- better yet, what if Marlene Ware gives me a complement?* I entered Jacks and tried it on. It fit perfectly! All I had to do now was run back across the street, get my money refunded, and buy the black hooded one.

When the college student saw me returning, he gave me a befuddled looked. I handed him the box with the receipt telling him (in my stuttering manner) that I had decided not to buy the coat and wanted a refund. He looked at me with contempt. His face turned red and he yelled:

"You people, are going to just have to take responsibility when you purchase an item. No, no, no. I will not refund you your money. You will just have to keep it."

"But, but, sir," I said, but he only pointed with his finger to the exit and told me to leave. I left feeling that I had no control over my own money, and now the coat did not mean anything if I could not enjoy wearing it. I walked out of the store and across the street to Jack's Outlet, stared at the black coat, sighed, and walked home mumbling to myself. When I arrived home, my sulking and mumbling caught Bunny's attention. He was in the kitchen having just completed konking Boochie's head and was in the process of putting his renowned finger wave patterns on Boochie's hair. Without even looking at me, he could tell something was wrong.

"What's the matter, Sugar Pie? Bunny asked, with a cigarette dangling from his mouth, squinting his eyes either from the smoke or from observing his work.

"I just bought this coat and the man at the store said I could not have my money back. And there's another one at Jacks that I like better."

"Hmmmm. Don't worry. Let me just finish up here and we'll go down to Montgomery Wards and talk with the guy. You got your receipt?"

"Yeah," I said.

I felt relieved. When Bunny said he would help you; he put all of his efforts into owning up to his promise. When he completed Boochie's hair, he handed him a mirror, and a broad smile of approval spread across his face. Out of all of Bunny's hoodlum friends, no one gave Boochie a hard time. He looked like he was in his late twenties, but he was a mere teenager like Bunny. He admired Bunny's leadership and would do almost anything for him. They both cherished their konked, patent leather look, finger-waved hair and their knack for doo-wop, street corner singing. And, I can say this now, when Boochie turned around and looked at me that night, my impression of him was a konked, finger-waved, badass, Mighty Joe Young. When he was upset, his massive build was not to be taken lightly. Boochie's skin hue was very dark. His

114

broad muscular shoulders and arms bulged out of his T-shirts. But I knew him to be quiet, mild mannered, and with a good sense of humor (Years later he would kill a man during a card game.)

Bunny said we would drive to Montgomery Wards. I was surprised that he could drive and more surprised that he even had a car. He wasn't even old enough to have a driver's license or learner's permit. The car, a burgundy late '40s something Mercury looked expensive and in great shape. I think Bunny and his gang "acquired" the automobile from one of the smaller communities outside Columbus. He said that Boochie, Little Ronnie, and himself had saved enough money to buy the car in cash. When we arrived at the store, I led Bunny to the salesman. Bunny, very much a gentleman, spoke to the salesman handing the box and said in his usual soft voice,

"Sir, here's my little brother's coat he just bought here. He works hard on his paper route and he wants to get his money refunded. The box, as you can see, has not even been opened, and here's the receipt. Why don't you just give him his money back, okay?"

The blond salesman sighed, looked grudgingly at Bunny, then at me, and began to wave his finger in Bunny's face when the most amazing thing happened. Out of nowhere, Bunny whipped out a small black snubbed-nosed pistol and shoved it hard in the salesman's stomach in a way so that no one could see the weapon. The salesman's face flushed, turned an ash color. He started stuttering and was about to throw up his hands when Bunny said in a very cool and soft-spoken voice,

"Put your damn hands down and give him back his fucking money. Is that such a problem?"

"Nnno, Sssir. No problem here." Although there were some people in the store, uncannily no one paid attention to what was going on in this section of the store. I stood there dumbfounded and could have defecated a gold brick right then and there. Boochie, in the aisle, swept his eyes from side to side, surveying the store's interior. When the salesmen opened the cash register's drawer and began to count out my exact refund, Bunny boldly reached inside the drawer and said,

"Hell, if you don't mind, we'll just take *all* of this for all the trouble you caused."

"Well, nnno sir. I dddon't mind."

Bunny took one of the Montgomery Ward's shopping bags and stuffed the cash inside. Boochie, for some reason, casually picked up an enormous pair of women's cotton underwear, held them up to his waist, and started laughing.

"Damn, would you look at these motherfuckers here." He held them up in the air and then placed them across his waist like an apron and began laughing. "These are what you call 'Motherfletcher' drawers. You think your mama can fit into these?"

Bunny quickly replied, "You know I don't play that dirty dozens shit, man. Maybe *your* mama can fit her fat ass into them. Here, make yourself useful. Take a bag and put some clothes inside. Grab a couple of those pants and quit playing around."

Bunny stuffed the pistol back inside his jacket pocket and slowly backed away from the stunned salesman. He snatched another large Montgomery Ward shopping bag and asked Boochie if he liked the sport shirt and held it up to his chest. Boochie nodded and Bunny grabbed an armful and stuffed them inside the bag. Next he stopped at the table where men's dress pants were neatly folded and grabbed another bag and stuffed rolls of trousers inside the bag. Boochie stopped, lit a cigarette, blew out the smoke and continued his shopping spree. I followed them in a daze, wanting to get the hell out of there, but they took their time "shopping"--holding items up to each other asking for each other's approval. They were very discriminate about certain items that were meant for them. Next, it was the ladies section where they indiscriminately snatched bras, skirts, sweaters, and other female items of various sizes and colors. They took their good old time while I was sweating profusely. Intentionally keeping a slow pace they kept shopping, and once in a while looked back at the dazed salesman. Hell, they even waved at some cute girls and puffed on their cigarettes until we got to the exit and walked casually out the door. By the time we left Montgomery Wards, they had managed to carry out several shopping bags full of clothing items, an undisclosed amount of cash, and were thoroughly satisfied that the things they picked were quality items. The whole event seemed too surreal for me. It didn't happen, I told myself.

"Now, Sugar Pie," Bunny said to me as he drove the Mercury back home, "You don't tell Mom about this, okay? (How in the world could I ever explain to anyone what had just taken place-- surely not Mom.) And don't tell her that you saw me driving. She's got enough to worry about with the divorce and everything." (Mom, had just divorced Willie, and had sequestered herself in her bedroom for long periods of time.)

I had been witness to something that was theater, felony, and school. It certainly was a memorable performance and Bunny played a role I've never seen him in before. He was undeviating, cunning, cool and undoubtedly in control. Certainly what he did was, in fact, criminal and there's no denying that issue. Nevertheless, it was easily preventable, had the proper respect been given. But it wasn't, and logic and rationale went out the door.

I think the ordeal was an educational experience for the young salesman. In his eyes, I was merely a nuisance from a subculture, and a hindrance to his sales commission. I believe that the experience helped dilute some of his General Custer complexes. I have replayed that scene in my head hundreds of times. Bunny, who always acted much older than his years, did so out of a sense of cause and effect that produced a reaction. Unfortunately, he had to deal with his demons at an early age simply because he looked older. Bubbles, Willie, Miss Orf, and God knows who else, caused him to grow up faster than he should have. But deep down inside, he was still a kid who wanted to do kid things. Bunny reacted so strongly to the Montgomery Ward incident because he saw me brokenhearted by the salesman's ration of haughtiness. The worse thing the salesman could do was to provoke and humiliate me in front of my big brother. And just as I felt I was Virgil's protector, Bunny felt the same for me. I'm very fortunate, though, that no one got hurt. And, as time went by, I upheld Bunny's defiance to arrogance, chalking it up as a token of his character. From that moment at Montgomery Wards, I held the ultimate respect for him. I grew more emotionally appreciative of his "big-brotherness" and relished his being there for me. And I wanted to be molded in his image. He was my Hopalong Cassidy, Lone Ranger, Cisco Kid, and Big Chief all rolled up in one.

****

During part of my high school years at South, when Mom was married to Jack Lovingood, her fourth husband and fifth marriage, developers were interested in a small track of land that included four houses on Parsons Avenue. These homes on Parsons Avenue concealed our small-framed house and the turn of the century outhouse situated in our backyard. After the Parsons Avenue homes were sold, they were demolished to pave the way for a future gas station, exposing our small dwelling to the busy Parsons Avenue public. Now it seemed the whole world knew of our poverty, and I actually believed that we were the poorest people in the world. I endured the snickers from other students and the out of place Appalachian-looking outhouse. For me, going to South High School was an invasion of my privacy. I felt naked. The Parsons Avenue bus carried many of my South High classmates that stopped only twenty-yards from our outhouse. One morning, a girl I was attracted to, spotted me carrying the honey pot in the middle of one of my dashes to the outhouse. I could have died right then and there.

Going to South High School, the school that boasted several famous graduates such as the relatives of Eddie Rickenbacker, famed Air Force General Curtis LeMay, and a couple others, was primarily to accommodate my mother. It was her idea that her children graduated from there. She believed South offered a better education than East or Central High School because South's students, at the time, were predominately White. That was the mind-set back then. She had no idea what misery and humiliation I went through each day, and when I complained, she merely repeated that I was getting a better quality education. I did get a good education, but at a price. She also made Bunny go there, but he quit after a couple of weeks.

By now, Bunny too had become a source of concern. He was constantly getting into trouble, and his name made the local news several times. A few teachers questioned me if I was related to him. So, I was very happy when Virgil came to South a year after me. He was a source of comfort. We both went out for the track team. Our team members called us the "TB Twins" because we were so skinny. They said our arms and legs looked like licorice sticks. I grew increasingly self-conscious and felt like a social outcast. My inferiority complex became more severe, and my stuttering made it harder for me to be open. I felt ostracized from the few Black students there who had their own long established cliques. Social life at high school did not exist for me. I didn't date and was never invited to go to parties. I went to my Senior Prom alone, stayed a few minutes, left, and walked home but decided not to go in so early. As I came nearer to where I lived, I stood looking at my house from across the street, and reflected. Turning away after awhile, I walked to Livingston Park a few blocks away. No one was at the park at that time of night. I sat alone in one of the playground swings feeling foolish wearing a white dinner jacket and tuxedo pants. Unsnapping my bow tie, I looked up at a Van Gogh *Starry Night* sky and cried my heart out, asking God why was I born poor?

****

Mr. H. D. Swain, South High's principal, closely resembled Liberace when he did not wear his thick, horned rimmed, bi-focal glasses. Like Liberace, he combed every strand of his thick chestnut colored hair into place. Efficient and business-like, Mr. Swain had a look that was stalwart and efficient. I soon learned that he was also a racist bigot. Mr. Pearce, my 10th grade biology teacher, was still on his lunch break when a girl sitting next to me dropped her plastic snap-beads on the floor scattering them around my seat. Since she was setting next to me, I helped her with the task of picking up each colorful plastic pearl bead and then snap them back together. She stood up after snapping the last one back on, and needed help putting it around her neck. I was standing behind her, and snapped the two strings of beads together around her neck when Mr. Swain stopped in mid-stride in the hallway outside the class. He gave me a cold glare and then pointed his finger, motioning for me to come to him in the hallway. I figured he was probably going to lecture me about my recent tardiness in the mornings, so I braced myself, and went into the vacant hallway. In a calm manner he said, "I don't want to ever catch you touching a White girl again. Do I make myself clear?"

"What? This is crazy? I said to myself." The little favorable impressions I had of the man evaporated at that instant. The episode further distanced my feelings about South High, and I wished my mother had witnessed Swain's comments. I just lowered my head and went back inside the classroom. By then, Mr. Pearce had return, ready to teach the day's biology lesson. A friend later told me that a couple of years back, a German girl had a Black boyfriend, and Mr. Swain called her into his office telling her he had no recourse but to talk with her parents about the situation. The next day her German mother came to the principal's office along with her stepfather, a huge Black Army master sergeant.

Bunny despised South High School and for good reason. He probably would have had plenty of White girl friends and might have slugged Mr. Swain for his racist remarks. As it turned out, Bunny dropped out of high school and became a full-time juvenile delinquent. He progressively got into more trouble. This obliged Mom to often appear in court to battle his cause. She also had to pay his bail on many occasions. She plea-bargained with judges and social workers to stop Bunny from going to jail, so much that it seemed like she was on a self-destruction mission.

When Bunny turned seventeen, he married one of his girlfriends because she was pregnant and gave birth to his first daughter, Pudding. Mom incorrectly thought this would make him become more responsible and that it may cause him to change. Like the rest of the family, I hoped that the marriage would work out too, but I actually felt sorry for him because Bunny was a free spirit, a mustang who didn't need to be corralled. He did try though. He was able to get a job working at the Yardley Plastic factory on the third shift, but he still yearned for the freedom of the streets. He stayed at Yardley only for a few months before he continued to get into trouble.

Me at age 11/12 during the time of Yahoo's
rampage of Columbus' Black youths

The Yahoos

Chapter Ten

"For as to those filthy Yahoos, although there were few greater lovers of mankind at that time than myself, yet I confess I never saw any sensitive being so detestable on all accounts, and the more I came near them, the more hateful they grew while I stayed in that country." *Gulliver's Travels,* by Jonathan Swift.

THE TERM YAHOO has nothing to do with the Internet or computers. It derives from Jonathan Swift's satirical masterpiece, *Gulliver's Travels*, where on one of his voyages, he describes talking horses as the only intelligent life form in a strange land, as compared to the debased, insipid humankind-like creatures, the Yahoos.

I choose the name "Yahoo" to describe the Columbus Police Department and a few of their officers during my early years growing up in Columbus. I witnessed many of their hypocritical, burlesque, racial arrogance in action. It can only be compared to Nazi Germany or the defunct, apartheid regime of South Africa. I grew up being afraid of them for good reason. Most White families cannot fathom the notion of the police as the boogieman, but in fact, during my youth, many were just that.

I would find it difficult if my past does not include some genuine injustices from a few of Columbus' law enforcement and state officials. Their actions make one wonder who, exactly, are the real criminals. This is not to say that the sum-total of Columbus' police officers are Yahoos. Indeed not. I have relatives and friends who are on the force and who serve the community honorably. Rather, this simply is intended to shed light on Columbus' past police problems and the White media who, in the past, had a tendency of turning a deft ear and manipulated the facts of those renegade Yahoos who took the law in their own hands in the Black communities and later on taking it to the college campuses.

The Ohio Sentinel, a defunct weekly Black tabloid and The Columbus Call and Post, both featured pages full of images of Blacks who had been beaten by The Columbus Police on a regular basis. It was a known fact that if one was Black and incarcerated, he was used as a punching bag, and if one were a Black female, other things happened. Rolls of photos displaying battered, swollen faces of Black men, women, and White women, who dated Black men, latticed the Sentinel's pages. It was a grid of horror that was routinely printed on the pages of these Black tabloids, but the White media conveniently covered-up these atrocities. The newspapers that I carried as a paperboy, the Dispatch, Citizen, and Journal Night Green, had no grotesque images of the truth.

[To substantiate this fact, one only has to try and find any evidence of this by inquiring at the Ohio Historical Society or the Columbus' Main Library newspaper morgue and request microfilms of the dominate media during those Yahoos' years of mayhem. What's equally amazing is the nine-year void of The Ohio Sentinels and Columbus Call and Post's tabloids. They are missing or misplaced minority microfilm media that substantiate those horrible years. A decade of African-American journalism documenting yahoo's atrocities is mysteriously missing from public resource archives? For the most part, negative imagery of Black males took center stage in the White press.]

The Columbus Police Department's grave history of racial profiling and police brutality was much worse than in many Southern cities, and this prompted my mother's real concern for her growing sons. With only a handful of Black police officers during my youth (perhaps about five on the whole force) my mother gave us important basic training on how to survive White policemen--especially during interrogation. Like most non-White mothers in White dominated societies, I'm sure that Nelson Mandela's parents imparted similar survival wisdom to him and could probably tell similar stories.

Besides the police survival preparations, Mom taught us to be kind and considerate, especially to adults.

"Don't assume that you know a lot. Play ignorant. Don't roll your eyes and never talk back to a policeman. Refer to them with a humble, 'yes sir' and a 'no sir' whenever questioned. I know you may want to retaliate and resist, but that's what they want you to do. Play dumb. And never, never run from them, but do as you are told and always walk away. Remember your telephone number and come home as quickly as possible."

It sounds very pathetic and sad that there is such a double standard in this country. Unfortunately, many American Whites have no idea that this type of thing occurs; but for Blacks it is an essential survival lesson. Mom drilled this into us on a regular basis. When we got older, (even as adults) she would say that we should never be caught in the company of White girls. She told us horrible stories of Blacks boys who had dated White girls in Columbus and what the police Yahoos did to them. Bunny, however, had a mind of his own and dated whomever he pleased.

There were a number of other items we adhered to for survival that no White kid ever had to deal with. Some of that changed in the '70s, when many White college students were labeled niggers by the cops during demonstrations on college campus communities at Ohio State, Ohio University, and of course, Kent State.

Meanwhile in schools, we were told something completely different. We were told that policemen were friendly who performed important duties in the community and that we could trust them. If there was a problem, we were to find the nearest policeman and report the trouble. They were there, so our teachers repeatedly told us, to protect and serve. But even at an early age, I was suspicious of them because Mom taught us one thing while the schools taught something completely different. Mom taught us how to *survive*, not only from the criminals, but also from the Columbus

Police Yahoos. Her teachings actually saved my life on several occasions.

One never hears of a White parent giving police survival contingency plans to their children. It is, however, prevalent in Black homes. As a Black youth, I thought of the Columbus police as being similar to the Nazis SS. I never heard the word "pogrom" until I was in graduate school. When I read its meaning, my thoughts immediately brought back memories of the Yahoos. Like their Nazi counterparts, they brutally killed (murdered) Blacks for the most minor infractions. It seemed like it was a sport. For instance, an eleven year-old Black youth, who was around my age at the time, was shot and killed after he broke into a school's milk machine one weekend after playing basketball. The *Dispatch* said that the Yahoos simply shot him because he resisted arrest. The coroner's report, however, indicated the trajectory of multiple bullets came from an angle that indicated that the youth was on his knees. Simply put, the kid was on his knees pleading. It was like an execution-style slaying. Furthermore, he was shot with an unauthorized weapon, the Yahoo's personal .38 Cal. automatic carbine. He unloaded a full clip from the automatic weapon, riddling the kid with bullets as he pleaded for mercy. The Yahoo was acquitted of all charges. His employment with the City of Columbus was uninterrupted. The White media downplayed the whole event. This same cop later tried to kill me at the age of twelve for an offense that I did not do.

I was put in jail and almost killed for simply jogging as a youth. I was on Mohawk Junior High School's cross-country team and had been running one snowy evening when suddenly, several police Yahoo cars pulled up. They all (about six of them) jumped out and pointed their revolvers at me. It was a serious Kodak moment and I felt like I was on the wrong end of a firing squad. I remember I was close enough to see their pistol's gray lead bullets inside the cylinders of their weapons. For some funny reason, I was impressed and confused at the same time. This was not happening to me.

"What do I do now?" I asked myself. "In the movies guys put up their hands. Is that what I'm supposed to do?" So I raised my hands slowly in the air and the next thing I knew they had slapped handcuffs on me! I was actually so skinny that I could have easily gotten out of them, but that proverbial bubble above my head, the one with my mother inside it, told me to keep them on. Appearing from out of nowhere, an old, toothless, white-haired White hag, perhaps in her late fifties or sixties and wearing a soiled apron, pointed her long contorted index finger at me saying to one officer:

"He's the nigger who beat up my husband and took his cab."

"What? Me--beating up her husband? Stealing a cab?" I wanted to laugh at the absurdity of it all. What a farce! I thought to myself. In the first place, I was a scrawny twelve-year-old kid who wouldn't think of fighting an adult. Besides, I only weighed eighty-eight pounds. Second, I wasn't reared that way. Besides, I never drove a car in my life and wouldn't know what to do with the damn thing if I had stolen it. Nevertheless, those mental midgets believed her. In addition, the same cop whom I believe shot the twelve-year old kid now looked at me and said, "So you like to run, huh?"

"Yes sir, I'm on Mohawk's track team," I replied proudly.

"So if I take off these cuffs, you'll run for me? I just wanna see how fast you can run."

A horrible realization came to me: He **is** probably the one who shot that twelve-year-old Black kid. The impending scenario he wanted was obvious. I may have been young, but I wasn't stupid. The expression of evil on his face was something I'll take to my grave. I was surprised at my composure of confronting this demon of death. Shivering in the cold still wearing handcuffs behind me, I looked around me at the array of police lights reflecting eerily off the night snow as cops puffed a mixture of smoke and frost. I couldn't help but think of how it must have been for my captured ancestors by a greater force. Nothing much has changed. In life, we all have our moment of truth. This was mine. And at that point in my young life, things from then on took on a new meaning. I redefined myself, not by choice, but by force and instantly I knew that my life would *never* be the same because of this moment. For me, this was the day *Howdy Doody* died as I realized that evil exists and is real. There are people who hate others simply because they are different. In silent rage, I spun around and looked at the nefarious policeman, and I wanted to be an adult just for just one minute. But the only thing I could do was to envision spitting sputum on his bovine face. Looking at him with loathing in my eyes, I abruptly remembered Mom's training. *Don't look defiant. Be humble.* So I deflected my stare away from him, bent my head, and gazed down at the snow-covered ground, knowing that I would survive this if I applied all of Mama's training. I willed myself to survive.

One of the younger levelheaded policemen with enough common sense stepped in. He suggested taking me to the downtown police Yahoo headquarters for a statement. The present scenario was even too tense for him. His racist superior officer wanted blood. He smelled blood and wanted to murder again. Everyone could sense it.

At that time, unfortunately, killing a Black by the police Yahoos would undoubtedly have been considered justified if you read it in one of Columbus's newspapers. It would have indicated that I probably resisted arrest after being detained for assault and battery of a taxi drive. I would have been just another notch on a gun handle, another Black kid murdered by the Columbus Police Department. Luckily, the younger police officer's logic won out. I sincerely believe he saved my life.

Sitting uncomfortably with my hands in handcuffs behind me in the backseat of a police car, hearing the crackling of the police radio was an utterly helpless and surreal experience. During the ride to the Yahoo station, all of my mental faculties gathered to question the events that had just taken place, while at the same time the environment played havoc with my sanity and senses. Glaring lights, shiny metal badges, and stale smoke filling my nostrils; and the bitter taste of bile on my tongue as I sat pondering my fate--it was all too unreal for a boy who was just jogging. Conjuring up all my mother's training, I let myself go limp and mentally prepared my body to be beaten-up. (*Go limp, don't resist. The blows will hurt more if you resist and are tense. Remember they beat Jesus too… . But Mom was Jesus beaten-up at my age?*)

The ride to the police station was short. It was only a couple blocks away. When we entered the station, I saw a Black police officer mopping the floors. He looked at me in disgust and I wanted to say to him that I didn't do anything. (*Hey, why are you here mopping the Yahoo' floors? Why aren't you out there protecting your children from the **real** criminals?*) I screamed inside my head.

I was ushered to a small room with chipped paint and cheap green tiled floor to be interrogated. The Yahoo who wanted to shoot me was my interrogator. He lit a cigarette, inhaled deeply, twisted his mouth, and blew a stream of smoke from the side of his face and started spitting out bits of tobacco from his tongue. As we both sat there, I stole a look at him and noticed his pale green eyes that were the color of pus. Once more he inhaled deeply, but this time he blew a bellowing cloud of smoke in my face. I looked at him forcing back a laugh because he looked like the pale-purple insect in Walt Disney's *Alice In Wonderland*. I winced and fanned the smoke away with my hands.

"Here's a statement that I want you to sign. If you confess and sign this statement, I'll give you a smoke."

When I told him that I didn't smoke, he tried to coax me to have one anyway. *(What a dumb-ass!)*

"Look, you know you did it. We tracked your footsteps in the snow to the scene of the crime."

"The footsteps you tracked were not mine, sir." I said. (*He's full of shit*), I thought. Very politely, I tried to explain the illogical absurdity of it all. Surely any moron could see the ludicrousness of how could an 85-pound, 12-year-old kid, who has ever been in trouble before, beat up an adult cab driver and steals his taxi? I didn't even know how to drive! I started coughing from the smoke in the small room and repeated that I didn't beat up the cab driver or take his taxicab. I then told him (as Mom had taught us) that I wanted to make a phone call home.

When I called home, I explained to Mom what all had happened. The first thing she asked was, "Are you all right?" I told her not to worry, that I was okay. I tried not to cry, but I think I did anyway. She said she would catch a cab and come down there immediately. Mom came down to the police station, but I didn't see her because they were already processing me for lockup. I spent that night in juvenile jail, and six more nights there as boys my age masturbated under their blankets and were beaten up in the mornings for minor violations. I applied all of Mom's training by eating all my food, getting as much rest as possible and keeping inconspicuously to myself. I knew that Mom was doing all she could do to get me released.

During visitation hours, it was a pleasant relief to see Mom and hear about all her efforts to get me out. All that I could think about was the embarrassment at school and the shame I caused my family in the neighborhood. After my release, and for the remainder of my life, I would have a bitter loathing for the Columbus Police Department and their insipid racist tactics. My young life almost came to a tragic end simply because of the arrogance of authorities and just because I was a Black junior high school jogger. My loathing for them seethed for a long time.

The Columbus Police Department did not have many minorities on their force. One of their excuses was that minorities could not pass the police civil service exams. What a crock! And the media bought into it. The media inadvertently substantiated many of the police Yahoo's wrong doings by not covering or examining the truth of many of the horrendous crimes they perpetrated. Many Whites on the force, at the time, came straight from the most racist areas of Appalachia or other parts of the South with little or no urban knowledge. Rumors circulated that many of them were Klansmen. But there was one Black police officer named Inspector Austin who was smart, perceptive, and full of integrity. Somehow he rose through the ranks during the time of unsympathetic segregation in the police force. When it came time to appoint a new Chief, he took the exam and received the highest score than anyone taking the test. He should have been promoted to the position, but the powers-that-be in Columbus' City Hall could not see a Black man in that rank so they "created" a bogus position of "Inspector" to deny Austin the coveted Chief's position.

****

There have been many other incidents with the Columbus Police that validate their "Yahoo" title. In 1963, for example, I had just flown to Columbus on a two-week leave from USMC Base,

Camp Pendleton, California. I had recently been promoted a Marine Lance Corporal wearing my Summer Tropical uniform when Virgil picked me up at the airport after a long four-hour flight. Virgil, a junior at Ohio State University, had just bought a beautiful lime green 1957 Plymouth, with its fishtail rear that had a push button transmission. It was gorgeous and I couldn't wait to take it for a spin. We arrived at the new house Mom had purchased on Carpenter Street, near Livingston Avenue, only a couple blocks away from South Lane. It was a welcome sight, this big brick house with one large bathroom upstairs and an extra shower in the basement. We even had grass on the front yard and two large urns that had plants in them as you came up the steps. I hugged Mom and she wanted to prepare a meal for me, but I had other plans. Virgil let me borrow his gorgeous lime green '57 Plymouth and I was off to see Louvinia, our childhood friend whom I'd been writing since bootcamp.

On the corner of Parsons and Broad, I stopped at a traffic light, waiting for it to change. There was a police car on the opposite side across the street that remained in place well after the light had turned green. I waited and waited and it had occurred to me that perhaps his vehicle had stalled. Not wanting the light to change again, I made a left signal, turned and headed west on Broad. I glanced in the rear view mirror, surprised to see the police car's red lights flashing. The policeman motioned me to pull over. What happened next didn't make sense. Keeping my hands on the wheel, closing my eyes, I inhaled deeply, releasing frustration and conjuring up another one of Mom's teachings--self-control. I tried to explain the situation as calmly and politely as I could, but it was no use talking. There was no rhyme, reason, or logic for what was about to take place next. Instead of handing me a ticket, he asked me to get out of the car, which I did obligingly. Then he turned me around and leaned me against the car, spreading my legs with his nightstick, and patted me down like a common criminal on one of the busiest streets in Columbus. I was not so much embarrassed for myself, but for the uniform that I was wearing. I stood there stoically as the Yahoo put handcuffs on me. Although I could have easily disarmed the Yahoo and bashed his pointed head in, I remained polite and calm. I had not a drop of alcohol in my system or was I indignant when I was being harassed. Soon a van and a tow truck arrived, and I watched from inside the van as the Yahoo tow driver unceremoniously manhandled Virgil's beautiful '57 Plymouth, and hauled it away.

I had been in Columbus less than an hour when the Yahoos escorted me to the aroma of piss and sour vomit of the "drunk" tank holding cell with intoxicated derelicts lying in their own waste.

One derelict lay passed out, snoring loudly, and sleeping comfortably as he floated on urine on a stainless steel cot next to a foul-smelling stainless steel overflowing commode that didn't have a toilet seat. The smell of my immediate environment was nauseating, and I didn't want to touch anything not only because the place was filthy, but also because I didn't want to soil my clean tropical uniform. I had always been an immaculately dressed Marine and felt proud of the uniform I wore. The ordeal was dehumanizing. I could only absorb my sizzling anger at the Yahoo's arrogance, and I prayed that some dark night I'd meet the arresting Yahoo in a dark alley.

Used to standing guard duty at Camp Pendleton in the hot sun for long periods of time, I decided to do the same in the cell. I stood at parade-rest with my hands behind my back, knees slightly bent, legs spread shoulder length apart, and with my feet planted firmly on the floor staring straight ahead. I stood there motionless for at least two hours, looking blankly out beyond the jail bars. Some Yahoos passed by my cell and looked at me with bewilderment. I tried being in another world as I meditated on the mantra of my mother's wisdom. Finally Virgil came and bailed me out. I was due to go to court in the morning, but at that moment, all I wanted was to see the girl I had unintentionally stood-up. By the time I got to her place, she was gone.

The next morning, the judge dismissed the case saying, of all things, that he liked Marines. Nevertheless, I had lost valuable leave time and Virgil's beautiful '57 Plymouth was impounded that cost me $50.00 of the precious leave money.

"What utter assholes," I thought to myself. "There's a war brewing in Southeast Asia and I just might have to go there with many of my friends and here I am only minutes landed at the airport, still in my uniform yet another of Columbus' so-called finest decided to dampen my spirit. Who in the hell is the enemy anyway?"

****

Those who were familiar with Dr. Allen knew him to have been a quiet, polite and dignified man. I don't know where he came from, but his mannerism implied a Southerner, a true gentleman to the core. His tailored suits fit him impeccably on his tall, thin frame, which always included a fedora. He wore a pencil thin moustache under his Cherokee nose and his close-cropped, wavy hairstyle gave him the appearance similar to Duke Ellington. As a matter-of-fact, their resemblance is quite remarkable. Wherever he walked, men tipped their hats and ladies smiled at him. He was the epitome of style and grace. Dr. Allen's fashion was a throw back of the late '30s and early '40s—the "polite" Jazz years of America. For me, being in his presence was like being in a military staff officers' meeting. You knew he was in command and you felt good about his control and self-assurance similar to that of a General. He indeed was one of the most impressive men I've ever known and one of Columbus' most influential Black citizens.

Dr. Allen had been a flight surgeon during World War Two and served with the famed Tuskegee Airmen in North Africa and Italy campaigns. He told me tales of his war adventures still retaining his pride of the famous squadron he had been assigned to.

Perhaps it may have been because they did not have any children that Dr. Allen and his wife, Lillian, took extreme interest and volunteered his time, money, and energy to charitable organizations such as The Big Brothers Association. I remember Dr Allen bringing in a distinguished speaker from Baltimore, Maryland, on behalf of the Big Brothers Association in January 1969. I was now in the Air Force stationed at Lockbourne, Air Force Base, just outside the city. I was a medic and slated to be shipped to South East Asia (Thailand) in March. In any event, Dr. Allen wanted to treat the honored guests and their wives to a late night hospitality meal at Jack and Benny's diner, located in the heart of Columbus on Broad and High. The diner was frequented by many police officers

132

who stopped in for coffee and a friendly chat with the waitresses. That late winter evening, Dr. Allen and his guests had been patiently waiting for quite some time for their order to arrive. He decided to inquire about their order, went to the counter, and politely asked the waitress if their order would be coming soon. When he approached the waitress about his order, two Yahoos who had been talking to the waitress and drinking coffee became belligerent and seized Dr. Allen. Perhaps the Yahoos misunderstood his intentions. It may have been Dr. Allen's Creole wife, who could pass for White, or his well-dressed appearance provoked a racist reaction from the Yahoos. More than likely, it probably had been the Yahoo's way of showing off to the waitresses.

Whatever the reason, it should not have transpired the way it did. Even when Dr. Allen tried to explain himself, one of the Yahoos hit him, knocking him on the counter. When Dr. Allen tried to defend himself (as best a late middle-aged person could) it became a mêlée because the Yahoo's partner joined in. When Dr. Allen's wife and guests attempted to intervene, one of the Yahoos warned them not to interfere or they too would be arrested. The out-of-town honored guest speaker, his wife, and Dr. Allen's wife stood there horrified as the Yahoos dragged Dr. Allen outside to their van and proceeded to beat him in the snow. He was beaten so badly that one of them said that they ought to take him to a hospital. But before they threw him inside the van, they removed his belt and dropped his pants to his ankles. This tactic was designed to give the impression that the person in custody was inebriated and resisted arrest. At the emergency room, Dr. Allen, swollen, bruised, and tattered stood there. The nurses and physicians on duty were stunned at how this could have happened to one of their own. The Yahoos had taken Dr. Allen to one of the hospitals where he was on staff. Realizing their predicament, they began to worry and started scheming up a story to cover their asses. Dr. Allen did not go to jail, instead his wounds were treated and he was sent home.

Late that night, I got a call from my in-laws explaining the incident. And that same evening, another set of Yahoos had beaten up a noted Black dentist. I went over to see my friend Dr. Allen and held back my rage, as he lay restless in bed, bruised with both eyes closed-puffed and face swollen and battered. He explained the story to me saying how ludicrous the whole incident had been. All this provoked an inquiry. Dr. Allen and his wife stated that they were going to inform the NAACP. I said that was not enough. That morning, I got on the phone and called all the media I could. I was surprised when the three television stations came and interviewed him at his bedside as well as the radio stations. Even the conservative Columbus Dispatch had an interview with him. Finally, the people got a chance to really see the result of the Yahoo's racist activities.

Dr. Allen's incident remained to be very upsetting for me not only because he was a friend, but also the fact that I would soon be leaving to be part of a very unpopular war. What was the purpose? Fight and die for *this*? Furthermore, a very unsettling question kept popping in my head: *Who was the real enemy? The Vietcong or Columbus' Yahoos?*

A day or so after Dr. Allen's news story got out to the community, hundreds of demonstrators with placards, Black and White, marched on the city hall, the police station, and the mayor's office. It was a time when there were many marches and protests, and I was given looks of bewilderment and admiration as I took an active part in it wearing my Air Force uniform. We marched straight to the mayor's office demanding an explanation, but he wasn't anywhere to be found. I remembered the times I had been incarcerated there as a kid and the time when I was a Marine standing at parade rest in a filthy drunkard's cell, all for things I had been accused of but did not do. If I had a burning torch, I would have burned the City Hall down to the ground that morning, as I was to leave the very next day for the War in Southeast Asia.

It was a long flight and my mind was crammed full of issues about the Yahoos of my hometown. Later, in the sweltering cramped confines of my room on the base, I read the cherished letters my wife wrote to me explaining the results of the trial. She mailed me news clippings of the court hearings and the lies and cover-ups from the Yahoos. Later, she wrote and said that the Yahoos were not indicted because a Black man, who was supposedly a witness, testified on behalf of the police. Everyone knows that trick. They paid a Black witness with bribes/leniencies of some sort and then compel them to testify against another. The whole thing was a sham and a travesty of justice. Yes, I loathe the Columbus Yahoos for that and all their other atrocities and the media that supported them. But most of all, I abhor them for taking away my childhood security.

Recently, though, Columbus has appointed a Black police chief [I think he is the same one whom I saw mopping the floor that night of my childhood incarceration] and even elected a Black mayor. *Black Entertainment Television* (B.E.T.) named Columbus as the best city for African-Americans to live. Times have changed indeed. I am inclined to believe, however, that those changes have had a lot to do with the FBI's post-Hoover investigations of the Yahoos stemming from the many complaints of concerned citizens like those of James Moss, a former Black police officer, who had the courage to report to the U.S. Attorney and the FBI the enormity of Yahoos' criminal abuse and inhumanity to Columbus' minority citizens. Today, even the conservative *Columbus Dispatch* seems to be interested in an egalitarian approach to the news.

In July 2003, two Black inmates were set free after twenty-six years of confinement in Ohio's penal system for a crime that they did not commit. The Yahoos withheld evidence, lied to the courts, and paid informants to falsely accuse the two young Black men. Twenty-six years imprisonment for a crime they had nothing to do with. CNN news reported the travesty of justice to the world and the judge, who released the men, apologized. But how can an apology give back twenty-six years of pain of imprisonment for something the Yahoos trumped up just to make it look good for their own careers? In essence, the two men, now in their fifties, had their future stolen.

U.S.M.C. Uncle Sam's Misguided Children

Chapter Eleven

THE THOUGHT OF JOINING the United States Marine Corps after high school in 1961, at the tender age of seventeen, fooled everyone, including myself. I only weighted 116 pounds. The Navy doctor who gave me my enlistment physical said I had to weigh at least 124 pounds. He scratched his head and said that if I wanted to be a Marine that bad he would *give* me the extra eight pounds on my physical.

My first day at bootcamp is something I'll never forget. Everything was new to me. It was the first time I had left home, the first time I had flown in an airplane, and been completely on my own.

After arriving at San Diego airport, recruits gathered around near a door that said: "Recruit Waiting Area." The Marine recruit started teasing the Navy recruits in a friendly manner, but all of us had a look of vague expectation on our faces. Soon a driver of a "cattle car" (a trailer/bus that looks like a horse trailer pulled by a truck) told the Marine recruits to get on board. We were all very excited and started chatting as we entered the cattle car. After we were all loaded on, the driver, a Private First Class, stuck his head inside and said he didn't want to hear one peep from any of us. He then slammed the door shut, climbed inside the truck, drove off to The Marine Corps Recruit Depot and we did not say a thing during the twenty-minute drive.

The DI's met us as we got off the cattle car, and I was immediately impressed with them because they looked elegant in their tropical tan uniforms, high polished shoes, and their smart Smokey Bear hats that dipped into their faces. All the other recruits looked to be the same age as me, and I could tell that most were frightened by the DI's silence. Then with monotone voices, they coolly but efficiently instructed us to line up according to their rosters listing our prospective DI's. It was like the calm before the storm. After our DI's formed us into platoons, they then took over with a reserved vengeance.

"Hello, girls, I'm Staff Sergeant Tavarossi and I will be your DI. You will be in Platoon 246. You will always remember your platoon for the remainder of your sorry ass lives." He began to walk slowly up and down the platoon, looking each of us directly in the face.

"I will be your mother, your father, and your god for the next twelve weeks. What I see in front of me, however, is a bunch of cheap civilians, shit-for-brains, young fucking American scumbags. You are not worthy to even look at me. And from now on when we look at you, you had better not make eye contact with us, you fucking maggots. Because, from what I see, you girls couldn't be a pimple on a Marine's ass."

The other DI's were introduced and walked behind Tavarossi with their own agenda. One recruit, out of his good nature or nervousness, was smiling and Tavarossi walked up to him, pressing his face in the recruit's and began to yell,

"What the fuck are you smiling at? Are you queer for my gear? Wipe that smile off your face before I kick your ass right here in front of God and everyone else. Where in the fuck are you from, *boy*!?"

"Texas," said the recruit.

"Who in the fuck said you could speak? Did I give you permission to speak to me, asswipe?"

"Nnno Sir."

"Get down and give me fifty you Texas-ass faggot. There're only two things in Texas, queers and steers, and I don't see any horns on your head. And for now on--this goes for all of you--the first thing that comes out of your mouths is, 'sir' and the last thing you say is 'sir'. Do you girls understand that? "

"Sir, Yes Sir!" we yelled in unison.

"And, if I ask you a question, and your answer is affirmative, you say: 'Aye, aye Sir!' Is that clear?"

"Sir, aye, aye Sir!"

"Now form a line, you maggots. Asshole-to-belly button. Double time, march!"

It was a pathetic circus. Guys were tripping over each other, stepping over the fallen, and those who had the misfortune of bringing luggage were the worse ones as we ran asshole to bellybutton to the barbershop where they cut off all our hair. We looked like onions. That type of bantering and performance went on for twelve weeks. Actually, Willie had already conditioned me in the "Sir" usage and my long distance running experience in track at Mohawk and South helped me immensely.

Learning how to kill became an art form and I found a transcendent taste for handling weapons. I had a fascination for seeing things get blown-up. I liked the visual effects of red tracers crisscrossing the night sky and the explosions of blinding white phosphorous silhouetting backgrounds into definitive negative spaces. I listened with awe to the distant sounds of a night firefight resonating popcorn being popped. The smell of freshly spent ammunition smelled sweet to me. In the evenings, I sat on my footlocker and sharpened my bayonet with great care, slowly rubbing the blade over stone and spit, trying desperately to cut floating toilet paper with it. And I especially enjoyed bayonet practice. It was one of my greatest pleasures. The Marine style of bayonet fighting is like boxing. Holding my M1 at port, arms in a boxer's stance, I saw myself as Joe Louis punching, jabbing, and stabbing.

"Listen up, girls, your rifle is your best friend. It is like your girlfriend back home--who is probably fucking your best friend at this very moment. They have to be cleaned and lubricated. If your weapon ain't clean and lubricated, you can really forget about little Susie back home, because your ass will be dead. Do I make myself clear, you shit-for-brains?"

"Sir, Yes Sir!"

At night, we slept with our rifles in our narrow bunk beds. We took our M1 rifles apart, cleaned them, polished the wooden stocks, and brushed sand and dust from the chamber and barrels. And if an unlucky private dropped his weapon at any time, "his ass was grass and the DI a lawnmower." I remembered my rifle serial number and the names of all of its moving parts. I knew its muzzle velocity, expertly calculated the windage and elevation of my target, and knew the exact slack of my trigger squeeze, even surprising myself every time I shot off a round. Soon, I was shooting expert at the rifle range. Being small-framed, I could weave my body into impossible firing positions holding my rifle sturdy with its sling wrapped tightly around my arm. There was an excitement as I controlled my breathing and heartbeat, while concentrating on my target, squeezing the trigger and--bam! Seeing the white spotter go up indicating a bull's eye was my reward. It thrilled me even more when a drill instructor smiled saying,

"Out fucking standing Private Hollingsworth. Nice shooting. Maybe we'll make a goddamn Marine out of you yet."

My marksmanship was so good that I later became a rifle instructor. Envisioning that Columbus racist cop as my target motivated me. Through my M1 rifle's peep sight, I saw him as my target. He provoked in me the art of killing. Becoming a Marine was taking hold of me and I took pleasure in hearing our DI tell me that I was becoming a teenage killing machine. I meant business--a Black Marine's version of Audrey Murphy. All I wanted to do was to kill the enemy—whoever it may be.

Martial arts were a crucial part of bootcamp that I enjoyed. Asian Marines, probably from Hawaii, taught us hand-to-hand combat. Some of the things they taught seemed extreme, like using our fingers as eye-gougers, and after gouging out an opponent's eyes, we should squish them in our hands. If we were on shore liberty and saw an unknown Marine in a fight, we were obligated to team up with him and kick the living hell out of his opponent. There was no such thing as a fair fight as portrayed in John Wayne's movies. The only honor is winning by any means necessary.

A Black Marine named Doug told me his fantasy was being locked in a room with a Klansman and a straight razor. We were in the barracks preparing for the next day's inspection. Both of us sat on footlockers spit-shining our shoes, cleaning our rifles, and sharpening our bayonets. He told me that he had slashed the faces of two White sailors recently down Tijuana in a provoked fight. Coming out of a whorehouse, the sailors followed him, called him names, wanting to fight the lone Black man who wore nice civilian clothes. What took place, he said, was fast and deliberate.

"The only thing them crackers saw was a brilliant circling motion in the night--swish, swish. By the time they realized what was happening, they were in shock. They stared at each other through their own bloody eyes realizing what I had just done. They then screamed and ran down an alley pushing in the remains of their faces with their hands.

"Damn, man. Why did you have to use a straight razor instead of your fists?" I asked him.

"Because," he said, "in the mornings--for the rest of their motherfucker's lives--whenever they shaved, they'd think back at that foolish mistake. You see, Charles, I just don't give a damn anymore. I'm tired of those motherfuckers fucking with me. I just wanted to get up close and do damage. Hell, we learnt that in bootcamp, right? You know making it a personal thing like they taught us in hand-to-hand. I just gave those bastards my signature."

That night I dreamt about what he said: A personal thing. Pilots have a different kind of feeling for killing when they drop napalm and bombs. They rationalize that distance detaches them from the slaughter. But when you are up close, close enough to carve a man's face up, that's real personal, and it will haunt you for the rest of your life if you are not conditioned. I dreamt about the Columbus police Yahoo who wanted to shoot me. In the dream, I used my razor-sharp bayonet crisscrossing his face with the same coolness as he had when he had his pistol sights on my skinny thirteen year-old frame. I envisioned him being in denial of the painless cuttings from the cold steel that I inflicted on him as I slashed his face to ribbons. His denial ushered in enough time for me to strike several blows across his groin area, cutting off his little pink penis. Certainly, he would think this surely wasn't happening to him, just like I felt being tossed in his police car, trying to control my shock by repeating my mother's survival mantra. In my dream, I wanted him to experience the humiliation of it all--not having control of his destiny even just for a moment. I would want him to realize that the oozing substance in his hands was the visceral remains of his face. I'd spare him his life because death would be too merciful. But every time he would go to the bathroom to piss, he'd think of me. He'd think of all the Black children he had murdered while wearing the police uniform which was supposed to represent the protection of citizens. I dreamt that dream several times in my life, waking up in cold sweat each time. I wanted a personal relationship with that son-of-a-bitch.

****

I had finally arrived. The Marine Corps' promise of making recruits into men, no longer left any doubt about wishing instantaneously to become one. I felt I had proved myself by surviving one of the world's toughest basic training courses when other recruits, bigger and stronger than me, were sent home. After bootcamp, I went home on leave. I had gained thirty-six pounds of lean, hard muscle and prayed that the racist yahoo cop would cross my path. I had erroneously thought manhood was a destination by wanting to instantaneously be one. I soon realized that manhood is a journey--a lifetime passage. As Robert Bly so eloquently expressed in his book, *Iron John,* about the esoteric rites of passage and how a woman can raise a daughter, but her son, however will rebel at a prescribed age of reckoning if an earnest male is not there to lead him on the right path. It is a primordial initiation handed down from generation to generation in a variety of cultures in various forms. The Marines had fulfilled that part of my induction into manhood. However, deep down inside, above all the bravado and the thirty-six additional pounds, I was still *Sugar Pie.* I still had plenty of insecurities, and I was still a virgin.

There is a patch from my Marine Corps past that has stuck with me ever since bootcamp. And no matter how hard I try, or how much education I've received, I find it difficult to break. It's the bad habit of swearing. There is usually a catalyst of some sort stemming from a provocation from others or myself. The words sometimes slip out unrepentantly if I am highly aggravated. And I cannot blame this entity on Charlie, because Mom drilled us on using good language. The Corps conditioned me to defend myself by all means necessary and I think part of my problem lies in that fact. Then there is the social etiquette of barrack life and it's communal influence. The guys in the Marines are made up mostly of rural White and inner-city Black men from all across the United States with each having their own creative expression of swearing. And when you live with a group of Marines, cussing comes natural as the air you breathe.

"Where in the fuck are you going, dip-shit?"

"Fucking a-right, shit-for-brains."

"I'm going on fuckin' leave, in the mother-fuckin' morning and get me some real pussy, while the rest of you turd faces will be wackin' you winnies."

"Hey, pass me the fuckin' salt this way."

"Wow, did you guys take a good look at the new BAM (a derogatory remark denoting a female Marine a.k.a Broad Ass Marine) captain? She's one ugly bitch. I wouldn't fuck her with your dick."

The word "fuck" was a good part of our everyday vocabulary and it was difficult not to engage in a conversation without using it. When I went home, I found myself in some of the most embarrassing situations and most of the time I didn't even know what I had said until it was too late. Even today, I have to watch myself when I talk.

****

When my thirty days leave expired, I took the return train back to California. This was before the creation of Amtrak, a time when America had its last vintage of a railroad that worked. It was the end of a distinctive era in American history. The railroad routes and trains that carried people from city to city still had exotic names. I rode on the *El Capitan* going home and the name of the return trip train is now long forgotten. I purchased my ticket at a travel office in Oceanside, California and was given a colorful brochure with photos of relaxed passengers and exotic places like Flag Staff, Arizona and Santa Fe, New Mexico. I may have been one of the last passengers to make the run across the continent to Chicago because soon folks preferred flying. From Chicago, I took another train to Ohio. The three-day trip was pleasant. The polite passengers seemed to be in no hurry and I got a chance to see America from the ground, watching cities, farms, and Indian reservations roll by.

****

Camp Del Mar, California, located on the outskirts of Oceanside, is part of Marine Corps Base Camp Pendleton. It overlooks the Pacific Ocean where the First Marines Division and Force Recon train for amphibious warfare. My unit, First Force Service Regiment, Fleet Marine Force (F.M.F.) a.k.a. the Fighting Mother Fuckers, consisted of amphibious landing crafts, amphibious drivers, mechanics, and a few Ontos a small very maneuverable anti-tank track vehicles. there also was a contingency of aging amphibious "Ducks", relics of World War Two that were still operational. In 1963, after spending two years at Camp Pendleton, I

143

was reassignment as an honor guard at the Marine Corps Barracks in Norfolk Virginia, a few days after the assassination of J.F.K.

Coming from the Mid-West, the ocean made a tremendous impression on me. Captivated by its painted sunsets and ocean sounds, I almost cried when I saw the magnificent glory of it all along the beach. I wondered about all the islands and countries and cultures the Pacific held. During off duty hours, I wandered into town and took long walks on the beach till night, meditating on the waves, talking to the starry water, and thinking about my virginity.

Sex and The Cuban Missile Crisis

Chapter Twelve

WHEN FIDEL CASTRO *successfully took over the control of Cuba from Fulgencio Batista in 1959, I had just graduated from Mohawk Jr. High School. A few years earlier, Governor Faubus ordered Arkansas National Guard troops to block nine Black high school students from entering Central High School in arrogant defiance of* Brown vs. Topeka *ruling to integrate a 1954 Supreme Court decision, which ordered that U.S. public schools be desegregated "with all deliberate speed." When President Eisenhower became fed up with the racist Governor Faubus' superciliousness of the Governor's ploy, Eisenhower federalized Arkansas' troops and sent a detachment of the 101st Airborne to protect Black children to attend public schools. Also during this time Black college students formed "Sit-ins" in lunch counters in the South and participated in voter registration. A young Alabama minister organized a successful bus boycott in Birmingham, and bigot despots regularly made headline news. Castro, in the mean time, who had unsuccessfully sought help from The United States, but was denied, became a champion in most Black communities. When the United States shunned his help, it was with done with an arrogant smirk and Castro took a serious bent toward furthering communism. And during his talk at the United Nations, he stayed in Harlem. I've always had a strong reverence for him and our arrogance disturbed me in my pre-high school years. That arrogance still continues in other third-world countries, and to be honest, I respect Castro's integrity more than those racist, redneck politicians who are the same ones who continue to perpetuate the Cuban boycott. To me, the whole problem with our government's attitude toward Cuba and other small third-world government is [political] testosterone and bull feces. During the Cuban Missile Crisis, however, I supported wholeheartedly the*

Camelot Court. I so much cherished President Kennedy that I would have walked in a lion cage wearing a pork chop suit.

****

At the tender age of seventeen, I was attached to the Marine Corps First Division in an amphibious unit at Camp Del Mar and we frequently held field maneuvers on the vast rocky, rattlesnake, coyote infested areas of Camp Pendleton. We fired blanks at each other, simulating a virtual combat environment. It was just that, *simulating* as we played grownup cowboys and Indians. In October 1962, however, the Regiment prepared for a major field exercise consisting of some serious hardware like tanks, heavy artillery pieces, and amphibious tanks. It seemed odd, but we just took it in stride as simply another field exercise. I remember waking up one morning, looking outside my barrack's window and seeing a dozen or more Navy ships in the bay and the base bustled with activity. Something major was up. Later, we learned that Castro had Russian rockets in Cuba and Russian ships were sailing for Cuba loaded with more missiles. President Kennedy had told Premier Nikita Khrushchev to back off or face serious consequences. It seemed like the Russians were intent on delivering their goods and J.F.K. was just as determined not to back down. It was fast becoming that the old proverbial: What happens when an irresistible force meets an immovable object.

We were told that this was not an exercise but the real thing. We mustered regularly, having inspections like the dreaded "junk on the bunk" that displayed our field gear and M1 rifles. Everything was inventoried. Paper work became a headache for the officers and high noncoms, and Marines in my barracks had their ears glued to the radio or watched the news in the squad bay for the latest events. Marines whose wives lived far away phoned frequently. The tables where Marines played cards were now taken up with letter writing. The look on everyone's faces took on a serious disquietness.

A few days later, "Top" (the First Sergeant) read a roster of the men who would be on the first, second, and third assault waves

146

at a predestinated Cuban beach. My name was on the first assault wave team. We were to make last minute preparations and restricted to the base. Each day new names were added to various assault waves and amphibious vessels. I, however, was concerned about only one thing: I didn't want to die as a virgin. I had to find a female--any female would do just to know what sex was like. But the pickings were slim on the base. I had no problem with fighting and the possibility of being killed. Glory was what we were trained for anyway. But the older Marines, who fought in World War Two and Korea, said that we (the young ones) were combat virgins in every sense of the word. That we were just *young, dumb, and full of cum.* They told us that combat is not what we think it is and that most of us will probably shit or piss in our pants when the first bullet flew over our heads.

One older World War Two veteran, who lived in the barracks, had been demoted several times was basically an alcoholic. But we all respected and tolerated him for his valor at Guadalcanal, Siapan, Tarawa, and Okinawa. Often in his sleep, he would call out the name of his estranged Japanese wife, Icheiko. And when he came into the squad bay from a drinking binge at the NCO club or in town, he would lay on his bunk in the darkness speaking broken Japanese, crying and calling for Icheiko. It kept us all awake.

I remember one afternoon after chow, the old veteran told me that I ought to re-enlist and request to be station in the Far East like Japan or Okinawa simply because (according to him) Asian pussy is better than American pussy.

"How?" I asked.

"Because it is slanted," he said. (Hell, he made it seem believable.) I set there spellbound and listened and soaked up every word especially when other Marines, who had been stationed in the Far East, testified to the authenticity of his incongruous claim. I tried to hide my virginity like a thief, but in the barracks all the guys talked about sex and they now knew I was a cherry. The White guys talked about eating pussy and Blacks guys talked about getting a "snapper." I just listened, absorbed everything I heard for future reference. Slanted pussy, snappers, and the art of eating pussy--

147

indeed, I was young, dumb, and full of cum and didn't know shit from Shinola.

When I heard Top was looking for me to go pack my gear as part of the first wave to hit Cuba's shore (the most expendable and the ones with the most casualties) I was so skinny that I was able to hide inside my locker as my name was called. I'd be damned if I was going to die a virgin. Marines in my Company were very supportive keeping quiet about my whereabouts. They were aware of my virgin status and willing to cover for me as I hid, while another Marine Private First Class, volunteered to take my place. So, later that evening, I went on Cinderella liberty (a pass until midnight) with Corporal Ben Pullium to San Diego to see if I could get lucky. I was desperate and would have fucked a female gorilla if it wore lipstick and a skirt. I idolized Ben because of his demeanor and deep commanding voice. He was a model Black Marine from Gary, Indiana, who stood tall and commanded attention. I frantically wanted to go to Tijuana to get laid, but it was off limits. I kept agonizing about the possibility of some Cuban shooting me and dying a virgin. Shore Patrol and Marine Military Police were busy that night with loud speakers calling out the names of ships and units, ordering them to report back to their base or ship. We saw trucks loaded with Marines and Sailors being shuttled back and forth in the night. Finally, it was time to leave San Diego. We had gotten a few drinks, but unfortunately no women.

The next morning three-fourths of the base had left including the Marine who took my place. Some were on ships and some flew out from El Torro Marine Corps Air Base in Anaheim. I now regretted not going and wished that I had left with the rest of my unit. As it stood, the few Marines on the base had to work 12 hours on and 12 hours off. I never worked so hard in my life and no liberty was granted, and we were restricted to base where I remained a virgin.

****

After the Russians backed down, the world was relieved. The Marines who left were now partying in the Caribbean as the ships stopped off at various exotic ports. When the guys returned, they told me beautiful stories of love, adventure, and showed photos

148

of those lovely Caribbean women. (The only love I had had was with "Rosy Palm and her Five Daughters.") After the crisis, I decided it was time for me to know what all this fuss over pussy was about. When the military lifted the off-limits ban to Tijuana, I made a few excursions across the border with some of my friends to partake in the delights of lovely Mexican women, but I was still too shy. In the bars, the ladies descended on us like locusts and with their hands under the table, they fumbled with our cocks while we drank beer, trying our damnedest to be cool. One by one, a Marine would be escorted to a room behind the bar, leaving me alone buying watered down drinks with women desperately trying to sell their wares. I would sweat bullets trying to conjure up the courage to be led to one of the back rooms. My reticent shyness, however, eventually frustrated them as they huffed off saying something in Spanish, leaving me alone at the table as they descended on another John. The guys returned, one by one, flopped down, rumpled, relieved, with shit eating grins on their faces and ordered more drinks. Two weeks in the boonies made them thirsty and horny. They asked me if the girl I had been with was any good. I'd lie, saying how fantastic she had been in bed. I just couldn't get myself the courage to do it. I told myself that I was a "cunt-coward" and, I continued being a horny virgin. It would take about another year before I could drum up enough courage, in addition to a few shots of tequila, to be led by the hand of a seniorita to her behind-the-bar-chamber in Tijuana's infamous Two Dollar Alley. The cost of losing my virginity was $2.40.

****

The day John F. Kennedy was shot, there was a solemn heaviness in my barracks, and much confusion. Many Marines walked around dazed and in denial. I had just returned from the personnel office excited about my transfer orders to Marine Barracks Norfolk, Virginia. My excitement stopped when I was told that the President had just been shot in Dallas and the world waited to find out if he survived. It stunned and saddened me as well as many of the Marines in the Barracks. Most were glued to the TV, while some surfed the channels of their private radios trying to get

149

the news. I was surprised how rapidly the TV networks had broadcasted the news while the radio channels didn't have a clue to what had historically happened. They were still broadcasting their programs and playing top ten hits. It was a smorgasbord media circus in the barracks and confusion abound. The repeated imagery on the TV showing the President's violent recoil of his head, and then slumping in Jackie's arms followed by the chaos proved many of our fears. We all knew too well the results of what happens from the velocity of a high-powered rifle. Some Marines were desperately holding back tears; others resigned nervously to do mundane tasks like cleaning weapons, spit-shining their shoes as a masked attempt of controlling their emotions. Some Marines acquiesced and stared at nothing in particular while lying on their bunks smoking.

I remembered a few from Texas entering the barracks laughing at the situation. Everyone told them to be quiet so they could concentrate on the news when one made a stupid comment about Jackie. It was, at that moment, a blasphemous remark. An Italian Marine named DeMarco from Newport, Massachusetts, stood up with a few other East Coast and Midwest Marines and headed toward the Texans. A corporal seeing the situation intervened and broke off what would have been a serious brawl. The Texans claimed that they were only joking because the man who was in custody for the shooting the President had lived in Texas, and had been a Marine himself. The Texans said that only another Marine could shoot like that. The bantering back and forth eventually subsided. Serious feelings, however, were hurt that day, and it seemed like the Civil War had almost started all over again.

****

A few days later, my replacement arrived, and that evening, we all gathered around him as he told us stories of where he had been stationed and what he did. He said he was a gunner on a helicopter, and we thought that was a very cool and exciting job. The country were he had been stationed was a place most of us never heard, Vietnam.

"Where in the hell is that?" I asked.

"In Southeast Asia near Thailand, under China."

"Must have been great duty being over there with all that gorgeous slant-eye poon-tang running around," one Marine said.

"I tell you guys, that's where the next big one is gonna be. Over there in the jungles and rice paddies. I've seen a lot of shit and it ain't pretty. Believe me, I'm serious guys, that's place is a powder keg ready to explode at any time."

"Ah, shit man, all they need is a battalion of Marines and we'll mop that shit right up in no time flat. Hell, I could use some fucking medals on my chest. Shiiit. Fucking-a-right," said the nineteen-year-old lance corporal.

****

Within a week after the assassination of President Kennedy, I was in a taxicab heading for Norfolk Naval Base, Marine Barracks for honor guard duty. I knew it would be a chicken-shit, spit and polish assignment, but I was a corporal, which meant as a junior NCO, I had some privileges. And, if I kept my nose clean, I could make sergeant in about a year.

As the taxi approached, we noticed an event that was taking place on the parade field in front of the barracks.

"Damn, godamnit, he's doing it again!" the taxi driver said.

"What?" I asked.

"See that fellow in civilian clothes with his baggage?"

"Yeah."

"Well, they're 'drumming' him out. He did something wrong and he's not getting an Honorable Discharge and so that bastard Colonel, the C.O. of the Barracks, ordered this illegal bullshit. Last month, I drove a *Life* magazine photographer around the base for something and we just happened by chance come across one of these damn things The photographer told me to stop while he took some pictures and someone at *Life* wrote a story about it. The Colonel was told not to do it again, but obviously he has friends in Washington. He's a chicken-shit bastard who probably graduated from Citadel or VMI or some chicken-shit place like that.
"

We paused at the gate as the young man who had just been drummed out, walked slowly passed us looking morose. On the right side of his pant's cuff and his right shoe were wet from the piss of Winston, the barrack's bulldog mascot. We witnessed Winston hiking up his pudgy rear leg and piss on the Marine's ankle ad shoe while the Sergeant Major read the Marine's discharge. The Sergeant Major then ceremonially threw the discharge paper on the ground on the puddle of piss and pointed to the gate. The Marine picked up his discharge papers and walked slowly toward the gate as a drummer tapped a slow funeral march behind him. There were three platoons on the parade field that morning and as the condemned Marine passed each one, a platoon sergeant from each platoon ordered an "about-face". I never saw anything like it before. Here was an expulsion of a Marine who once worked, trained, and lived with his fellow Marines, who now had to watch them being ordered to execute an about-face as he walked past them to a slow rat-tap-tap of a drum. To me that was the most demoralizing thing I've ever witnessed in the Marine Corps. The incident went way beyond being chicken-shit. It was unsettling and shameful. I felt sorry for the guy, and I felt sorry for the Marines in the barracks.

When we were allowed to enter, I didn't feel especially comfortable about my reception to my new duty station. I got out the cab, tipped the driver, and collected my seabag and headed for the steps leading to the building.

"Hey, Marine!" said the taxi driver, "You keep your nose clean and watch yourself in there." He drove off before I could say "thanks."

My tour of duty with Marine Barracks Norfolk proved to be very eventful. I witnessed another drumming-out, this time it was that of a popular Black Marine from Richmond, Virginia. His crime was that he spent over thirty days in a civilian jail when he visited home. I discovered it proved easy to go to jail in the South if you were Black. I was even thrown in jail for "failure to move on" after being caught up in a race riot with the White Norfolk Police. I had witnessed them beating up a Black sailor on Church Street outside a Black restaurant on Thanksgiving Day whose patrons were Black sailors, Marines, and soldiers. I guess I wasn't moving fast enough for a cop who made the mistake of calling me a nigger. A group of about ten Black Marines, soldiers, and sailors teamed up against a platoon of cops and police dogs. I remember landing in a police van face down looking at a pair of scuffed spit-shined shoes and the guys "welcomed" me aboard. The Marine Barrack's Officer of the Day bailed me out that same night. He was a young White Lieutenant who seemed to be sympathetic. He told me what to do say when I had to go in front of the judge in the morning. The next morning in the courtroom, I heard a bunch of lies from the police and I was found guilty for failure to move on. I paid a twenty-five-dollar fine and left.

Racism didn't confine itself to the city of Norfolk; it also resided on the naval base itself. I recall vividly a Warrant officer waving a piece of paper, running on the lawn toward where some Black Marines and White Navy Waves played dominoes and cards.

"You people can't do this, it says so in this *herya paypa*." And then he began reading some Virginia legal gobbledygook as the Black Marines looked at each other and continued their games. The White Waves had heard it all before and one stood up, placed her hands on her thick hips and told him to go and fuck off.

Also during my tour of duty at Norfolk Marine Barracks, I had to participate as one of the honor guards and drivers during General Macarthur's funeral. I was also one of the guards for Senator Robert Kennedy and his wife during a brief visit in Norfolk. I remember that he was just as personable as his brother and a little thinner. He came over to me and shook my hand just as his brother did several years earlier, before climbing aboard an awaiting aircraft.

The events in Vietnam had begun to heat up rapidly. My replacement's prediction came true. Everyone now knew where Vietnam was located and Headquarters Marine Corps in Washington was asking for volunteers to reenlist with promises of promotions and other career opportunities. The tour of duty would be for thirteen months, but a Marine had to spend some weeks for jungle training before being shipped out. We were advised that it would be an excellent opportunity and many career minded Marines reenlisted. One Marine who volunteered to go to Vietnam had just completed his advance jungle training. He came back to the barracks with his brandishing new Buck Sergeant stripes and his new bride. He excitedly told us of his career plans in the Marines and encouraged all of us to do what he did. He received his reenlistment bonus pay and had the world at his feet. A few days later, we heard that his plane crashed at El Toro, California, U.S. Marine Corps Air Station. The plane was in route to Vietnam; all were killed. His was the first casualty that I knew personally, and there would be plenty more from the barracks as well as other places where I had previously been stationed.

I would have reenlisted also had I not been demoted to Lance Corporal for being AWOL (Absent Without Leave.) I merely walked my girlfriend to the front steps of the barracks and was accosted by a jealous fellow Corporal who had been Corporal-of-the-Guard that night. The nonsense stemmed from my taking evening college classes at Norfolk State College in town, and the Captain-of-the Guard supported my initiative. I wanted to take college courses so that I could become an officer. Although Marines were encouraged to advance their education, in reality, a lot of the NCOs (many high school dropouts) made it difficult for Marines to pursue a college education. Most of the officers were themselves college educated and encouraged the initiative. But, my fellow NCOs didn't like the idea of me taking classes. I was even teased for going to college. Actually, I enjoyed it and got a chance to meet girls. But due to my having to switch hours to study and go to classes, I was harassed and knew that I had to walk a fine line. So when the Corporal of the Guard saw me escorting my girlfriend to her car a few feet just outside the Barracks, he accosted me saying, of all things, that I was AWOL. Once again the chicken-shit of Marine Barracks prevailed. I was given a Captain's Mast, Article 15 (a minor court martial) and the Colonel reduced me to the next lowest rank and a gave me small fine. I didn't think furthering my education would result in my being "busted" to a Lance Corporal, but it did. With only a few months left, I now resolved on getting out.

July 9, 1965, the racist paper-waving Warrant Officer asked if I wanted to reenlist. Although a lot of things scurried inside

154

my head on what to say to him, (*You dumb cracker bastard*.) I merely replied with a simple, "No, Sir." However, when he signed my Honorable Discharge certificate, I waved my discharge papers in the air saying that I was drying the ink.

Redemption

Chapter Thirteen

THE MARINE CORPS was not the only military service that I would serve. It's like the first time you have sex, you'll always remember it no matter if it was good or bad. The Marine Corps provided an important foundation that would remain with me for the rest of my life. There's not a day that passes that I don't have some reverie about the Corps. The Corps indelibly becomes a part of those who have earned its lofty status. They told us in bootcamp that *once you're a Marine, you're always a Marine,* and out of all the military branches I served, the Corps initiated me into manhood. I learned how to be independent as well as a part of a team. I learned to accept challenges and look at myself as more than what I think I'm capable of doing. But most of all, I learned how to survive. I later entered U.S. Air Force and U.S. Coast Guard and applied my Marine Corps discipline to those branches of service.

After my tour of duty in the Corps, I returned home to Columbus in July 1965. It didn't take long before I began to feel I had outgrown the place where I grew up. I felt like a growing schoolboy in last year's trousers. Family, friends, and the city as a whole seemed to crowd me. I felt claustrophobic, restless, and uneven. No one expected me to get up and run, do calisthenics, or stand in line to eat. I felt uncomfortable when speaking because profanity seemed to slip past my lips at the most embarrassing moments. For years, Mom had waited my homecoming and she would catch me saying some god-awful things, then shake her head and look at me in absolute amazement. She wanted me to live in the big new handsome house on Carpenter Street in a nice residential neighborhood (now part of Columbus' ghetto). It had a huge porch, lawn, and most of all two baths (one upstairs and another in the basement.) I had been sending her a monthly allotment to help make her house notes even after she married Archie. At this time, Charlie was married to Mary. Though my mother and father lived only seven blocks from each other, it seemed an ocean away. Now retired, Charlie started raising poodles with his new wife, Mary who seemed to live in a delusional world supported by her lust for alcohol with Charlie's hard earned money. But he tolerated her intoxicated habits and behavior.

Like Mary and Willie, Archie too had a drinking problem. Seeing this I became frustrated and decided to accept Charlie's proposition and move in with him. Like my mother, he welcomed me with open arms and went out of his way to make me feel at home. That lasted for a few months before I discovered some of my hard earned money missing. I told Charlie and he said he would pay me back the amount taken. I said that he didn't have to pay for that "bitch's" crimes and he became angry and told me to leave. I was wrong and should have controlled my mouth, but I was extremely upset about being a recipient of thievery in my father's house. As I begin packing my things, he came into the bedroom looking brokenhearted and said he was sorry for what he said. I also apologized, but said that it would be best for me to move out. He felt ashamed for Mary's petty thievery and I told him not to worry about it, that I should move on.

I relocated into one of the apartment buildings where I once delivered papers as a kid. In my mailbox there were letters from cities like Los Angeles, Washington D.C., and New York trying to recruit me as a police officer for being an ex-Marine. I briefly considered it, but wanted to remain at home for a while to see if I could make some changes in my community and help Bunny with his situation. He had been incarcerated around the time I got out of the Marines. I worked two full-time jobs and one part-time to get money to pay his lawyer for an appeal. I worked as a lab assistant at Ohio State University College of Medicine during the days and at night worked at General Motors. General Motors paid very well, but they still had no Black foremen or supervisors. People told me that I was fortunate to be working for them anyways. On the weekends, I helped as a short-order cook working with my Aunt Dorothy, Mom's sister. When I got enough money saved, I paid the attorney in cash and I still can remember the look on his face when I handed the money to him. I think he was expecting rhetoric from me--or a plea to reduce the fee. I merely asked him how much and gave him what he needed. He drooled. My financial effort was in vain, however, because he lost the appeal. He did say that with a little more money he would have a better chance with furthering the case. I realized that his only motive was money and his actions were half-hearted. All this was around the same time General Motors decided to lay me off just after I gave my notice to my other jobs. I was frustrated, and felt that I might as well be back in the Marines. At least things weren't as complicated as civilian life.

Vietnam was really going full steam. Many guys that I knew were coming home in body bags. I'd cut out newspaper clipping of casualties of war of Marines I had been stationed with: Corporal James Allen, killed in Quan Nam Province, age 22. Sgt. John

Mitchell, age 25, had just re-enlisted and volunteered for Vietnam. The list went on and on. If I re-enlisted, I would be instantly promoted again, and be defiantly shipped out to Vietnam and probably to spend a couple of tours of duty in the bush. I was assured at least the rank of Staff Sergeant if I returned home vertical. I debated with myself about doing something more worthwhile with my life than killing people. I knew I could do that, but another part of me wanted the chance to see my skills as a humanitarian. I'd learned hundred of ways to kill, but I knew very little about healing. My job at Ohio State made me realize that I could use my talents in other, non-destructive ways. Maybe what I wanted was redemption. I couldn't bring James or John and the others back, but maybe I could save somehow some.

Jack Ferguson, a high school friend of mine, had been in the Navy and got out the same time as I did. He too was frustrated with civilian life. I didn't see him for a couple of months and then I got a post card from him in Italy saying that he had joined the Air Force. In the card, he said that the Air Force was like a civilian job, and he loved it. He suggested I consider it. I wrote him back and said that although I had been considering re-enlisting, I, however, didn't know what I really wanted to do. I had some options to consider and I didn't want to make any mistakes with my choices in life at the moment. However, I would keep in touch about my decision.

I decided to take the Air Force's entrance exam; I felt there was nothing to lose. When the Technical Sergeant finished grading my battery of tests, he said that he had never see such high scores before. I had almost perfect scores in every category. He asked my age and I told him that I'd be 22 in the fall.

"Why don't you consider the Air Force Academy?" He said. I was thrilled, but also curious.

"What do I have to do?"

"Simple, just enlist and you make an application. Hell, I wish I had your test scores. You can request any position the Air Force has to offer. I mean anything. How about it?"

"What about something in medicine?" I asked. "And can I be stationed right here in Columbus at Lockbourne, Air Force Base?"

"Man, you can do anything you want. Plus, being an ex-Marine, you'll be promoted in no time. I'm going to speak to the Major about you, man. You're special," he said. A major whose red hair contrasted with his blue uniform swore me in the Air Force. He shook my hand earnestly and said:

"I'm curious about why young men, such as yourself, would consider re-enlisting especially since there is a war going on. You've fulfilled your obligation in the Marine Corps, and I'm just inquisitive that's all. Could you just tell me why are you joining at this time during when a war is going on?"

I looked at the major, and I sincerely replied that I liked the late President John Kennedy's remark: *Ask not what your country can do for you, but what you can do for your country.* I could see tears forming in the Major's eyes as he shook my hand again saying,

"Welcome to the Air Force!"

My enlistment in the Air Force began immediately. Once again, it felt good being a part of some form of regimentation. I needed order in my life where I understood the rules. Having been issued a new uniform I set about learning a new military vocabulary, e.g., a toilet in the Marines is called a *head*. In the Air Force it is called, a *latrine*. There were other minor differences like not tying my necktie in a four-in-hand know as in the Marines but Windsor knot. Not having to say, "Aye aye, sir" when giving an affirmative reply. Essentially, I felt I had been put back in order again, and Jack Ferguson had been right, the Air Force was easy compared to the Marines. I fitted comfortably into my new life, as compared with the eleven months of civilian disappointment that I had just experienced. I now needed to specialize in something wholly different than killing or blowing things up. Becoming a medic would give me a chance to do something wholly redemptional, but I wanted more than being just a ward medic; I wanted to literally put my hands to use healing. Mom always said that I had hands of a surgeon so why not do something useful like becoming a surgical technician? My scores more than qualified me for the career field and I was immediately put into training at Lockbourne Air Base Hospital. I met an Ohio University student just prior to enlisting in the Air Force who would soon become my wife. Marrying would disqualify me from being admitted to the Air Force Academy, but I didn't care.

Valarie, my tall beautiful wife, came from an upper-middle class Black family in Columbus. The subsequent birth of our son, Eric, meant extra work. To make extra money to supplement my meager Air Force pay, I took evening positions in area hospitals working in emergency rooms.

****

My first time in the operating room was a nauseating experience. I had to bring in a little girl from the ward and get her chart ready for a tonsillectomy. The girl was about seven, and frightened. I talked with her as she held her doll close to for emotional support. We played and talked, until she began to trust me. When I pushed her in the chilly surgical suite, she began to cry. I pulled up a blanket so she could be warm. The ENT (Ears Nose and Throat) doctor and the surgical tech were already scrubbed. The surgical table and mayo tray was neatly arranged with shiny stainless steel surgical instruments, and before I knew it, the anesthetist had the girl intubated and asleep. My job as a new trainee was to observe and work with the circulating nurse. The ENT's hands were huge. He looked more like an Abrams Tank mechanic than a surgeon. He inserted a long instrument down the girl's throat, yanked out tissue while another instrument, held by an Airman Surgical Tech, sucked blood out from her mouth. I was not expecting this. Watching the procedure my stomach began slowly turning cartwheels along with my swirling, pulsating head, and I imagined my complexion changed into a couple of unnamed shades of maroon. The sea green operating room took on the pale color of puss and slowly began whirling into psychedelic paisley variations. Despite this, everyone was too busy to notice that I was getting sick. The mask I wore effectively hid my expression. Only my eyes showed through, but no one was watching me because they were too busy with the procedure. I conjured up all my strength to support my weakening knees. Every nerve in my body screamed for me to get the hell out of there, and now! I politely excused myself and went into the men's latrine, locked the door, sat on the commode, and vomited, defecated, and pissed, all at the same time. I became one huge perforated tube eliminating bile, waste, and other assorted body fluids from all my portals. Hell, even Marine Corps' bootcamp had not prepared me for anything like this--and I was seriously wondering if all of this was a big goddamn mistake.

After a half an hour, or so, locked inside the latrine, I came out shaken. I went into the surgical lounge where physicians, scrub nurses, and techs smoked, read, and waited between surgical cases. A young airman sat alone, calmly smoking and reading a newspaper. He had been the surgical tech who assisted on the little girl's tonsillectomy case. He glanced up at me wearily and I tried to make small talk by asking how the little girl was doing. Taking a couple long draws on his cigarette, he introduced himself and said the kid was in the recovery room and doing fine. I then confided my traumatized feelings as well as my latrine episode.

"You'll be all right." He said. "I remember my first time. I did the same thing. Hell, they could butcher someone now and it wouldn't bother me."

Somehow, the word "butcher" did not agree with my stomach because it started doing cartwheels again. With that, I excused myself, and walked briskly back into the latrine. I must have been in the latrine for another thirty minutes, once again debating my future. I guess I lost ten pounds that morning. As I was puking my guts out, I wondered if my reply to the red haired Air Force major about Kennedy's remark, *Ask not what your country can do for you, but what you can do for your country*, qualified me as a real patriot. Afterwards, I told myself that it was just mind over matter. If I could only leave the sanctuary of the latrine and return to one of the surgical suites and touch some blood, then I would be all right.

I left the latrine, and went into the surgical suite, peeping in several rooms to see which one had the bloodiest surgery taking place. I found one where a doctor was performing a vaginal hysterectomy on a 39-year-old Black female. I walked in and forced myself to watch. With gloved hands, I picked up the bloody sponges off the floor and counted them as was required. I took the

161

bloody instruments and rinsed them, before returning them to Central Supply. I placed a cyst ridden uterus specimen into a sterile container for the pathologist's frozen section. I labeled new specimens and placed them in separate sterile containers. After surgery, I helped clean and move the patient to the Recovery Room. I purposely touched her blood with my ungloved-hand, looked at it, rubbed it between my thumb and forefinger, and vowed to myself that I was going to make it. Subsequently, it got to a point that any human anatomical parts, no matter how deformed, mangled or bloodied, didn't bother me. Now I too could watch someone being cut up and eat a meal afterwards because I *had* to.

****

After a couple of years at Lockbourne, I got orders to be transferred to a Royal Thai Air Force Base in southern Thailand. It was home to a few squadrons of U.S. Air Force B52 bombers that bombed targets in Vietnam, Cambodia, Laos, and other designated targets deemed necessary for the Nixon's needs. I was attached to a hastily fabricated military hospital as the NCOIC (Non Commissioned Officer In Charge) of surgery. I made rank fast because I enjoyed my job and took pride in knowing that I helped someone. Although, there are many stories about my tour Thailand, the most interesting ones, however, took place in the small hamlets. I also took it upon myself to learn conversational Thai and try to involve myself with the culture of the people. Actually, I learned my Thai from the children who seemed eager to talk with me. I discovered that I had a tongue for Thai and it came in handy. The Thai people were just as curious about me as a Black American as I was about them and their culture.

As part of a medical goodwill program, a medical team of doctors, dentists, medics, and nurses conducted medical treatments programs in the small villages and hamlets. We helped dispense medicine, gave inoculations, performed minor surgery, instructed midwives, and I also acted as an interpreter. The children in these hamlets would swarm around me and put their arms next to mine and say: "See, you same-same me. Dum, dum poochie [Black

162

man]." Whenever I had a chance to sit down, I could expect small hands reaching for my head to rub my short regulated Afro. I knew they did it out of curiosity more than anything, and I would allow them to do so as we chatted in Thai. Sometimes old grinning women with black teeth from chewing beetle nuts would walk up to me, rub my head, laugh, and mumble something in Thai. I was the Pied Piper whenever we entered a new hamlet and it was always the kids who were the first ones to approach. The sun caused my skin to turn darker than usual and I guess it was because of my skin color and hair, plus my ability to speak Thai, that they felt a connection and trust in me.

In one particular village, I remember a mother came carrying her daughter wearing a filthy, infected bandage on her ear. Since I served as the translator the doctor asked me to ask the mother why hadn't she changed the dressing? The mother said that the last time when the Americans came some months ago, they put the bandage on. The problem was that they had neglected to tell her to take it off in a few days. When we took off the dressing, the child's ear came off with it, along with some crawling maggots (actually maggots were a good thing because they ate the pus.) We wound up taking the girl back with us to the base hospital for treatment.

****

Clad in bright orange flowing robes, the barefoot Buddhist monks with their shaven heads, walked placidly and fearlessly from village to village with a sense of grace and dignity, chanting and asking for alms. They were absolutely remarkable. I encountered many of them in the bush. They reminded me of the Hari Krishna people I had seen in airports, and later on college campuses. I have an enormous respect and admiration for their sense of devotion. Once, coming into a hamlet, I saw a parade of about ten of them. Among them to my surprise was a Black monk. The bright orange robe he wore contrasted enormously his dark skin. Head shaved and barefoot, he paraded along with the rest of them towering like a giraffe in complete harmony. Stunned, I walked up to him and looked at him wanting to get to know his story. I knew that he was a brother GI who probably came over from Vietnam on

R and R [Rest and Relaxation] and "got religion." I had a million questions to ask him, but he only graciously smiled at me in a knowing way and continued with the others chanting in absolute bliss.

I had on another occasion seen a White Buddhist monk trotting along in the bush with other orange robed monks in a state of bliss. These individuals had been once GIs who just one day laid down their weapons, gear, and ended up in a monastery. I would suspect this might explain a few of the MIAs. I had seen some strange things in the bush, and it wouldn't surprise me that many GIs were converted to an exotic religion or fell in love and simply stayed. In the beginning, I felt that I would fear the jungle and the strangeness it offered, but actually, for some odd reason, I felt a sense of comfort. I had a deep primordial awareness in the bush. The foliage's arms extended to welcome and protect me. I had no fear whatsoever—even at night I walked in complete peace. Perhaps one of the reasons may have been because I "felt" my mother's prayers. I literary felt her praying for my safety and I felt protected. It's difficult to explain this, but I think most veterans know exactly what I mean; you just have to experience it to understand it.

****

Since I had become accustomed to my job and made rank fast, I seriously considered making a career of the Air Force. It all seemed so easy and perfect. Besides, I now spent almost eight years on active duty including my tour of duty in the Marines. This made it possible for me to retire in another twelve years. However, my wife back home had other plans for me. She wanted me to get out, return home, and to go to college. I enrolled at Ohio State University prior my discharge when I was in Thailand. One of the surgeons whom I worked with was from Dayton and graduated for Ohio State. He recommended me to the College of Medicine in the School of Allied Health Science to study Medical Illustration from the drawings I did in Thailand. I was subsequently accepted and The Eighth Air Force granted me an early discharge on condition that I begin my studies immediately. Two days before Christmas in 1969, I was back in the "World"--a GI's expression for home.

As a non-smoker, I felt sick on the thirteen hours flight back to the World. I felt miserable as I choked on GI smoke in the cramped confines of the aircraft. I tried holding my breath and covering my mouth, but it was a ludicrous attempt because all around me guys were lighting up and puffing happily away. When we landed, I pushed myself through duffle-bag-toting GIs, groping and squeezing along the narrow aisle to the aircraft's door, and finally catapulted myself outside into the fresh California air. I inhaled deeply, coughing, relieved to be on solid ground and breathing clean air. I hated that flight. I hacked up mucus oysters from my smoked filled bronchia and spat under the aircraft's wing. I watched GIs kissing the tarmac as they came off. On the other side of me, another plane was loading GIs outbound for South East Asia, and making ready to taxi off. We all suddenly froze when we saw airmen unloading shiny coffins from our plane's cargo bay onto awaiting conveyer belts pulled by forklifts. And I thought, *How fucking poetic!*

Flashback and the Path
of Least Resistance

Chapter Fourteen

*J*ANUARY 6, 1970, central Ohio was experiencing one of the coldest months I ever remembered. So cold, my nuts seemed to shrivel up to the size of raisins. Bending forward, I trudged through the wind and blinding snow to get to my 8:00 a.m. anatomy class when suddenly, I heard a distinct thump a few feet ahead of me. It sounded like a distant mortar round leaving its tube. The glaring whiteness of the morning snow caused me to squint my eyes and I saw a black object on the frozen ground not far from me. I instinctively glanced up and saw another dark thing fall from the sky and it too made a thud sound when it hit the hard snow. They were ravens--beautiful ravens falling clumsily out of the sky landing one by one with periodic thumps. They had frozen to death in flight. This part of the campus, near the Oval, around a grove of trees, was raining ravens. Small black tufts littered the snowy landscape looking like large clumps of coal in a sea of milk. I held my books on my head for protection and continued trudging through the fresh snow, stepping over fallen ravens, when I inadvertently caught my reflection on the large window of the bookstore on Neil Avenue. I stopped dead in my tracks. What I saw startled me. Behind the intermittent puffs of frost fanning from my flared nostrils was a pair of vacant eyes staring back. They were the eyes of an exhausted man in a steamy tropical terrain wearing dirty, sweat-stained, camouflage jungle utilities. The most conspicuous part of the ghostly figure was the two olive drab field medical packs solicitously clutched in his hands. The image appeared like a shadowy phantom, distant and far removed from the existing winter landscape. It was not the reflection of a shivering twenty-six year-old Black man bundled up in a parka with white ice-crystals forming around his mouth and two-week-old beard. No, the perspiring figure peering back at me gave the impression of someone who was uncertain of his immediate surroundings.

I suddenly became frightened. Could the image I was looking at be just the reverse true picture of myself? Instead of being a bystander witnessing a sub-tropical phenomenon, was it *I* who was actually back in the bush staring back at a dubious figure in a snow covered campus landscape? Indeed, I often pictured wintry scenes enough to escape the blistering heat during operations. God, I thought to himself, which hallucination is real?

****

A year before, I had left my wife and an infant son Eric behind to go to war. When I returned home, my eighteen-months old son didn't recognize me. It broke my heart when I reached out for him, and he shrugged away from me, crying to the awaiting arms of his mother. I realized I would have to win him over with patience, love, and my presence. In the evenings, I'd creep into his bedroom and watch him sleep, holding his fat little hands. During the day I tried catching up on being a father.

Having been home for only two weeks--coming directly from the jungles of a structured military life of discipline and death, to a freezing winter of student life, taxed my mental senses. It was too much, too soon, too fast, and too overbearing. I often would wake up still thinking I was in the bush. Once, I actually awoke after hitting my wife in my sleep. I tried hiding my war-mind, but you can't hide from yourself. War changes things. And yes, a part of me had it cozy in the Air Force while my brother Marines were in hell. And, although I had taken on the new challenges of trying to redeem myself by learning how to heal rather than kill, it still was war. In a sense, killing is simple. There is no responsibility in it except protecting yourself or your own. In reality, killing is just a matter of *you* or *them*. *You* against *whomever*. Trying to save a life, however, has other loads of complexes and responsibilities. It is the training, skill, timing, luck, and several other things all factoring into keeping your patient breathing, from bleeding to death, and from going into shock, all in that order by all means necessary.

Coming home for many veterans meant sanctuary. The dreams of some, however, became nightmares where guilt slowly gnaws away, itching like jungle rot. Some immediately melted down within days of returning home, while others had, as me, what is now known as a *delayed reaction syndrome*. My delayed reaction (like many veterans of South East Asia) occurred ten years after I came home. It seems guilt has a way of dispensing itself in time capsules adding a little bit at a time in one's thoughts until an eventual meltdown. There were no ships that took a couple of weeks to return home on thereby providing time for reflection on issues of associated guilt, life, future, and most of all, redemption--it simply was a sickening thirteen-hour flight from a steaming mosquito-infested place with strange landscape, strange architecture, strange customs, exotic homogeneous people, only to land onto a cold wintry familiar called home which appeared more eccentric than the place I left. The only item that made sense was Jimmi Hendrix's rifts, and the console of another Vietnam Veteran's time.

I grew a beard and let my hair grow into a huge Afro that haloed my head. I donned bell-bottom pants, walked in the highest platform shoes I could find, wore colorful shirts with beads around my neck, and sported a peace sign for a belt buckle. This became my new uniform. I drove a red 1968, Triumph TR 250 while my wife drove a new blue Mustang Convertible with a white top and chrome spinner wheels. And I experimented with pot. And, like everyone else at the time, I inhaled as often as I could. I began to enjoy this new sense of expression and freedom, and I took all the advantages of my new civilian life. But, in reality, I was hiding behind layers of extravagances.

My major was Medical Illustration and I worked full time at General Motors. I would leave campus and drive directly to the end of west Columbus and punch-in working second shift until midnight. At work, all the supervisors were White. My position was the worst position in the factory, Cleaning Equipment Specialist. It entailed crawling in the dirty ducts and cleaning out the soot, grime and metal shavings. It also required cleaning out the various grease pits throughout the plant. I had to wear hip boots, rubber gloves and shovel out old grease and metals. The job was disgusting, but it paid well and I knew that it would end as soon as I graduated.

My courses included Mandarin Chinese, human anatomy, histology, embryology, and other science course requiring many hours of study. (I took Chinese because I wanted discipline and a foreign language would force me into good study habits.) That did not include the long hours spent in the drawing studio and surgery. Once, just before an anatomy final exam, I hid my books in the large coveralls pockets I wore at work. I tried to find areas away from my foreman between cleaning jobs and consume as much as I could from my textbooks. The restroom proved to be the most convenient place, but I would be exposed. On one of my breaks, I went there, closed the small door, and sat down on the commode without undoing my trousers. I got lost in the study forgetting the time. I had just turned a page when I sensed I was being watched. Looking over the edge of the book, I saw a pair of black winged-tip shoes. Since workers wore steel-toed brogans, I knew I would be in trouble. As my eyes slowly moved up the gray pin striped trousers onto the swinging door (that looked like a western solon door) I saw the grim expression of my foreman. He didn't say anything, but pointed his finger at me motioning me to follow. The whole thing reminded me of the Captain's Mast in the Marine Corps when I got busted for essentially for being a college student. Being a college student, at that time, and working in a blue-collar environment wasn't the most ideal situation. Most laborers hated college students and claimed us to be closely coupled with the communist party. I was summarily chewed-out and written up. I had no defense except to tell the truth that I was studying for an anatomy final exam, to which the foreman had no interest whatsoever. Once again, I got busted while a college student, but this one was my own fault. I'll accept that. So, like we used to say in the Marines, I got my ass-chewed out really good. Afterwards, I went about cleaning grease, soot and metal shavings and I marveled how Charlie having spent over half his life a working in such an environment could do it.

After work, I went home and stayed up and studied until it was time to go to class. I passed the final, but could have done better if I had more time and more sleep.

I accelerated my studies by taking as many courses as I could per quarter and attending summer school completing my bachelors' degree in two and a half years. I made the Dean's list several times, but my overall average was not the three-point or above that I wanted. Again, like during my elementary and secondary school years, work took away much of my academic time.

****

Riot Yahoos wielded their batons with skill on the head and backs of students (males and females) and professors. I recall seeing on television news, the arrest of a well-known Black Ohio State professor who had been protesting for a Black Studies curriculum. During his arrest he was ruthlessly mishandled, handcuffed, and knocked to the ground Rodney King style by several Columbus Yahoos. There was little to no resisting, he only shield his face with his arms while taking blows from batons. I recognized one of the racist Yahoos who was doing some of the worst beatings. We had been stationed together as Air Force medics at Lockbourne Air Force Base in Columbus. He was an easy-going mild-mannered guy and I liked him. But seeing the way he handled the professor tied my stomach in knots with anger. He went overboard and I thought to myself, what kind of training did the Columbus Yahoo Department have to turn out such individuals? There still were not many Black policemen on the force with the city going through a selective process recruiting Whites from out of state and rural areas, asserting the tired racist claim that Blacks cannot past their test. The absurdity of that statement is not only racist, but also insipid. If that was the case, why did so many Black men go to other cities and get on their police force? Is Columbus' exam more difficult than, let's say, New York's or Chicago's? Columbus has one of the best public schools in the nation and Blacks rated high in academics, especially compared to the individuals the police department was hiring. Essentially, it was good ol' boy mentality and the effort for

170

recruiting minorities and women came later--after, of all things, campus unrest and Les Brown's avocation for Blacks to vote and protest for their rights. Brown, a local disk jockey who aired on the predominantly Black Community, eventually became a state legislator, television talk show host, and motivational speaker.

An ex-Navy freshman I knew got arrested by a Columbus Yahoo for wearing his old Navy peacoat. The Yahoo claimed he was breaking the law by wearing the Second Class Petty Officer Rate patch he earned while in the Navy. Not only was the veteran put in jail, but he had to rip off the Petty Officer Rate patch and pay a hefty fine. I jokingly told him, over a beer, *welcome, you're now a full fledge member of the nigger club now.*

****

To get to class, I had to frequently weave through crowds of cops and student protesters who handed out leaflets on a variety of issues. Students were demanding change but the powers-that-be in Columbus, as well as most of the country, was very ultra conservative. Often, I recall seeing men with short hair--looking very much out of place--take pictures of student demonstrators. I once saw a student stoop down in front of my path to pick up a brick and hurl the damn thing through the R.O.T.C. window. He wore a bandana around his head, and I marveled not only at his accuracy, but also at his brazen act. I would never do something like that, but it let me know the tenacity the students had for change.

And change came not only in violence, but also in peaceful demonstrations. My all-time hero, coach Woody Hayes soothe an angry crowd of students, one afternoon while nearby nervous National Guard troops stood poised, as barefooted braless girls, wearing long paisley peasant dresses, placed flowers in the gun barrels of the troops. Students would also gather as a troubadour sat down and strummed a few cords from a guitar as others sang along. With all the commotion on campus, there also was a sense of freedom, goodwill and love. I felt I was in the presence of history in the making. Something seemed fresh and alive. Everywhere, there was music, flowers, and a lot of good times. Also on several occasions, I witnessed Yahoos agitating and provoking students into

171

an eventual chaotic situation. Students were being indiscriminately targeted for senseless infractions.

Then Kent State happened and all hell broke loose. The agony of the incident had a rippling effect all across America and the world now looked at the White House differently. Even as Kent State provided fodder for the Columbus racist Yahoos, there seemed to be a growing weariness in their concerted efforts. The handwriting now had been written on the wall. That day at Kent State, a tide had turned. Prior the Kent State incident, protesting Black students on Black college campuses in the South (Southern University in Louisiana, and South Carolina State University) had been ceremonially assassinated by local White Yahoos with little or no media coverage except the Black media. The media surreptitiously swept the event under the rug making it back page news. (I didn't even know about the killings.) It took a predominately White school's carnage of White students to grip the nation's attention. Kent State forced me to see, for the first time, how I had been seen from the eyes of the people we were killing in Southeast Asia.

Grad School

Chapter Fifteen

I HEARD SOMEWHERE that ninety percent of Vietnam veterans had broken marriages that ended in divorce. By 1978, I was part of that statistic. I also heard that forty percent of the homeless were also Vietnam veterans. Those numbers frightened me. I knew that my chances of being homeless were high if I resorted to drug or alcohol abuse. I was much stronger than that. No amount of drugs or alcohol was going to have control over my life. But I had seen a lot of guys strung-out at the various Veterans hospitals. They sat in the waiting rooms glassy-eyed, smoking, rumpled. I felt sorry for them and we often exchanged war stories. Many were on street corners pan handling for change. I dropped in spare change and looked at their eyes knowing that at one time they were strong, proud, and brave. The GI Bill saved many lives, so why didn't these guys take advantage of it? At thirty-five, I began to feel life was slipping by too fast and I had to *do* something, *be* somebody before it become too late. In 1978, I was accepted to several schools but opt for the University of Cincinnati's (UC) M.F.A graduate program in painting and drawing. I wanted to become a painter and perhaps an art professor. I applied and received a Dansforth Scholarship toward a M.F.A. degree. It had been five years since graduating from Ohio State and I had worked at Hampton Institute's School of Nursing as their first medical illustrator. I also taught Comparative Anatomy as a fluke. A nursing student came into my studio one afternoon asking if I knew anything about anatomy. I looked at her textbook and told her that anatomy should be studied with a partner and to use flashcards. She came with another student the next day and I tutored them. When they both received A's on their tests, the next thing I knew I had the whole class crammed in my studio and a message from my supervisor informing me that for now on, a part of my job would be assisting the biology department teaching nursing students anatomy. I should have known better than to volunteer for because one of the cardinal rules I learned in the military is not to volunteer for anything. But I did enjoy the task for it provided me my first teaching experience. And I thoroughly enjoyed Hampton and the Tidewater area, as it was hallowed ground for me because my grandfather's roots were there. After working there three years, I left for New Jersey to freelance. While living in East Orange, NJ, I worked for a Black Newspaper, a substitute teacher, and freelance medical illustrator in New York. I took night art classes at Montclair State College where I became very interested in abstract expressionism. My painting professor suggested that I should seriously consider getting a Master of Fine Art (M.F.A).

****

Unfortunately the dean of UC's Masters of Fine Art department and I did not have a good relationship from day one. I arrived on campus after a twelve-hour drive from New Jersey, stopping for a few days in Columbus to see my sons. It was spring semester; I had been admitted into the highly competitive program, and I was excited. I parked my car still loaded with my belongings, near the art building, and bounded up the stairs to meet the dean. After making a favorable impression on the two department secretaries, who had told me that the dean would be returning momentarily. I drank coffee and we chatted about the drive and my life as a medical illustrator in New York and New Jersey. When the dean arrived, I stood up, stuck out my hand to shake as the secretaries introduced me. But the dean did not return my handshake. He only glared at me with his hands on his hips and said in a gruff voice:

"Where in the hell have you been?"

I was stunned by the tone and condemnation of his voice. Immediately my racism radar picked up all kinds of bad signals. He

174

reminded me of Mr. Swain, my old high school principal wearing the same Liberace hairstyle. I was in no mood for this--at least not at this point in my life. I did everything I could to stop from ramming my fist in his face. However, I remained cool, calm and collected. "I think we have a miscommunication problem here," I said calmly looking right into his eyes retracting my hand. "It is my understanding that the semester starts next week, so I came a week early. If there had been a notice about me coming sooner, I didn't receive it, and I didn't see anything in my letters or brochures about any classes starting early."

"I have another student ready to teach your classes," he said.

"What classes?" I replied calmly.

"You are supposed to teach undergraduate students."

"I received nothing in my communications saying anything about teaching here. My fellowship does not require me to teach. Perhaps you have me confused with someone else. However, if you would like, I'd gladly teach because I enjoy teaching," I said.

That confused him and I noticed the two secretaries who kept themselves quietly preoccupied, stopped and smiled at each other. I had already sized-up this clown as a racist-ass and it looked like it was going to be a long two years.

I did enjoy teaching at UC. It seemed a natural for me, and my relationship with the undergraduate students flourished. Occasionally, however, my radar often sensed the dean's presence. Through my peripheral vision, I would catch his shadow concealed behind the door listening and watching my classroom instruction. I just pretended he was not even there, but I rather enjoyed his listening anyway. There had always been good ambiance in my classes as I enjoyed each student. My job was to elicit creativity and I was mature and experienced enough to do just that. Teaching art is like teaching love. You only have to put your heart into it. I was the only Black graduate student and the first one in seven years. The students and my graduate peers were great. Most of them were fresh out of undergraduate college, in their early twenties. They were just beginning to live while I was a generation and a war ahead of them.

My situation with the dean, however, began to deteriorate further, when another incident occurred where he raised his voice at me once again in the presence of his secretaries. And once again, I absorbed his verbal blows, this time because I was partially stoned from the previous night of carousing with some graduate students on the strip. I stood there probably wearing my best Louis Armstrong grin. After his verbal reprimand, I simply walked out of his office and headed to the student lounge for a cup of strong java to clear up my hangover. Surely, all of this must have been a hallucination of some sort because I couldn't believe what just occurred. After about an hour or so, I reported the incident to my provost who asked what I wanted to do. I told him that I wanted a conference with the three of us. About three weeks later, I got a call from the provost to meet with him in his office.

I purposely came to the meeting five minutes late. I wanted to make sure the two chatted a while before I arrived. The provost sat behind his desk and mentioned to the dean that I had called this meeting. The dean was eating from a box of Cracker Jacks. He seemed small in the provost's office and his pale Pillsbury Doughboy's face hid uncomfortably behind his neatly trimmed beard. But with all his facial vulnerabilities, there was an evil in his lizard eyes. I told them thanks for allowing this meeting and that I wanted to get something off my chest. Sitting next to the dean, I turned my seat around directly facing him and said:

"I called this meeting here because I want the provost to witness what I'm about to say."

I put my face very close to his just as my DI's did in bootcamp, and in a low voice I whispered:

"I decided to take two years out of my life to come here to earn an M.F.A., and from day one you've been treating me like dirt. I'm not a child and not even my daddy talked to me like you do. I'm thirty-five years old and an ex-Marine, and please hear me clearly: for a chocolate chip cookie I'd kick your ass right here and right now. As long as you have a hole in your ass, don't you *ever* talk to me like that again, do I make myself clear?"

I heard something rattling and noticed it was the Cracker Jacks he held in his hand.

"I said, do I make myself clear?"

"Yyyes, yyes," he said.

I glared at him for an extra moment and turned around facing the dean. Afterwards, the dean, made an everlasting impression on me because he too gave the dean an ass-chewing substantiating my fellowship grant money, making it perfectly clear that my funds came from another source and that, essentially, I was doing him a favor teaching at no cost to the art department.

****

Within a few weeks, I was scheduled to have my first evaluation of my paintings from the faculty of the art department. I had no idea that the chair of the painting department was a close friend of the dean. But I came to discover that even academics have "good ol' boy" clubs. The painting chair told me that my works were "eclectic," and that they showed a *lack of understanding of art*. I looked at the faces of the other professors, who were seated solemnly. Many felt uncomfortable and couldn't look at me; others looked around as if they didn't want to be part of what was going on, but it would be to their best interest not to protest the hypocrisy because they were up for tenure. I could tell that they were not going to say anything on my behalf. It was indeed, strange, that in private they told me that my work looked exceptional. As I sat there listening to the painting chair degrade my work and me, I remembered the vow I made to myself when I got off the plane from Southeast Asia, and I finally stood up and said:

"Okay, I heard enough. I will not be a victim of your *Inquisition*. This is a farce. It's obviously a prejudged review and you're just pissed-off because of what I said to your boss. This is not an evaluation. It's a sham. So, if you don't mind, I've got things to do."

I then walked out of the room. In a few days I was given a

formal typed-written evaluation saying that I "failed" the evaluation. It was the first time in history, I was told, that a graduate student failed a preliminary art evaluation. I was told in the letter to paint in the graduate art studio (or "the barn" as it was known by the students) with the other graduate students instead of at my studio in my apartment where I listened to Miles Davis, John Coletrane, and other jazz and classical music. I was not in my early twenties, but in my middle thirties, and I certainly was not interested in listing to Punk Rock music that was being constantly played in the opened space of "the barn." Painting in the school's space with other graduate students' music had previously influenced my work, which was my prime reason for seeking another painting space in the first place.

Furthermore, I was told by the chair not to have exhibitions in galleries in the city. It was odd because it was my prerogative to exhibit. It was good for the department, school, as well as myself. The whole situation seemed targeted unjustly against me since other students were exhibiting and selling their works in galleries in the city as well as other places on a regular basis. I, however, disregarded most of their sanctions, and did what I pretty much wanted. And by doing so, my paintings improved and I developed as an artist. In general, though, my time as art student was an uphill battle during most of the time at University of Cincinnati's art department, but I felt confident in my work and refused to become discouraged. My bitterness took form in my creativity, and I used it to paint constructively. Whenever I would complete a piece of work and bring it to "the barn," I'd get plenty of oohs and ahhs from my graduate peers and a few from sympathetic faculty. After the incident with the dean, I received very few A's and plenty B's although I knew that my work was exceptional and deserved a higher grade. I got a C in a printmaking course from a young instructor I regarded highly. I enjoyed his classes and learned a lot, but evidently, he was playing politics in order to gain tenure. I felt betrayed and his giving me a "C" was the first one I had ever received in any art course in my entire life. I took one of the prints from that class to a self-framing shop, and a girl who worked there was so impressed with it that she offered to buy it for seventy-five dollars.

****

During my ordeal with UC, I emitted myself into Deaconess Hospital, one of the many hospitals near the school. For weeks I had been coughing up blood and defecating black stools which are an indication of blood in my digestive system. I knew these were symptoms of a stress ulcer. Obviously, the stress *(this was also an indicator of AgentOrange exposure that I was not aware of back then)* at the art department had taken its toll even though I thought I could handle most adversities that came my way at my age. I was now an adult. I didn't have to *wish* myself to be one at a given moment. Now with this hole in my stomach, how really fragile we are as human beings. Any my only relief from stomach pain was to drinking a lot of milk and Maalox. After a day or so of testing in the hospital, a physician introduced me to the surgeon who would be performing the operation in the morning. That night an orderly came and prepared me for surgery by shaving my abdomen and pubic area, and gave me an enema. I slept restlessly in anticipation for the ordeal of surgery in the morning. However, when my physician came to see me, he said that my student insurance didn't cover the cost of surgery and asked if I had any other insurance. I told him no. He dug deep into his white medical smock and handed me some medication and politely suggested going to the VA (Veteran's) hospital.

I was disappointed to say the least, but I took the medication and went to the VA Hospital where I filled out forms and waited in the emergency room for several hours holding my stomach, sipping on my blue bottle of Maalox. When it was my turn, I explained to the medical clerk what had taken place at the other hospital; he placidly said that the next available time for surgery would be in the middle of February. It was early September and waiting five months for a needed operation seemed like punishment. The previous physician told me that I had a class "A" personality--whatever the hell that was supposed to mean--and that I was ripe for

179

ulcers. I only knew that I was bleeding inside and help seemed impossible in the land of opportunity and the country that I had served. Sitting there, looking around at all the veterans from various wars, I felt a sense of betrayal. Just before my class "A" personality was about to explode in the face of the young intern, who must have sensed my frustration, said that a lot of Vietnam Era veterans were recently coming in at an alarming rate. He suggested that I see the psychiatrist who had been using Vietnam Era veterans in a biofeedback project. The intern claimed the success rate of the program to be very high. He gave me a prescription to see the psychiatrist in a few days along with more Maalox and some new pills for ulcers. We said our goodbyes and I walked out the hospital door clutching my guts like a stomach wound.

In a couple of days, I returned to the VA Hospital and went to the Psychiatry department. The first thing the doctor asked me was what movies had I seen recently. I thought what an odd question, and I told him I saw the current box office hits: *Deer Hunter, Apocalypse Now,* and *Coming Home,* all dealing with the Vietnam War. He said, "Um hmm. That's the problem. *Post Traumatic Syndrome.* Something new that I'm working on and have written and lectured extensively on the subject. I'm seeing a lot of you guys these days. Even though you've been home from the war for ten years now, these movies are now coming out cause you to relive the experience. The problem lies in witnessing the movie and reliving the war. I think you'll be a good candidate for biofeedback therapy. We'll start treating you immediately."

Three times a week I went to the VA Hospital's Psychiatric Department, walked into a dark room and sat in a chair that reminded me of a barber's chair. I was given a set of earphones, and the technicians attached wires on my forehead, arms, and fingers that led to various machines. I sat there blindfolded and periodically instructed to relax as I listened to assorted ranges of frequencies that generated from every twitch my body made and any negative thoughts were loudly transmitted to an amplifier and speakers. (I sat in the middle of a soundproof room, surrounded by speakers.) When I finally became relaxed, a gentle low audible hum was produced. If I scratched, licked my lips, or blinked my eyes, the

180

motion registered audibly in the room. And if I unfortunately sneezed, all hell broke loose in my ears. My job was to mentally maintain the soothing sound. The sound determined how much I could relax. I had to control the sound with my will.

The first couple of sessions were terrible. I did not know how to relax. I would think about negative thoughts like my divorce and leaving my sons. The situation with the dean in the art department didn't help either. After some coaching from the psychiatrist, I became better. My soothing thoughts were thinking of both of my sons' births. I clearly envisioned the night when my wife gave birth to my first son Eric when I was on duty as an Air Force surgical tech. There in the operating room, I assisted the physician and excitedly watched the delivery of my first-born. I remember his first cry—it happened when the doctor snipped off his foreskin with a small pair of Iris surgical scissors, giving him an uncelebrated circumcision. He made an earth-shattering cry and I felt my heart drop. It would be another five years when Charles, III (a.k.a., "Beetle"), my other son, came into the world. I was a medical illustration student at Ohio State and made a deal with the gynecologist to deliver him in exchange for drawing some illustrations for him. (Beetle's circumcision didn't take place immediately after his birth, but a week or so later and I was not present.)

Other soothing thoughts that worked for me involved the activity of painting. I visualized myself dipping my brushes on a palette, mixing colors and running the brush confidently across a taunt, white, freshly primed canvas as color, shapes and textures emerged from my brushes in front of me. I danced on the canvas, painting with both hands--as I often do--making music with colors, gliding on alpha waves and feeling close to God. I did these colorful abstract mind-paintings in the dark swirls of my subconscious. It seemed like an eternity and I wanted to hold onto each stroke, each splatter and texture so that when I got back to the studio, I could attempt to somehow reproduce what I had envisioned during the biofeedback sessions. The time spent in the biofeedback laboratory soothed me as I floated off on the sounds produced there. It was indeed soothing in my ears as well as my soul, and my ulcers and anxiety soon healed.

Meanwhile, in the art department, the dean was fired for *unprofessional* activities. Not only was he a bigot, but a thief, so it seemed, as well. He was caught red-handed, via security surveillance video, stealing art from the school. Security had set up the cameras thinking that some janitors or other grounds people were the thieves. They were surprised to discover the dean as the guilty party. The art he stole were sold to galleries in New York for a decent profit, and he was surreptitiously dismissed without fan-fair or noteworthy expulsion. The administration just quietly let him go. (*They might as well have given the bastard a gold watch.*) Within a few months after his removal, he obtained a better position at the University of Buffalo in New York. There is no doubt in my mind, however, that if he had been anything other than White, he would have summarily been treated like a common criminal, expelled with earsplitting verbosity, and, of course, given some noteworthy punitive action. However, universal laws prevail because to my understanding the man's career went downhill having left Buffalo for a school in Michigan and then eventually back in Ohio to The Columbus College of Art and Design where he was also furtively dismissed.

In lieu of the blatant bigotry initiated by the dean and the subsequent residual effects toward me regarding his dismissal, by a few of his cronies within the department, I decided to take hold of my future. Although they certainly have a fine program including some marvelous instructors, certain attitudes dissipated my belief to continue there, and my health dictated a more important message. So after eighteen months and less than six months until graduation, I made up my mind to forfeit my M.F.A. program at U.C. for greener pastures. I left disappointed and fed-up with the school.

With my ulcers healed, I packed my paintings, art supplies, books, and other belongings that could fit into and on my Volkswagen bus and sadly said farewell to my friends and lovers. With only one hundred and seventy dollars in my pocket, I nosed the Volkswagen for Penn State University at State College, Pennsylvania. Richard Mayhew, a renowned African-American artist, was teaching there and I felt that I needed to experience some positive mentoring or sincere Affirmative Action. I did not transfer any credit hours from Cincinnati, which meant I must begin my M.F.A. all over again. But it was a fresh start, and I knew that I would do better than where I had been. I remember Virgil, my sage little brother, telling me once *that sometimes we have to take two steps backward to get four steps ahead.*

****

Richard Mayhew, as well as the other art department faculty at Penn State University, were internationally renowned artists. My time with Professors Richard Mayhew, George Zordich, and Yar Comicky was without arrogance or belligerence of any form, and my time there only nurtured my artistic yearning. The color palette Mayhew used and the teachings by Zordich and Comicky helped my research of painting and the history of abstract expressionism. They sincerely honed my classroom teaching abilities as well as studio and style of art.

During the latter part of my first year at Penn State, I began working on a series of automatic expressionistic paintings encouraged by Professor Comicky who said my brush calligraphy had elements of self-automatism. I hadn't a clue what he was talking about, only that automatism part. Puzzled by what he said, I asked him quizzically and asked what did he mean? He suggested that I research the history of automatism. And then he gave me the most important worth of information I received in all my years of schooling:

"Well Charles, if I tell you what it means, you won't go to the library and research it will you?" He smiled and walked away.

This was in 1981 before the Internet and computers were just becoming trendy. The one I owned was a cumbersome *Commodore* computer connected to my television and typewriter with a spinning daisy wheel and every four months another one came on the market making yours obsolete. In bars and video game rooms, *Pac Man, Ping Pong,* or *Space Invaders* intruded the spaces of pinball machines.

I went to the Library and looked for books dealing with automatic painting and found only a few with automatic writing and hardly any were available that made reference to art. Interestingly, all these books were written between the war years of the 1920s to 1930s. My inquiries lead me to a group of artists in Europe that included renowned artist and photographer Man Ray and the surrealist artist Salvador Dali. These groups of artists were passionately making art under the influence of self-automatism that came to a halt at the start of World War Two.

The notion of self-automatism began again after the war, but this time in America under the influence of Jazz, Bee-bop, and the writings of existentialism by the French philosophers John-Paul Sartre and Albert Camus. The art was called *abstract expressionism* and the American artists involved were Rauschenberg, Kline, Pollack and DeKooning, just to name a few. Like them, I experimented with non-objective automatic paintings with some measure of personal success. I read as much as I could about the existential phenomenology and tried to transcendentalize a painting method that I could call my own. The experimentation meant being completely alone. I meditated, prayed, danced, and tried to combine my subconscious mind to visual possibilities. As my mind opened, I realized that this was nothing new in the process of being creative. The Shinto artisans of Japan believe that a spirit resides in all things including non-living objects such as stone and wood. Western African tribes, as well as the Native Americans, also believe in the same concept,. They all believe that before one could produce a work of art, he has to make contact with the spirit residing in the material first. An African drum maker talks to a tree and begs his forgiveness for having to cut it in order to make a drum. The end result, however, would be a beautiful work of art that would be cherished by the drummer and honored by the patrons who heard its sound. Thus, I needed to communicate with my materials and explored what I learned in biofeedback. I made my frames, stretched and primed my canvas in a ritualistic manner. I usually painted with no one present in the studio in the still of the night and

I worked until the crack of dawn. It was during those moments that I produced some of my most influential works calling my method of painting: *Transcendental-Abstract-Expressionism* or TAE.

The Dance of TAE

Music sets the mood. It carries me away. I paint ambidextrously holding brushes in both hands. I paint in stereo and music flows through my brushes in colors. Each one has its own rainbow of notes, flowing harmoniously into each other as the audience applauds from the canvas. To the left is Fred Astaire, and the right, Ginger Rogers. They flow and mix into each other; tapping, sliding, gliding, and Dancing at the Ritz in each other's arms, embracing the cane, tossing the top hat...concluding with a kiss... A matador appears with a raised arm and swiftly slashes downward into the heart of the painting. He turns and bows to Mahler conducting the Fifty Symphony with both arms moving precisely to the melody's flow, forming a colorful choreograph of calligraphy of swirls, slashes, jabs, thrusts, and twists...Cheers and whistles of color, Jab, thrusts, twists, and punch. Mohamed Ali trading punches with the shadow and the Bear bleeds Cadmium red...Coletrain, Miles, and Dexter playing silent solos. Each having his own shade of blue; Blues flowing harmoniously into each other and the audience applauds in purple, yellow lemon yellow, lime and Hookers green, lamp black...

My research gave me the understanding that everything in the universe is deliberately, in some way, interconnected with each other; that there is a fine balance that keeps a constant pattern of change. I began to comprehend that color is alive and that life itself is like placing a mirror in front of another mirror. I heard sound in

185

three-dimensional tones and everything seemed to be a metaphor that had meaning to something else. Indeed, tangibility was clearly not as concrete as I thought. And the more I learned, the more I knew that I didn't know.

****

It was Kenneth Beittel who fostered my yearning to advance beyond a Masters of Fine Arts degree, and he encouraged me to pursue a doctorate in art education. He was the art education department's chair. One day as I was walking down the halls, he greeted me and I nodded in reply. I didn't have him for any of my classes, as my major was Fine Arts. The fine arts students had a cockiness about themselves, thinking that those majors in Art History and Art Education were essentially "wannabe" artists. We had the notion that if you can't do the studio stuff, you teach.

"Have you ever considered getting a Ph.D. in Art Education?" He asked me.

"What for? I'm getting a M.F.A. shortly and it's a terminal degree. I don't need to go any higher." was my reply.

Beittel was tall and lanky with thinning, white shoulder length hair. He reminded me very much of Reverend Johnson of my youth on South Lane Street. Both soft-spoken, polite, he had a way of looking at you with accessing gentle eyes. His dress was extremely casual, often working in sandals, and you could occasionally see him wearing a colorful bandana around his head like an Apache. He leaned against the wall and said,

"Who told you that you don't need to go any higher?"

I said that everyone knows that you don't need a Ph.D. to teach if you have a M.F.A.

Then he said the most remarkable thing that I will always remember:

"*Who* said that *you* don't need a Ph.D?"

Lights went on in my head. I stepped back and squinted my eyes and stared into this man. He was different. There's more to him besides his laid back demeanor. This tall hippie of a man was one of the most respected individuals on campus as well as in the world as I came to discover.

"Step into my office and let's discuss your future over a cup of tea," he said.

I followed him into his bare office and we sat on a Navaho rug on the floor drinking herb tea. His office furniture consisted of only a desk with little correspondence, two chairs—one for his guests, the other behind his desk. There were a few potted plants suspended from the ceiling, and a beautiful large painting hanging on the wall that he said his wife painted. His office gave an ambience of a sanctuary. It is said that there are a few people who influence us positively in our lifetime. Besides some members in my immediate family, these influential individuals were the artists and scholars at Penn State's art department. Zordich, Comicky, Mayhew, and Kenneth Beittel. Beittel was the one who first told me about his mentor, Viktor Lowenfeld, the noted psychologist and art educator. I was so intrigued about the fascinating stories he told me about Lowenfeld's life that I eventually wrote my dissertation on him.

Years later, someone asked me what did I thought of Kenneth Beittel. I told her that for me, he is Socrates, Buddha, and Christ all rolled up into one. His influence on me changed my life, and my reason for going beyond my dreams.

****

There is a painting hanging in The African-American Studies Department at Ohio State University entitled, *Zero*. I painted it during my visual exploration when I was a graduate student at Penn State. The upper third of the painting is painted realistically and the remainder lower portion is abstract. It is dark, gloomy, and has texture emphasizing environmental desecration, war and death. The upper portion has a Black Marine's portrait painted and he's wearing dress blues and is looking straight at the viewer. On his right side is the following text:

187

We used to call him ZERO, a name he hated. If there were anyhay [sic] of saying I'm sorry he would have heard it a thousand times by now. His real name was James Allen and he was from a small town in Ohio. Some of the guys used to tease him about his rural ways. But like me he was a poor black kid who joined simply because there were few jobs available. And like me he would send money home. He told me that the only suit he ever owned was the one he got for his high school graduation. I remembered when he got his Marine dress blues. He felt so proud that he wore them home on leave. He never had a girlfriend and was 23 and still a virgin...Allen was killed in a fucking place called Quang Nam, Vietnam. His head was blown off by enemy artillery fire. I went to visit his mother and his younger brothers and sisters, who lived in a run-down tenant house. I lied and told them that he was respected by all the guys and that he had a lot of girlfriends. Looking back, I realize that being black and or poor, in this country, is an asset for war.

Penn State University's main campus locates in a town called (of all names) State College. The main strip and its tributary alleys are filled with bookstores and bars. On Friday nights the town becomes alive with students carousing from one bar to another, and house parties flourish with *Rolling Rock* Beer kegs placed in a corner of a room or on a back porch dispensing their brew from spigots into plastic cups.

Penn State people party until the early hours of the morning. It was on one of those Friday nights after leaving a party early that I started painting Zero. I just had an urge to paint and left the party at the chagrin of some friends when the party was just beginning to get interesting. Once inside the graduate student's studio, I set up my area in preparation to paint. I wasn't drunk but I had a nice buzz sufficient enough to be creative. It felt good being alone in the studio, and I began painting in my usual ritualistic manner with no idea where the painting would take me.

Halfway into the work I became frustrated and my mind, for no apparent reason, drifted back to my Marine Corps days. I started thinking about Corporal James Allen and remembered him as a Private straight out of boot camp and how other Marines at Marine Barracks in Norfolk teased him because of his rural ways. His uniform seemed perpetually rumpled and his shoes lightly buffed instead of the regulated spit-shine like that of other Marines in the barracks. He was like a square wheel on a fine automobile. Other Black Marines tried in vain to get him to shape up, but it was useless.

Allen was likeable enough but he had a very stubborn streak. Perhaps it was his way of coping with his own inadequacies in a hard ass, spit and shine Marine Corps culture. Whatever it was, he maintained his own course of action and lived with the consequences afterwards. It was a White Marine who dubbed him "Zero" from the character in Beetle Bailey comics. Initially, I laughed. It was more spontaneous than anything else--like an impulsive response when seeing a funny footage of Laurel and Hardy. My initial laughter came from out of nowhere and afterwards I felt bad because the name stuck with him in the barracks. The fact is that Allen actually looked like a Black version of the cartoon character Zero in Beetle Bailey's comics. Eventually, Allen was one of those who volunteered to go to Vietnam, either for higher rank or just to get away from the barracks and his ball and chain nickname. By the time he volunteered for Vietnam, I was Honorably Discharge and back in Columbus. I learned of his death about three months later when I picked up the *Columbus Dispatch* from a trash container in an office I had been cleaning and saw a clipping with Allen's picture in the daily "casualty of war" section on the front page. I worked part-time as a janitor upon my discharge. Setting aside my push broom, I collapsed in a vacant chair behind someone's desk and read. His was the second article in a period of two weeks I had read of a Marine I had known who had been killed in action. Sgt. John Mitchell was the other.

Alone in the studio, I remembered. Fifteen years had passed and now alone, except for the ghosts of dead Marines, I painted *Zero*. Fifteen years of subconsciously suppressing grief and

189

guilt had flown by. Into this painting I poured my grief on canvas. Time and space cumulated to this fixed moment. I cried all throughout the remainder of the painting process. I couldn't help it. My tired eyes burned with tears and turpentine fumes. Several times I had to stop painting. I just stood and wept.

I decided to paint texts on the painting because I wanted Allen's story verbalized. I exhausted all I could do visually. My hands automatically inscribed and painted bits and pieces of past Marine Corps moments. I didn't care about my grammar and misspelled words. This was an emotional "draft copy" outcry, and I had to get it all down at *this* moment. The text became symbolic and I decided to leave it as it was (bad grammar and all) because my feelings were pure. It became my emotional outpouring of hurt, forgiveness, and healing. In essence, it was an epitaph not only for Allen's valor--as the American Legions would expect—but also acted as a symbol for his humility, and I guess for all the Allen-types who had fallen in wars.

****

After my discharge from the Marine Corps, I had the pleasant opportunity of meeting Allen's mother. When I knocked at her door, I was expecting a middle-aged, white-haired woman, but stood face-to-face with a young attractive woman, probably in her middle thirties. Clinging to her apron was Allen's little three-year-old sister. She was surprised when I told her that I knew her son, and standing on the porch in the open doorway we talked. Mrs. Allen did not look at me while I spoke vaingloriously about her dead son. All during the brief conversation, she kept her head bent, either out of shyness or sorrow—-or both. I never saw her again after that.

A few weeks later, I met Sgt. Mitchell's parents, who also greeted me at the front door. Once again I wasn't invited to come inside. John's father, a bespectacled man, peeped out the door that was only opened wide enough where I could hand him some photos of John. Our conversation took place on their porch where I gave them a couple photos of John and myself when we were instructors at a rifle range in Virginia Beach, Virginia. One photo showed him shaking my hand when I received my Marine Corps Good Conduct

Medal; the other was in front of the Marine Corps emblem that we made out of concrete.

I remembered the time we drove together to Columbus in his '61 Chevy for Thanksgiving holiday. His folks lived somewhere in the Short-North area then. Mom had just bought the new home on Carpenter Street, and I was proud of it when John dropped me off. When he came to pick me up on our way back, I told him that Mom had baked us a couple of sweet-potato pies. Sweet-potato pie was a new treat for him like many Northern White people, but when he ate a slice, he was smitten. So there it was in the *Columbus Dispatch*, a brief article along with a picture of an American flag-draped coffin and Marine honor guards at the gravesite a few weeks after Zero was killed. All I could think about was the drive back to Virginia and him enjoying Mom's pie. I also considered doing a painting of John, but the one I painted for Zero had already emotionally drained me. John's painting would have to be left for another time. When I completed painting Zero that early Saturday morning, I stood back, assessed it, and was startled because the face I had painted was not Allen's, but my own.

****

The Process

VISITORS TO A PRISON *find the experience humbling from the moment they enter the parking lot. You are sensitive to the confined and find the occasion similar to visits to funeral parlors—surreal and sad. The razor sharp barbed wire that surrounds the compound gives the impression of Christmas tinsel ornamentation. And, as you walk toward the entrance, you see doldrums of prisoners staring as they work or mingle around the compound looking at you like pet store puppies. Besides their stares, the guards stare. They have a different stare, the kind that makes you feel like an intruder. You feel awkward and out of place. And, there is a feeling that things are in reverse order. You are the inmate carrying news, lies, and illusions of an outside world. Walking through the process line, you confront another dilemma-- the dehumanization of the "pat down" experience. The idea of other people touching you, having you emptying your personal contents into shallow trays, exposing them to the world, leaves you feeling vulnerable and naked. But, to see your loved one, you surrender a part of yourself over to a person you do not even know, or perhaps like, filling out forms hiding behind a smile and doing what you are told.... "Next!"... .*

Orient Correction Facility

Chapter Sixteen

(10:05 a.m.)

*B*Y THE TIME the preacher was speaking his final words at Flo's graveside, I was already gone. Enough had already been said. What more could he say about Flo that I did not already know? I left the ceremony in the middle of the eulogy and headed south on highway 71 for the Orient Correctional Center, twenty-five miles away, to visit my brother Bunny.

I wanted to spend some time with Bunny before returning to Lincoln University in Pennsylvania. He had been incarcerated for more than half his life for a crime of which he has yet to be proven guilty. A newly appointed warden, wanting to flex his muscle and make an ostentatious impression on his superiors, as well as the inmates, used my brother to set an example. He refused him a pass to attend Flo's funeral. We are not Catholic, but a Catholic priest chaplain had the common sense to intervene and repeatedly tried to get the warden to change his mind. His efforts were in vain. Moreover, the Protestant fundamentalist born-again chaplain did not attempt to contact the warden on my brother's behalf. Compared to the more educated Catholic priests, many of the born-again Protestant chaplains employed in correctional facilities are politically motivated and lack education. Their spiritual pronouncements espouse emotionalism and pontification, rather than spiritual logic. As a result, the sudden news of Flo's death coupled with the new warden's decision caused Bunny to snap. The warden placed him in solitary confinement, a.k.a., *the hole*. Bunny was to remain there in his grief for an undisclosed period.

****

I abhorred the stench of cigarette smoke, and even as a child I would find various ways to avoid it. Bunny enjoyed blowing smoke in my face as well as Virgil. He delighted in watching us frantically fan our hands as we rushed outside groping for fresh air. One of the things I remember, as a non-smoker, on visiting Bunny in jail, was the stale pungent smell of cigarette smoke in the visiting rooms. During his many years of confinement, he had been transferred to several correctional centers within the Ohio Correctional system and the visiting rooms of all of them seemed to have the same stale smell of tobacco smoke. Swirling pools of smoke circulated around visiting infants, children, wives, mothers, grandparents, and friends. Most of them begrudgingly tolerated the smoke, while others joined in the ritual. Someone, usually ashen with thin red circles around the lining of his eyes, invariably started a chain reaction cacophony of coughing and snorting. Bunny would have liked to have quit smoking, but couldn't since most inmates rely on tobacco as a form of currency.

After going through the ritual of being patted down having the contents of my pockets emptied, I walked through a maze of

195

metal detectors to then fill out a series of forms. I was given an invisible stamp on my right hand that, when shoved in a black-light box for the desk guard to see, displayed a bright bluish design. After this, I was escorted to a very small room partitioned from the smoke and clamor of the main visiting area. The room actually looked more like a confessional booth, but without a door you could close for privacy. The wall that faced me was Plexiglas from the waist up. The booth was designed for those who visit inmates locked in the "hole."

There was a low chair in the booth and, on the other side, behind the Plexiglas partition facing me, a concrete wall painted a dreary institutional gray. I tried to imagine inmates arriving from the hole and entering the narrow aisle that ran along one side of the wall to the small private booth with thick Plexiglas partition. Tiny pinholes drilled in a circular pattern in the glass like a telephone receiver were situated way too high for communication. A short person would have trouble talking through it.

Feeling claustrophobic, I wanted to get out in open space again. I needed fresh air. I have always tried to hide my fear of enclosed places. When I brave elevators, I panic when going above the twelfth floor. My worst nightmare, though, is of being locked behind bars. The few brief experiences I have had of being locked-up instigated feelings of complete rage, like being a trapped animal. I respected Bunny's ability to cope with the same inherited fear.

First came the rattle of heavy chains clanking, then a quick sliding and dragging sound. I could hear the shuffling of feet and a rhythmical sound that reoccurred every three seconds. When I finally saw my brother, he was bent forward at a forty-five degree angle. A short chain was attached to a pair of handcuffs on his wrists and to the shackles on his ankles. He came in with a White, shotgun-toting guard. I wasn't expecting this. That scene awakened the spirits of all my ancestors inside me. He looked like he had been spiritually beaten up. It was the same look years ago when Willie broke him. That moment in time defined the pure meaning of pathos. Standing up, I wanted to scream! I felt like the creature in Munch's painting, *The Scream*. If the warden had come in my view at that moment, I would have willingly sacrificed my left testicle for an opportunity to place my hands around that son-of-a-bitch's (red) neck, squeezing it with all my might. But all that I could do was lower my head and muster up all the courage inside myself to convey to my brother Bunny to have strength. I tried to smile, wanting very much to trade places and take his burden. He was Christ carrying his cross. I couldn't even touch him or carry his load. When I looked up at him and met his eyes, a torment arose from the depths of my soul. Every atom in my being cried out. The smile on his face betrayed him, as I'm sure mine did. This ordeal was worse than Flo's funeral. At least she was in peace. The pain in Bunny eyes was non-terrestrial. He tried to conceal it from me.

"Hey man, how's it going?" I said, searching his face through my tinted bi-focal lenses, trying to conceal my emotions.

"It's going all right," he replied in a hushed voice returning my shallow gaze. "How was Flo's funeral?" Bunny spoke in whispers. It was uncommon for him to raise his voice. He had a naturally soft, mellow flowing voice, whose soft cadence was a lot like Mom's. Even when agitated, he remained calm, low and relaxed. His soft voice was one of the things the girls had always liked about him. It was good listening to his voice.

"Flo's funeral was last night." I said. "I just came from the cemetery because her burial was this morning, less than an hour ago."

"You know I was just thinking about her. It's hard for me to believe that she's gone," he said, his head bent and looking at his handcuffed hands as they rested on his lap.

"Yeah, me too."

"I mean she didn't deserve to go like that," he said.

"What the fuck was on that niggas mind? He didn't have to waste her like that."

"Bunny, he probably just went bananas. He had Alzheimer's, you know. At least that is what was diagnosed along with prostrate cancer."

"Alzheimer's and prostrate cancer?" Bunny paused sighing. "I guess he knew that he didn't have long to go and probably wanted to take someone with him."

197

"Bunny, I can hardly hear you. Can you speak up?" He bent forward, closer to the thick Plexiglas window that separated us, and spoke a little louder. I leaned forward, turning my head to the tiny pinholes on the glass. All this, and the noise from the visitation room behind me, made it hard to hear him. Moving closer to the glass he pressed his lips and asked: "Is this better?"

I leaned forward, pressing my ears to the glass and said, "It's a little better." I hesitated with my next question as I found myself looking at the shotgun the guard was holding. I wondered why the hell White authorities have to do things in excess. Bunny, bent over in chains from his head to his feet, was broken. The Guard glanced away, looking at his watch. It was probably time for him to go home. "Hell," I said to myself, "he's just another link in the chain. He probably has his own problems."

"Bunny, when will you be getting out of the hole?"

"I don't know. But I'm okay," he lied.

"What is it with this new cracker warden? I mean he could at least have let you view her body at the funeral home," I said.

"Sugar Pie, don't get me started. He is just one of those mother fuckers who want to make an impression with the head office."

I felt uncomfortable sitting in this tight confinement. I couldn't help but notice the dark fading bruised ring around Bunny's neck where he tried to hang himself several months ago. He had wanted a transfer because he had been ill treated at the previous prison. The guards there, he claimed, were a bunch of rednecks who constantly provoked him into trouble. It was strange for me to realize Bunny was being provoked. Age was catching up on him, and his physique was not as strong as it once was. Bunny was growing old and was not capable of fending for himself as he had when young. I knew that strength and cunning were important assets when incarcerated, but the realization of what it must be like to be confined twenty-four hours a day always watching one's back hit me straight in the face. It is a powerless feeling seeing a loved one incarcerated. The system strips him of everything even the prisoner's dignity. It is important that outside family support them no matter what.

I looked at Bunny's hooded, deep-set eyes, remembering the past when he crooned and doo-wopped on street corners with his friends, and how he defended me at Beck Street Elementary School from big George Miller's intimations on the playground. I remembered our shooting marbles in the backyard and Willie's whippings. All of these childhood visions rushed into my mind in the tiny booth as I peered at my big brother Bunny behind the thick Plexiglas partition. The fading bruise of his suicide attempt still circled his neck. The difficulty of trying to hear him in the cramped confinement of the booth only further fueled my anger at The Columbus Police Department for his predicament. I thought of when they told Mom, "Somehow, someway, we're going to get him."

****

A year or so before Flo's death, Bunny met a woman named Hazel through an inmate, and soon a vigorous correspondence developed that blossomed into love. Hazel became very attentive to Bunny, as much as one can through Plexiglas, and under the constant imposing stares of prison guards. During the holiday season, inmates were allowed to receive care packages. With great care, Hazel took responsibility for choosing the holiday package selections. She organized family members, getting them to donate new shoes, underwear, new batteries for Bunny's Walkman radio, canned food, and other assorted items that were on the prisoner list.

When she visited Mom, Hazel posed her in bed and took pictures of her, which she would show to Bunny when she visited him. Hazel was equally attentive to Mom, and during her frequent visits would comb and brush her hair, care for her. I consider Hazel to be a saint. Bunny knew that she was a good woman and he wanted to marry her, even if he was still incarcerated. Things like that had been done before, and he felt close to Hazel. He wanted someone on the outside to care for him in his aging years. He once told me that when he got his parole, he would settle down and open a small diner. But when Bunny made the request for marriage, the warden took it upon himself to do yet another inconsiderate thing. He denied it. This was yet another blow to Bunny and once again, he felt utterly helpless. You could see it in his eyes when you visited him. Sadness clung to Bunny's eyes in dark circles.

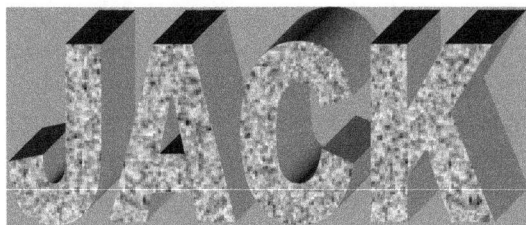

Chapter Seventeen

JASPER "JACK" LOVINGOOD started courting Mom about a year after her divorce from Willie. Jack was not as tall as Willie was but he was very muscular and broad in the shoulders from working various construction jobs most of his life. He was one of the most intelligent individuals I would ever come to know, past and present. His IQ was over 160, and he would read volumes of books at a time. I once remembered him reading *The Fall of The Third Reich,* which he began on a Friday evening, and by Sunday afternoon, he completed all the volumes. He was a walking encyclopedia.

Jack had been recently released from prison and was trying to make it on the outside. He formed a baseball team for teenage gangs, and it was Bunny who introduced him to Mom. One look at her and he flipped. He came over every night with bags of groceries, and had even taken us all out to eat in a restaurant—something that we had never experienced before. He also took a keen interest in our education. He was extremely intelligent. He was not militant, but it did not take much to provoke him if a wrong was being done. It seemed to be a shame that with such talent, he had to wind up in prison.

It was a breath of fresh air meeting Jack who was not an alcoholic or an abuser of children or women. His only passions for drink were a few beers or "brownies" as he called them. Usually on hot summer nights Jack would sip his brownies while listening to his vast music collection of 33 RPMS that ranged from classical to jazz. He was the one individual who introduced me to the world of jazz. And I still appreciate his knowledge of jazz and thank him for making that idiom a part of my life. When he began to date Mom, I was around twelve or thirteen years old; I remember coming down the stairs one night to use the toilet. As I glanced in the dim living room light, I could see Jack on his knees holding Mom's hand, displaying a Shakespearean show of affection. I knew that he loved Mom but soon I would discover that he had a flair for bizarre dramatics. He would, for instance, fake fainting and collapse on the floor spread-eagled and not move for hours. He did this on several occasions when he first started courting Mom. The first time this happened, we began to call the emergency squad when Jack miraculously woke up and asked us what had happened. After several of these thespian performances, we began to ignore them. He was good. I mean he would lie there without flinching for a long time. We would try to awaken him by shaking and other means until we just started ignoring him. We would ignore him and step over him, as if he were a piece of unwanted furniture. Eventually, he would come out and once again ask what had happened. His fainting spells, however, were still puzzling to my curious 12-year-old mind. Were they real or was he just faking? I had to find one-way or the other, regardless of the consequences. It would be worth knowing. So I suggested to Virgil that we pee on him the next time he fainted to see if this would get his attention. We couldn't wait. The next time he fainted, we would be ready. I believe it was on a weekend when Jack came over and went into one of his famous dramatic fainting spells. He collapsed on the living room floor and Virgil and I took our positions on each side of him and started unzipping our trousers. When he heard the sound of our zippers unzipping, he was like Lazarus. He never had any more fainting spells in our house again.

Jack told me about the CCC camps that he was a part of during the Second World War, and how he helped build the roads throughout the Mid-West. He also told us history of Black people and about things left out of history books that were never taught in school. Books and Jazz albums were his passion and it was also his shortcoming because a few years after he married my mother, he went to a federal prison somewhere in Indiana for mail fraud. Jack read law books and knew that an individual could make an order from a magazine ad and was not liable to pay. He had figured it out that when you make a mail order for a subscription for a record album, that if the bill was not paid within six months, the company would merely write your account off as a loss. So, after the book or record subscription ran out, he would change the name on the account and start over again. We had a record and book collection so vast that he started selling them to record and bookstores. Our record collection on Jazz was so extensive that he called WVKO the local Black radio station, and discussed his collection. They invited him to come to the station and spin a few of his platters. He enjoyed playing the role of a DJ for an evening, airing certain cuts to my mother.

Jack told us that there were plenty of intelligent people locked-up. Perhaps the greatest minds—especially Black men's mind—were incarcerated. He said that the worse fear that the White man had was to see an educated Negro. Indeed, Jack's keen insight and intelligence had ignited my desire to learn.

Mama and Willie, my stepfather circa 1949

Mom

Chapter Eighteen

THE DRIVE to the convalescent center located on the far east side of Columbus was uneventful, compared to the drive to Flo's burial service only a few hours ago. I was too busy trying to calm my anger about my visit to Bunny and everything else that was crowding my mind at the moment. I remember the large hand painted banner that stretched across the pulpit at the church the previous night during the funeral service. It read: "We are at war with Satan." It seemed appropriate then because I was at war. My enemies were the criminal justice system, the abusive behavior of the Columbus Police Department, my unresolved memories of Willie's abuse (that still haunted me after all these years) and everything negative that had been thrown at me in life. With Flo still warm in her grave, Bunny in leg-chains and dumped in isolation in some cold Ohio prison hole, and a redneck warden wanting to show his subordinates and prison inmates how big a prick he was, I was definitely at war. Satan had always represented the ultimate evil and it seemed the sign over the pulpit was dead on. I was at war, and have been perhaps all my life. But where was the justice? Actually, as I grow older, I still don't really know what the word means living in a so-called democracy. I only know that if you have money, you are more than likely to get by with murder than a poor man who steals.

So the forty-five minute drive to the Yorkshire Convalescent home where Mom was, whisked by in a matter of minutes. I always got a funny feeling every time I went inside the place. It was not the smell of sweat, urine, or feces permeating the halls, although Yorkshire is a decent, clean, and orderly place. That

204

is not the waste I am referring to. What I smelled was human waste--individuals whose lives were used up, in accordance with the societal definition of old age. America is a *disposable* culture. We are conditioned to throw things away when items are used up. From diapers to disposable razors, it all ends up in the trash. We throw away things merely as a matter of convenience. Unfortunately, that seems to be the same situation for human lives. The end result of many seniors simply implies that their lives have been used up so their kids deposit them to the nearest nursing home. Shelly, an art student punk rocker girlfriend of mine at Penn State, would often say, "Life's a bitch, and then you die."

They were just words that meant nothing at the time. For Shelly, they were merely tongue-in-cheek words, usually spoken out of frustration at the outcome of one of her paintings. I heard others say it too, but I never gave into its philosophy because it seemed too incompatible for my taste, a temperament representing the ultimate negative. "Life's a bitch and then you die?" Bull crap. I have always tried to celebrate life no matter how hard things got. But if you are an incapacitated patient in a nursing home, you might give some credence to Shelly's philosophy. These residences had at one time led productive lives. Now due to an accident, old age, or sickness, they find themselves at the mercy of nursing attendants, technicians, and dietitians. It was a difficult decision for my siblings and me to place Mom in a nursing home. We can remember her saying that she would not want to be placed in one, but she wanted to remain living at home until her last days. When, however, the strokes' scar tissue enveloped much of her mental acuity, it left her also blind. The advice of her doctor was to have Mom sent to a nursing home, came as a shameful relief as well as regret for us. We certainly did not have the financial means for a 24-hour nursing care. That was virtually impossible. To try to pull together as a unit meant a hardship on all of us. Asian families in Asia have it down to a science. Their family units are tight-knit organizations that have for centuries functioned with elders properly being taken care of by designated members of the family. Trying to compare them is like comparing a minnow to a whale with the only similarity that they both live in water. My family is close, but like most American families, we never prepared for anything like this until it was too late. So we were left with some hard facts and decisions. Flo, Virgil, Dottie, and Sandy made the bulk of them because I was living in Montreal at the time. The decision for placing Mom in Yorkshire proved to be a good one, and I believe she would have been pleased with the level of care she received. Her only complaint was that she wanted to know why she did not eat. She was unaware that a tube, which had been surgically inserted into her stomach, was feeding her. Mom's food, which hung from an IV pole, looked like, and had the same consistency peanut butter.

When I visited Mom at Yorkshire, I closely observed others--elderly people sitting idly alone in the hallways propped up with pillows in a wheelchair looking, waiting, and staring at you as you walked by. Others lying in bed stared into nothingness. The lucky ones, could amble around and those with good mental acuity nonchalantly watched TV, played cards, Monopoly or chatted to each other in the lobby to pass the time away. All of them, however, had one thing in common; they all waited for visitors. It's pathetic thinking of those whose family members never visited their confined relatives. Maybe it is because they are in denial, not of their loved ones' circumstances, rather their own mortality. Once seniors are deposited, many families simply put them out of their minds. The out of sight, out of mind adage is put in practice with those families burying their heads in the sand. They also often complained about the financial burden of caring for the welfare of their parents.

Certainly, nursing homes make you very aware of your own inevitable old age and demise. Many patients, however, are very mentally cognizant, but their bodies may be too old to participate with their mind. Some have excellent physical acuity, but their minds are on another level. And all nursing homes cater to terminal illness and death. Death is no stranger to them, and one by one, the residents watch each other die.

It takes a special person to work in those homes. The underpaid nurses, aides, and technicians at Yorkshire seemed really concerned about the care of the residences. They are angles and many residents grow to embrace them as family. I recall when I was an Air Force Medic working part time at the University Hospital as an orderly; a very young and pretty patient lost the use of her legs in an automobile accident. Her once beautiful muscular legs withered and had the flexibility of a rag doll. She was married, but her husband rarely visited. I often wondered what her future would be like if she simply gave up. Would she end up in a place like Yorkshire? During my shift and when I had some time to spare, we played Rock 'n Roll trivia. She was good. Otis Redding was her favorite singer, and I could just imagine her dancing.

****

Once I visited Mom on Mothers Day, expecting to see many residents' family members visiting their relatives and I was surprised to find very few visitors. I was carrying a Mothers Day card and a bouquet of peppermint carnations. Little white haired women in wheelchairs immediately swarmed around me and started tirelessly chattering about the flowers and the card I held in my hands. Taking a few moments to wish them all happy Mothers Day, I tried to depart and head toward Mom's room, but the rolling horde of white-haired women in wheelchairs deliberately blocked my path. They encircled me and the scene reminded me of one of John Wayne and Ward Bond's movies. I was trapped in the chatter and saw no way out. They wanted to know whom I was going to visit, and their questions flew at me from all directions.

"My what lovely flowers. Can I smell them?"
"Did you drive in from Cleveland?"
"What does your card say?"
"Where did you pick up the flowers?"
"Do you always give her peppermint carnations?"
"What part of Canada?"
"How do you like my brand new slippers?
  My daughter sent them to me. Pretty, huh?"
"Young man, are you married?"

I took my time and spoke with them all, wanting to give each a flower if I had enough to go around as I inched my way down the hall toward Mom's room. The sad thing was the look in their eyes, which conveyed that they would not receive any visitors with flowers or hand delivered cards that special day. I felt sorry for them and pitied their children.

****

Being recently blind, Mom would radar her head to the sound of my voice. The nurses took away her false teeth and it seemed strange seeing her without them because it made her face look smaller and her chin more pronounced, but her smile still illuminated, even without teeth.

The strong medications she took caused her not to acknowledge my presence most of the times, but I always identified myself and she would smile and call me by my nickname, Sugar Pie. Her medications also made her sleep a great deal and I would never awake her. Often when she was awake, she had a very venerable look that some blind people have when they stare vacantly into space. At those times, I wanted to hold her forever. If I pushed the bed table out of the way, or walked to the opposite side of her bed, she still would be looking at the spot where I had previously stood. And when someone spoke to her, she would turn her head in the direction of the voice. She went to great lengths to give others the impression that she still could see, and that everything was all right. Mom wasn't in denial of her blindness; it was just her way of trying to let others believe she could cope for our reassurance.

"Sugar Pie, is that you? How's Lorrie?"
Even though I informed Mom that my second wife, Lorrie and I were separated, she would often ask about her. She, like other members in my family, felt a close connection with Lorrie. One reason may be that they shared the same inimitable Appalachian culture. Lorrie was born in a coal-mining region of West Virginia and lived in southeastern Ohio. Her father, a coal miner, was drafted into the Army and stationed in Brooklyn. This explained Lorrie's strange mixture of Jewish-Irish-Appalachian heritage. This blend made her extremely sensitive to cultural matters. They shared an Appalachian sisterhood for each other of culture, wisdom, and a raw spiritual earthiness. Even though Lorrie's status had elevated

from that of a coal miner's daughter to a (Ph.D.) college professor, she would unconsciously regain her Appalachian accent when talking with Mom. I believe my mother would never entertain the thought of Lorrie not being an intricate part of her family, even if all Mom's mental faculties were skewed or not.

After a casual exchange of greetings, Mom sometimes turned her head away from me abruptly as though she was embarrassed about her current condition. Later, she would simply close her eyes and fall to sleep. When she was asleep, I would never wake her. I would hold her hands, which had lost their fleshiness and gently rub her forehead. We never told her about any of deaths of the family fearing it might set off a seizure. The consequence of telling her about a family member's deaths was too high a risk. I've seen her in a couple convulsive seizures and it would always be sudden and very frightening. So we kept their deaths from her. It was strange, however, whenever their names came up during a conversation and we had to talk as though they were still among the living.

****

I had a custom of visiting Mom in late evening hours when it was quiet. I would stand close to the bed rubbing her forehead. I was my mother's sentinel, her guardian, and her usher to any impending death angel if the time came. It was a special time for me, and if she were asleep, we would quietly converse about anything and everything. When she first became a patient there, we talked about any subject from the distant past. Mom could relive it all in vivid detail. Things I had long forgotten. Flip, our old dog, who had been dead for twenty-five years, and for whom Mom had a special affection. A few times, she told me to feed him, remembering the exact color of his dog dish. She would tell me I should wear my boots when I walked in the snow, as if I was still a boy. I would reply in the present as if we were still living on South Lane Street, and attending South High. I tried to talk softly, so as to not to disturb the other patients. It didn't really matter because you could usually hear shouts and loud self-conversations among patients in other rooms throughout the convalescent center.

****

A strange incident occurred at Yorkshire when I visited Mom one winter evening. It was long after most visitors had left, and it was unusually quiet on the floor except for the periodic and raucous conversations an elderly lady across the hall was having with herself. The only light in the room was the light emanating from the door that opened into the hallway. One of Mom's roommates, whose name I shall say is Mabel, had a bed across from Mom. When I came during regular visiting hours, Mabel would always inform me about Mom's condition. She would tell me that she had been sitting, or if the doctor had visited, and who Mom's other visitors were. Mabel was very astute and had reasoned very well. This particular evening, she was staring at me intently without saying a word. I was beginning to worry about her, so I smiled, and suddenly noticed a very odd thing. She was propped-up on a couple of pillows and her right hand was under the blankets moving rapidly between her legs. The movement caught my eye and I was taken aback. My first response was disgust, but then I thought why should I be so upset? As I looked at her, I noticed for the first time that she must have been a beautiful woman. I could see behind the placid layers of aging, a beautiful woman. Perhaps I reminded her of her husband, lover, or first love. I don't know, but I took her masturbation as a compliment. Standing in the middle of that quiet and darkened room, I spread out my arms in an open gesture and told her to enjoy herself. She rose up from the pillow and the blankets' motion became more rapid until finally she rolled back her eyes, shuddered a moment, and laid back on her pillow. Exhausted, but with a broad smile on her face, she slept.

****

Thinking about Mom laying still, her eyes staring into space, I recalled the days of my youth, remembering all her vitality and beauty. Stroking her hair brought back many detailed memories I had completely forgotten—like the time she saved Virgil's life and mine. I probably must have been around four or five at the time. The incident occurred after she had placed some of Charlie's .38 Cal. bullets in the burning trash container after cleaning the house. I recall her cleaning out the dresser drawer and becoming upset with the blue-black revolver that she held like it was a dead mouse. Obviously, Mom knew nothing about weapons or bullets. She did know that they kill and perhaps she was thinking of the safety of her cowboy-playing sons. Thus, after sweeping the floor, she dumped them along with the trash in an old metal oil drum and lit it and went back inside to continue cleaning. Bunny was around carousing the neighborhood somewhere; Sandy was asleep in her crib, while Virgil and I played in the backyard. Our playing was interrupted with the sound of "popcorn popping" and whizzing noises flying around us. We thought we were going to be treated to some nice hot popcorn from the iron skillet Mom used to pop the corn, but the sound was coming from the trashcan. Attracted to the sound, Virgil and I started walking toward it. Suddenly, Mom came running out of the house and yelled for us not to move. We stopped. I was thinking she was coming to play with us. She walked straight toward us with the popping and whizzing noise buzzing all around us. When she came close enough, she immediately positioned herself in front of us and stood motionless. She told us not to move and stand very close behind her and to keep our head close to her thighs. We waited holding on to her dress pressing our faces on her soft buttocks, even when she suddenly jerked. But she remained standing still with her arms tightly behind her, holding us close. After all the popping and whizzing sounds stopped, she walked us into the house, clutching her thigh. The front of her dress was drenched with her blood. She got on the phone and called Charlie. Hanging up the phone she took a bag of sugar from the kitchen shelf and poured a huge amount into the gaping wound of her thigh. I noticed the red ooze through the sugar and it would be years later that I realized that Mom took a bullet *for* Virgil and me. The impact of the bullet on her thigh aligned where my head would have been as she shielded us from harm.

Charlie came rushing home from work and swept up Mom

in his arms and nervously packed more sugar to the wound and told her to hold it while he carried her to the car. He took the wheel of the old Plymouth with one hand and held down on the horn with the other dodging cars, running red lights and stop signs, heading for Grant Hospital about eight blocks away. I watched him carrying Mom into the Emergency Room as Virgil, Sandy and I looked on. In the waiting room, Charlie mumbled something to us how he told Mom to pack the wound with sugar because that would help control the bleeding. We had no idea what he was talking about but we understood his need to talk. A doctor came out and talked to him saying that he never heard of sugar being used as a method of dressing before, but it was very effective and said it probably saved her from losing a lot of blood, but the baby girl she was carrying didn't make it.

****

I also remembered the first time Mom took me to school. It was 1947, the year of the Roswell incident when a downed alien flying saucer reportedly crash-landed in Roswell, New Mexico. I was four years old and probably in the back yard discovering my own universe. Playing in the backyard dirt, observing the colors of ladybugs, tobacco spitting grasshoppers or chasing butterflies (I was extremely fascinated with bugs) when Mom came and took me inside. She had the galvanized tub already prepared with warm sudsy water. I thought how strange it was being bathed in the middle of the day. Why was she bathing me alone without Virgil? As she washed me, I noticed she was smiling. Something was up. She was acting strange. Then she produced a brand new light blue short-sleeved shirt, a pair of navy blue shorts, and a brand new pair of white shoes with white socks. Something definitely was up, but I felt good from all her pampering and attention she was giving me. She said that I was a very handsome boy, and that we were going for a walk.

After I was dressed, she took me by the hand, and we walked up Parsons Avenue. I felt special. I remember a car full of White guys slowed and started honking their horns. They leaned out of the windows, wolf whistling and saying obscene things. It was a routine occurrence, and Mom nervously squeezed my hand as we turned off busy Parsons Avenue and headed west into the shady oak canopy of Beck Street. Polite White people with neat homes and well-kept lawns mostly inhabited the neighborhood. These were places where I seldom ventured. As we walked, Mom mentioned that I was going to be starting school in the fall. I remembered asking her about Virgil, and she replied that he would be coming the following year.

The principal of Beck Street School was Mrs. Cummings, a tall White woman with thick legs who wore a dark suit with a long skirt. She greeted us with a serious smile as we entered her office. She gave us a tour of the school and showed us where my room would be located. I was impressed with the tile-decorated floor that had various numbers and the colorful letters of the alphabet emblazoned on it. The room was inviting with tall windows that allowed the light to bathe the colorful floor. Mrs. Cummings seemed sincere and proud of her school, and I find it amazing that I can still recall in detail much of the texture and color of that day.

Although Mom only went to the eighth grade, she put a lot of emphasis on education. Just before her last stroke, I asked her what she would have been if she had completed school. To my surprise, she replied a school administrator. I believe Mrs. Cummings made an enduring impression on her.

Stroking Mom's forehead there in the nursing home, we talked and relived the past.

****

Even at the age of 83, Mom still possessed a quality of feminine beauty as she slept quietly in her nursing home bed. Looking at her sleeping, I recalled a time when I witnessed men on their knees begging for her hand in marriage. I witnessed both Jack and Archie on their knees asking Mom to marry them. Their marriage proposals were among the most incredible occurrences I have ever seen and I wonder if Charlie got down on his knees to propose.

During the time Jack and Mom were married, Archie began writing to Sandy on a regular basis. Archie had been incarcerated in Leavenworth Prison after serving a ten-year drug sentence when he was in the Army. Perhaps he felt that his pre-adolescent daughter was now old enough to read and write letters on her own. Sandy may have felt obliged to return his correspondence being curious about a father she could not remember. His letters to Sandy displayed an obvious affection for Mom. He would mention how much he still loved her and would like, somehow, to make it all up to her. Of course, Jack was upset with all this, and made it perfectly clear that nothing would come between his marriages with Mom. I think he even wrote Archie telling him so, but unfortunately for Jack, he himself had to serve time in a federal prison. He was sent to a prison in Indiana.

About the same time Jack went into prison, Archie came out. In the state of Ohio, there is a legal decree that grants a spouse the right to obtain a prompt divorce if one of the married couple is imprisoned. It was 1961, and I had just graduated from South High School. I can vividly recall coming downstairs early on a Saturday morning to make a bowl of Post Toasties to nourish my skinny seventeen-year-old body. I recall that I could not sleep because of the anxieties I had of post high school graduation. What was I going to do with the rest of my life? Where would I find a job? Who would even hire me? Even though I enjoyed drafting in Mr. Moler's class and my work was outstanding, it was the White boys that he talked to and referred for jobs after graduation. Here I was, a high-school graduate, and scared as hell, trying not to make too much noise on this late June morning. By this time, Bunny was married and lived with his wife Bertha in the Lincoln Park Projects in the far Southside. I was now the man of the house and felt responsible. It was a position I felt I deserved. I wanted very much to prove myself, if only I could get the right job. From the kitchen, I heard the low whisper of an unfamiliar male voice coming from the living room. I went over there slowly to investigate, and to my surprise, I saw Archie Armstrong, Sandy's dad, whom I hadn't seen since I was seven, wearing an oversized overcoat while bending on one knee holding Mom's hand. Was he proposing to her? Sandy had mentioned that he was to be released soon, but this scene caught me by surprise. He was posed in the same Shakespearean way Jack had been some years before. Perhaps, I thought, all federal prisoners practiced this routine while incarcerated. Or was it that they had an affinity for Shakespeare? At any rate, they seemed oblivious to my presence. I was invisible. They seemed to be in a state of suspended animation.

Mom was smiling looking radiant in her pink frayed terry cloth bathrobe. To me she looked like a lovely teenage prom queen. A man I had not seen in years was now in the living room, diminishing *my* position as the man of the house. I didn't want my mother to have to suffer again from another man. I didn't want to see her hurt or abused ever again. Now that I was finally maturing, I felt that my scrawny arms were quite capable of defending her from any harm, physical or mental. I was finally becoming a man. And in what must seem like some bizarre psychological Oedipus complex, she my mother-queen and I her son-prince, all I wanted was to thwart and ward off evil. Standing there alone in the kitchen, I didn't know who was the most pathetic, Archie or me. The inevitable was happening and I felt my life slipping out of my control and away from me. And I knew, at that moment, what I was going to do with my life. I was not going to work in a factory like the high school counselor recommended. Of course, he recommended that to all the Black male students who were not athletes or eggheads. My father and uncles had spent a lifetime in those factories, and I could not disappoint them by following in their footsteps. I decided I was going to join some branch of military service. The Marine Corps sounded challenging enough, as did the chance of going to California. Seeing Archie begging Mom to marry him gave me the hopeless feeling that I was in a place where I no longer belonged. I sat down, finished eating my Post Toasties corn flakes, and pondered the Marines Corps' promise of turning a skinny seventeen-year-old into a man.

Flight

Chapter Nineteen

(1:37 p.m.)

AFTER LEAVING MOM at the Yorkshire Convalescent Home, I felt like I could drink a fifth of *Maker's Mark* whiskey all by myself. In the nursing home Mom looked like someone else. There was another life form inside her body causing her to deteriorate, grow old, and act strange. Where was the beautiful, wholesome woman I had known who was full of life? Only looking closely into her eyes could I tell that there was my mother behind them. The rest of her was completely altered. When I touched her, she called me "daddy." Mom never spoke about her father ever. In fact, I don't even know his name because the object of her affection had always been her mother. But as I stood over her, stroking her thin strands of silver hair, and feeling the warm skin of her forehead, she cooed like a baby. I played the part of father to my mother.

Today's events were all too heavy even to contemplate. Flo, Bunny, and Mom's condition left me emotionally impotent. It seemed I had no control over any situation, and life was slowly oozing from me. Everything was beyond my reach. I felt powerless and alone. I decided then to catch the next flight back to Lincoln University, PA.

****

I lay back on the airplane seat and contemplated the day's events. I would never forget them. No dream could possibly top this. I looked inside my briefcase and noticed my students' papers that needed grading. At least for a moment, I thought, I could have some control reading and making marks with red ink. I could make a little difference in their futures. But how was I to know what *my* future would bring? How was I to know that on a November Sunday morning, three years from now, I would get a call from Virgil saying Bunny had died of a massive heart attack in his cell? Or five years forward I would get another call from home telling me Mom had died. Both instances would rip out a part of my soul. Bunny, my hero would die in prison at the age of fifty-six. He would be the third brother who died at the same age. And he died while incarcerated, something he feared. It was his worst nightmare. He told me once that nobody wants to die in prison. His death was not caused by a massive heart attack, as stated in the coroner's report. Bunny died simply of a broken heart because all hope was drained. He finally got his parole.

Mom's death, on the other hand, was something we all conditionally came to grips with when she first entered the convalescent center years before. Actually, we were impressed at her ability to survive, living as long as she did in the confinement of that environment. It gave us strength knowing that she was a fighter. It was my sister Sandy this time that called and gave me the news. After speaking with her, I laid on my bed watching mental motion pictures of the past spin before me. I saw myself holding her hand as we walked down Parsons Avenue to register at Beck Street Elementary School in the early August afternoon. I remembered the way she cried when I left home, when I left for the Marines, her face full of tears, pressed on the kitchen screen door watching me as I took a cab to the bus station. And I recall her crumpling to the kitchen floor from the blows of Willie's fist as it crashed onto her beautiful face. My pillow would be wet from the tears of remembering all those things about her. Finally, I rolled over on my stomach, buried my head in the pillow and let her go. Later lying there in the quiet stillness, I smiled remembering her singing.

Somewhere, twenty thousand feet over Pennsylvania, I looked out the window at the reflected image of my face. It strongly resembled the image of Charlie. Peeking through the clouds below, I saw the snow-covered ridges of the Allegheny Mountains. And meandering parallel with them moving eastward like a serpent, lay Interstate Highway 70.

The End

Epilogue

S INCE MOVING to New Orleans, I don't go home as often as I would like to. Whenever I do get the chance to return, I always pay a visit to my childhood neighborhood on the Southside. Now chipped with age and blackened by time, the road of South Lane is still neatly lined with red bricks. And I marvel at just how small and narrow South Lane and Beck streets really are. South Lane, my boyhood stomping ground, is essentially no larger than an alley. Perhaps it has always been just a small alley, but as a child I remember it being big and ringing with life from the previous, vibrant residents. Most of the people I knew who lived there are long gone. A real estate company recently renovated Reverend Johnson's, the junkman's house, and tried to give it the appearance of a cottage like those homes further inside German Village proper. They painted it, of all things, a canary yellow and placed a purple wreathe on the front door. It seems totally out of character, and to me it looked junky. Reverend Johnson would roll over in his grave if he saw what they did to his beloved home. And with a price tag probably fifty times its original cost, he would include a double somersault flip.

The hallowed ground of my childhood home where I grew up is torn down and is now a Marathon Gasoline station, with automobiles rolling in and out where I once played and dreamt. Ziegler's Drug Store on Beck and Parsons where we purchased RC Colas and comic books from a tall good-natured Jewish pharmacist by the name of Red is now an adult bookstore. And Bobb Chevrolet bought up most of the real estate in the area and tore down all of Layman Avenue's beautiful homes. They cut down the large handsome elm, sycamore, and maple shade trees and transformed that once beautiful working class neighborhood of Layman and South Lane Streets into a red light district, a ghetto of cars and fast-talking, slick-dressed pimps, selling automobiles instead of flesh.

****

The early morning hours of December 2, 1982, my phone rang near my bed. As I reached out for it, a strange thing occurred; I clearly saw the Tarot Death card from the night before when I had visited Margaret, my German girlfriend's home. We both were graduate students at Penn State in art and Brigitte, her French roommate, wanted to perform her skill of Tarot reading on me, so I let her practice. After receiving three Death Cards one after another, she looked at me and said it wasn't good, but then recanted and said that the symbol meant many things besides death.

The voice on the other end of the phone was Virgil's telling me to drop everything and come home immediately because Charlie suddenly had become very ill. The drive from Penn State to Columbus, Ohio, normally would take me about seven hours, depending on the road and weather conditions, and Pennsylvania's notorious speed traps. Fortunately, the weatherman said the exceptional warm spell we were experiencing would break Mid-Western and the Eastern Atlantic records for December. This allowed me to drive to Columbus in six hours praying and talking at full volume to myself. I drove straight to Grant Hospital in Columbus and went to the ward Virgil said Charlie was in. I told the desk nurse that I came to see my father and had just driven straight from State College, Pennsylvania. She took a register and I glanced at it seeing Charlie's name was ruled through. I had a suspicious feeling seeing his name, my name, ruled-out, I felt light-headed. But having worked in military hospitals, I rationalized that he had been transferred to the Intensive Care Unit. The nurse said she'd be right back but was gone for a long time. Eventually, a Black nurse's aide came and sat behind the desk. She smiled and looked at me and asked where I drove in from. I told her State College where Penn State is located, and we chatted about the unusual weather and compared Penn State and Ohio State's football season. Very politely she interjected and said that my father had "passed" early that morning.

"Passed?", I said. "No, he can't be. My father, Charlie, dead?"

"Can I take you to the hospital chapel where you can be alone?" she said. In the chapel, I thought how utterly unprepared I was for this. My mind drifted to my eleventh birthday wish. The least I expected was to be there with him in his final hour.

Virgil had lied to me. He told me later he had lied because he didn't want me to be upset during the drive. In the meantime, Mom remained sequestered in her bedroom for a week and refused to attend the funeral. She just lay prone on her bed in the darkness oblivious to the clatter and the blue blur emanating from her television set. I realized she missed his presence and nightly phone calls, even though they both had remarried and lived separate lives. It was obvious to me that my father loved my mother until the day he died.

221

Charlie was an undemanding person who was satisfied with the bare essentials of life: a cigar or pipe, chewing tobacco, a newspaper, some change to play the daily numbers, a simple garden of cabbage and collard greens. All his life, he worked hard, and after forty-seven-years of working weekly rotational swing shifts, he retired from Federal Glass.

****

As a kid, I wanted Willie to die. Willie, however, was already a dead man way before his ultimate demise. I didn't discover that until years later when, as an adult, I realized that the man simply had problems. He had cancer of the soul, an incurable self—induced disease that nibbled away at him, bit by bit, until there was nothing left but a shell. He was a walking zombie full of abomination, consumed with the only pleasure he lived for-- drinking. In the fall of 1979, years after Mom divorced him, Virgil called me and said that Willie was at Grant Hospital dying of stomach cancer. He and Mom had been divorced for years. Virgil wanted me to drive there with him to visit Willie. Virgil and I both had decent jobs. I worked in upper administration with the State of Ohio and Virgil with Western Electric in the human resources department. He has always been a good dresser, and his slim body conformed to all of his expensive suits. When we arrived at the hospital, I recalled how Charlie and his brother dressed when they took Poppy from the house and placed him in the awaiting hearse. It had been years since I had last seen Willie and when I walked in the room, I did not know what emotions I was going to have. He was asleep and alone when we entered his small hospital room. I noticed his feet protruding from the covers extending off the bed. I also noticed a series of intravenous tubing connected to his thin arms. A stomach pump stood low on the floor next to the bed, pumping chartreuse colored bile into a bag. Another bag holding his urine dangled next to it.

Willie now had a full head of white kinky hair. Other than that, he still looked the same. I looked at Virgil and said that I would probably enjoy yanking out the tubing and all other inserted life

222

supporting devices in him. Virgil's compassion was far greater then mine. He said that I had to forget all the things that had occurred in the past.

"Just simply look at him with different eyes. Here's the tyrant who mistreated us, but look at him now. Doesn't he seem so helpless and fragile?" He said.

"Yeah, just how I like for him to be. I want to wake him up and peer down into his face and say: *Hey motherfucker, look it's me Sugar Pie, and I'm grown. And guess what? You're dying of stomach cancer, you bastard. Does it hurt?*"

Virgil looked at me shaking his head, half amazed half amused and said, "You're going to have to forgive all that Sugar Pie, and it's not good holding all that inside yourself."

"Yeah, I know you're right. I can't believe that I still have held that bitterness inside me all these years. I mean I wouldn't hurt him in his condition, but I just want him to know what he did to us. That those years caused a lot of resentment and hatred because of how he treated us."

"Probably we ought to say a prayer for him. Maybe that will help you too. Do you want to pray with me?"

I looked at Virgil who had already had his head bowed and I saw how devotional he looked. I felt moved. I too bowed my head as Virgil softly spoke; somewhere in his words, I peeked at Willie, stretched out and still asleep in what would be his deathbed. And at that moment, I forgave him. A few minutes afterwards, Willie opened his eyes and looked up at me. He was surprised and said, "Sugar Pie, Virgil? How you boys doing? My, you boys certainly have grown. And you look good too."

"We're all right Willie, can't complain," Virgil said.

"I'm doing fine too Willie," I said. "How are they treating you here?" And so, we chatted about the old neighborhood, friends, and the family. It was light talk without any complaints about the past. Willie died not long after that. It was a private funeral. I did not go. Not because of any resentment, that was resolved. I just had no reason for going. My closure with Willie took place in the hospital. Dottie took care of all Willie's arrangements. After the funeral, she mentioned it was just a small service with only a handful of mourners. Virgil had it right all along. He has this deep compassion for people. He always has. I am not like him in that respect. I have a tendency to hold a grudge for a long time. It's hard for me to turn the other cheek. But I have, Virgil, my little brother to guide me. Who knows what mental madness was in Willie's whiskey degenerated head whenever he got the notion to beat us. But the blame goes far beyond the bottle. Obviously, he had his demons. Growing up in Georgia during a time of horrendous Jim Crow conditions that surely must have taken its toll.

****

The last time I saw Jack Lovingood was when he was taken to prison in my junior year at South High School. His presence in my life was brief, but the quality of his being made a deep impression on my life. His capacity to want to learn more instilled in me an everlasting trait. And like so many really intelligent Black men who had to find other means to justify a need of survival, they eventually are caught and end up locked behind bars. What an immeasurable waste of talent in this country on individuals who are incarcerated for having to do wrong in order to survive. I have no idea where Jack's whereabouts are now.

****

Mammie, Charlie's first wife, died quietly during the middle 1970s of natural causes. Her demise had been less than a decade after she retired her placard and picketing post in front of the Neil House Hotel.

****

Archie Armstrong, Mom's last husband and Sandy's daddy, died in September 2002, of lung cancer. His niece, during the eulogy, commented on his robustness saying he was like the Energizer Bunny who just went on and on.

224

****

Five weeks after Archie died, Bunny's daughter Pudding was taken from a crack house in an ambulance and died a few days later. She was forty-one and had not fully recuperated following the murder of her son, Wee-Wee, a few years back. Like her father, she too died of a broken heart.

****

During writing the revision of this book, my brother Virgil developed, at the age of 50, Alzheimer's disease. I couldn't write much about it because the illness is progressive not only to the individual, but to his family. It hurts to watch him slowly loose contact with existence in his life as he slowly dissolve. I thought it would have been insensitive of me to write about it while he was going through the dilemma. At the beginning of the book, in 1997, he assisted me in developing the characters as well as recalling moments of our childhood. One of the sadist moments for me was when I visited him one evening when he was attempting to read the Bible (as usual) and said to me with tears in his eyes, "*It doesn't make any sense anymore.*" I asked him what he mean by that? You read the Bible all the time, and at your church where you are the assistant minister, it's your voice that the congregation loves to hear because of your eloquent voice.

He said that the words didn't make sense anymore. And that he would re-read the page several times, but the words were just *words* that were jumbled in his head. Later, I visited him and he had the Bible in his lap reading it upside-down. Virgil, the most intelligent of all my siblings, is in the last stage of the disease.

****

I don't go to my family's church, but I respect their beliefs. Many used to think I was a heathen and I may have been one in the past. I am extremely spiritual, and now my family seems to understand and respect my beliefs. My church is within.

Life's a bitch and then you die? Some would say it would seem so from all my life's tribulations, but again, I do not subscribe to that negative logic. It's absurd to do so. Indeed, some of us have had it worse off than others, but life is still wonderful and everyday is a gift. And for all the Yahoos—police and others who tried making my life miserable—they didn't succeed. I forgive them all. Life is too precious to linger on retribution, and it is too short to have any negative individual or thing take up space in my head. In spite of the many imperfections of life, I find a comfort in looking at the troubled past and appreciate the good things that come from living and loving. Perhaps Nat King Cole summed it up best in his lyrics in, *Nature Boy* by saying that the best thing we'll ever learn *is to love and be loved in return*. In times of difficulties and stress, I only have to close my eyes and feel the warmth of Flo's hugs, hear Bunny soulful doo-whooping songs, see Charlie smiling behind the stubble of his two-day beard, or hear the soothing voice of my mother singing. Her songs resonate the fabric of my soul, melt away pain, and always bring a smile on my face. Whenever I hear someone crooning Hoagy Carmichael's, *Stardust*, I think of her and home and how it used to be that seems not so long ago....

Stardust

And now the purple dusk of twilight time
Steals across the meadows of my heart
High up in the sky the little stars climb
Always reminding me that we're apart

You wander down the lane and far away
Leaving me a song that will not die
Love is now the stardust of yesterday
The music of the years gone by

Sometimes I wonder why I spend
The lonely nights dreaming of a song
The melody haunts my reverie
And I am once again with you

When our love was new
And each kiss an inspiration
But that was long ago
Now my consolation
Is in the stardust of a song

Beside the garden wall
When stars are bright
You are in my arms
The nightingale
Tells his fairy tale
Of paradise where roses bloom

Though I dream in vain
In my heart it will remain
My stardust melody
The memory of love's refrain

*(Best sung by my dear Mama, Nat King Cole, Willie Nelson, Perry Como, Frank
Sinatra, Dinah Shore, and a few others whose names slips my memory. *Stardust*
composed by HOAGY CARMICHAEL 1927 lyrics written in 1927 by
MITCHELL PARISH)

Acknowledgements

When a literary agent suggested that I make some negative comments about my mother (Mom), I decided to self-publish. Obviously she came from an entirely different environment from mine, and I suppose as a Black mother herself; she became too involved with the manuscript making irrational conclusions of my mother. In our last conversation, I allowed her to blow off steam as she waylaid my mother's character and after a few minutes, I politely hung up on her.

My first attempt in the world of self-publishing was with a P.O.D. (Pay on demand) or vanity press. After years of submitting manuscripts and a few thousand dollars later, the first edition was published. However, anyone who is acquainted with the writing world knows that once a book is in print, the errors seem to jump out of nowhere. So I asked the P.O.D. people to hold up the press while I make the changes. In the meantime another company bought out the P.O.D. people and things seem to go downhill from there. Even though I told them to hold the press until I corrected the errors, they went ahead and marketed the book anyway—mistakes and all. I then decided to dispense with the P.O.D people and do it alone.

****

Please know that I am the one who takes full responsibility for any errors in this book. I apologize for that. I do wish to acknowledge and give thanks to my family and friends who took the time to read the manuscript. Dr. Floyd Goodwyn, Dr. Gayle Duskin, Dr. Shengmei Chang, John Grande, Virgil Hollingsworth, Sr., Virgil Hollingsworth, Jr., Michelle Hollingsworth, Saundra (Hollingsworth) Davis, Dorothy (Howard) Stanley, Pat (Hollingsworth) McCall, and my sons, Eric and Charles Hollingsworth, III, and Ms. Elizabeth Marsden, Thank you all.

Sample pages of
My

Stolen Memoir
of
TheDayHowdyDoodyDied

Please know that **Book Two** was written 20 years after **Book One.** Although some say that time heals all wounds, it could also produce a lot of pain. The two memoirs are very different in many ways that some may say **Book Two's** message comes with a bad attitude. That, however, depends on one's interpretation. My suggestion for the reader is to put yourself in my skin and ask the question: *"why me?"*

At 63, I fell in love with an extremely beautiful Tunisian Fulbright Scholar 36 years younger than me who came to teach French and Arabic at the College where I chaired the Art Department. I had been divorced for about ten years from a previous marriage and felt a need for a steady partner to accompany my soon-to-be retirement life. My father Charlie, (see Chapter Seven: *Charlie)*, had the same idea when he married his last wife, Mary, which turned out to be a terrible marriage. As a result, I got married, and

230

like my father, I too experienced a horrifying marriage. My wife told me that she didn't think an older man could get her pregnant.

Furthermore, she said she only married me to get access to U.S. citizenship, and for some odd reason, she thought that I was rich. Worst of all, however, was that she didn't want a baby with my Negro blood. To make a long story short, I talked her out of an abortion and prayed that Mother Nature would step in, causing her to relate to motherhood (further details of all this is told in **Book Two**.)

Unfortunately, a few months after our beautiful daughter arrived, I became a single father at 65. However, my wife tried to *"Turn our daughter's future around"* (I don't want to go into any details talking about this--it hurts.) She was diagnosed with postpartum depression. Thus, raising my beautiful infant daughter Priscilla alone at age 65 turned out to be a blessing. I felt like a grandfather and a father at the same time. Being the father of my daughter was the only good thing that happened after my Memoir's kidnapping from AuthorHouse.

Eighteen months after Priscilla's birth, she was diagnosed as being Autistic. Besides being her father, grandfather, mother, cook, chauffeur, nurse, maid, brother, coach, child psychologist, etc. Personally, my writing and painting were put on hold. I put all my attention into raising my daughter. I had to stay healthy for her sake. I didn't have time to be sick. Although I haven't painted since I divorced her mom, my artistic endeavor taught her art to develop her reading skills. I homeschooled her using my Art Education Doctoral Dissertation as references for reading since art and reading are cognitively related like music is to math. Watching her learn and grow to where she became high-function, reading early in life. She became my Masterpiece, where our colorful, loving relationship was the pigment of my beautiful canvas.

****

Book Two also mentions other revealing stories of events that drastically caused attitude changes like those of the aftermath of Hurricane Katrina; I include photos contrary to those of the news media showing looting of grocery and drugstores. There was a purpose for stealing drugs such as medication for diabetic seniors and formulas for infants. Since the hospitals and pharmacies were shut down, those providing these provisions were usually youths in groups, which the news media mistook as gangs. Remember, it took President Bush five days to respond to New Orleans' devastation of Katrina as people were literally dying in the streets and abandoned nursing homes.

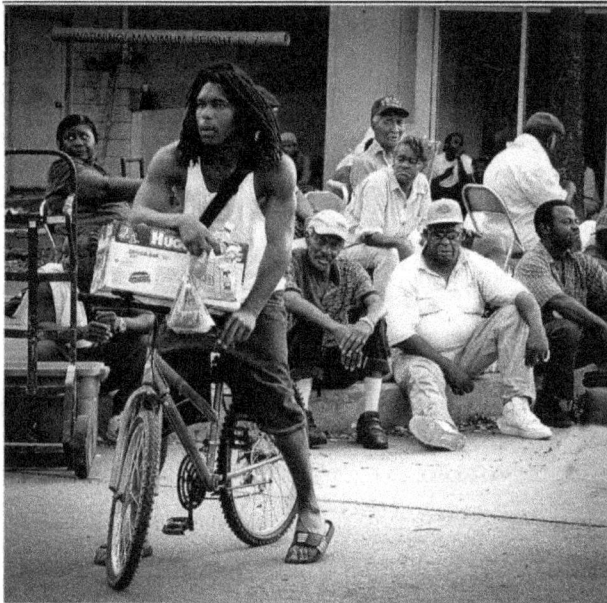

Book Two also discusses my experiences of being a Black American who proudly served in four different branches of the U.S. Armed Forces. The Army National Guard, the U.S. Marine Corps, the U.S. Air Force, and the U.S. Coast Guard Reserves. I started as a 17-year-old senior high school student as an enlisted Private in the Ohio Army National Guard who would later become a Commissioned U.S. Coast Guard Officer. I served nearly 40 years. However, in my last service, it was the U.S. Coast Guard where I experienced *"trickery"* in obtaining my Commander promotion when a senior board member claimed my paperwork wasn't submitted on time, which was a deceiving

232

lie. I hand-delivered it to them in person driving from my home in Lincoln University, Pennsylvania, to Dam Neck, Virginia, a 10-hour roundtrip drive with a little over 570 miles. They probably had their quota of nigger Officers. Again, in **Book Two**, the details are thoroughly discussed, and my intentions would be if there were a chance to meet in person.

President Donald Trump, even though he graduated from a military high school, his family's fortune and influence kept him out of the military during the Vietnam War. He made a statement during his canceled visit to the Aisne-Marne American Cemetery near Paris in 2018, saying that veterans being "losers," especially Vietnam (Era) Veterans. The white veterans I've talked with about Trump's statement was simply brushed off his remarks, and like him, using the news media as an excuse. However, we all know that if President Obama said something similar, there would be cries for his lynching. Indeed, the universe knows Trump's opinion on minorities. I, being a Black Vietnam Era Veteran, realize his statement makes me a *double-loser*—and in a sense, perhaps, he is right. As a Black U.S. Veteran, I do not receive the same benefits as my white veteran comrades. In the U.S. military, Blacks are historically seen as "expendable." This notion is seen when one is approved for the Medal of Honor. Look how many decades it takes for them to receive it, i.e., if he's still alive. Indeed, Trump's statement makes me a *loser, a double-loser* due to America's racism and the knowledge of being deceived by all my military services to include The Veterans Administrations.

I am offended because I was stationed in Thailand at the airbase, where we were told that it had no exposure to AgentOrange. However, forty-six years later, after having a batch of various illnesses, including kidney cancer, heart failure, hypothyroidism, and had two pulmonary embolisms, etc. I discovered that I had been exposed to AgentOrange, which is also why my daughter and son are Autistic and why my Grandson died. Yet, I do not receive any AgentOrange benefits. I feel guilty for having been the cause of their illnesses and my Grandson's demise. My White Veteran comrades who were stationed with me in Thailand, received their benefits. *Having been* exposed to AgentOrange, and not being compensated, especially for the sake of my dependents' medical benefits needs, is unfair compared to those veterans of the Dominant-Culture. Having been exposed to AgentOrange means I am **not** eligible for life insurance to benefit my special-needs autistic daughter, Priscilla.

Moreover, the Veterans Affairs (VA) has denied my benefits since 2015, saying my illnesses **are not service-connected!** Thus, I have to pay for my hospitalization, surgery, and medicine. I had to file bankruptcy twice to pay the VA hospital for my surgeries, treatment, and hospitalization expenses.

At any rate, thinking that the changes in my body were merely the process of aging, the truth came when Priscilla was five. I was at the Veterans Hospital on a treadmill, taking a stress test for my heart failure. The X-Ray camera attached to the treadmill accidentally slipped a bit, taking a photo of my lower right side. The accident displayed two tumors on my right kidney. That minor accident of the camera proved to be God sent. The tumors turned out to be cancers. After doing some personal research, I discovered that when one is exposed to AgentOrange, its toxic poison Dioxin attaches itself to their DNA. Thus, it is the reason for my daughter and son's autism and my four-year-old Grandson's death, along with a series of other health issues that I continue to confront. However, there are some ongoing miraculous outcomes published in my **Book 2 Memoir**.

****

I respect all my medical caretakers at the VA and civilian Hospitals' clinics and staff. However, my issues are with the politically racist-minded-redneck administrators in those government positions, who handle claims and benefits-- especially those who handle *my* AgentOrange claims. (Probably the same Coast Guard racist now retired, who deceived me from my Coast Guard Commander promotion.) Since 2014 when I discovered my exposure to AgentOrange, I was told by the DAV (Disabled American Veterans) to apply for medical benefits, which would help Priscilla's and my medical bills. Please read the statements under the photos **Pretty Priscilla** and **Lil' Max** without repeating this frustrating segment. It explains in detail my frustrations with that part of my life, which handles claims and benefits from AgentOrange exposure. For years, those bastards claimed that I was not contaminated by AgentOrange because the Utapao's Airbase in Thailand, where I was stationed, was only exposed around its perimeter. That logic is so insipid. First, one confronts the main gate, to enter or leave the base that is located on the perimeter. Second, AgentOrange is sprayed—airborne. Third, water is a good transmitter of particles and is naturally carried by the many canals that run through and around the base (my barracks was located next to one). Moreover, the drinking water, toilet, shower, laundry--even the water we scrubbed our hands with for surgery. And one mustn't forget the infamous monsoons seasons. Furthermore, although Utapao was a B52 bomber base, other aircrafts landed and took off from there including those that sprayed various herbicides containing Dioxin as well as barrels ready to be loaded and those stacked in various places on the base.

Three months ago, I requested counseling on my own behalf to help me cope with my frustration that subsequently lead to my post traumatic stress disorder all brought on by the Veterans Affairs politically attuned, racist administration offices. The stress, anger, and depression of witnessing my daughter dealing with her condition, my grandson's horrible death, as well my own medical situation puts me in a state of mind to do something extremely vindictive to those bigoted, ignorant racist rednecks within the Veterans Affairs. And, yes, I've gotten in trouble for expressing my deep frustrations over the phone about what I would like to do to those individuals if given the opportunity. That night, two police officers came to my house. (All this is recently expressed in **Book Two**. Indeed, I want the world to know how upset I am. Meditation, and prayers help, but the ideal that this is happening to me seems unbelievable.)

****

I devote this book (Book Two) to my beautiful, talented, now 12-year-old, darling daughter, Priscilla. When I'm no longer in this Three-Dimensional World, I want her to know that all my love for her will continue to exist in all realms.

(Daddy will always love you.)

(Priscilla, six-days old.)

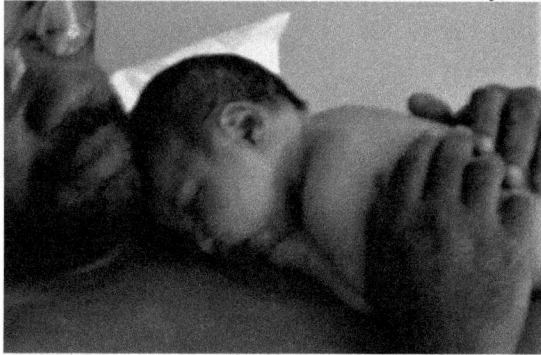

SPOTLIGHT ON LIFE

Graduation day took place at 1:01 A.M., June 21, 2008, the first day of summer at The Christ Hospital (Theatre) in downtown Cincinnati. When my daughter made her appearance onto the world stage, she did so to flying squadrons of cheering cherubs and a crowd of applauding Angels, all welcoming her arrival to the light. I was the first person she had ever seen as I handed her, her well-earned Divine Birth Diploma of Light. She received an ecstatic standing ovation. The image of her looking at me has no words to express that moment. A deeper connection was made when I spoke, and she recognized my voice outside of the darkness. Then she smiled, and her brilliance outshone all the Halos of the Angels and Cherubs singing in the audience.

236

Pretty Priscilla

This photo was taken 18-months after the one above living with me as her single-parent. Fortunately, she was too young to realize what her other parent had put her through. Unfortunately, I took this photo the same month as her diagnosis of Autism. Five-years later, I discovered my DNA caused her condition had been exposed to the deadly poison, Dioxin in AgentOrange when I served in The Vietnam Era War, which my Government kept hidden from me.

****

Look at both photos of me holding my Priscilla. In them, I was unaware that I had been exposed to AgentOrange at this time. Indeed, in **Book Two's** Memoir, I have a lot to talk about, and my tone is different than in **Book One**. Between AuthorHouse ripping me off, Priscilla's mom, and my Government deceiving me, my life's trust in America has ended.

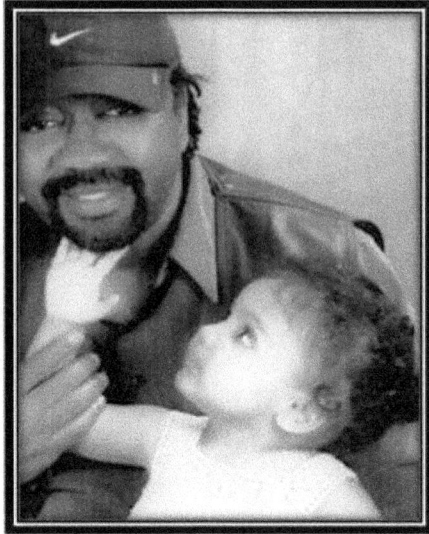

The Loving Touch

In the above photo, taken in the summer of 2009, I'm proudly posing with my beautiful 13-month-old daughter, Priscilla. She made me feel more like a wholesome 26-year-old rather than a 66-year-old retired art professor. Notice the tenderness in her way of communicating with me like her loving hand touching my face, and her captivated gaze seems to imply another dimension of time and space. As a consciously contented single-father, I am indeed truly blessed being her father. (My role of becoming a single father came from her young mother's mental issues and postpartum depression--a long ugly story.) Unfortunately, two months after this photo was taken, Priscilla was diagnosed with Autism--I was overwhelmed and astonished. One afternoon, with my fist balled up and tears streaming down my face I looked up at the ceiling and angrily yelled: "God, why her?" After a long pause, with my head in my hands, a relaxing Angelic charm came over me. A calm conversation took place inside my head advising me to give her art lessons. This would help her read as Divine intelligence is nature's universal life force called--creativity.

Years later in 2014, I learned the reason for my daughter's Autism. It was due to my exposure to AgentOrange during the Vietnam War 46 years ago. I learned too the war was the reason why my Grandson, Little Max died (please read below) years prior to Priscilla's birth. He was a product from a previous marriage.

238

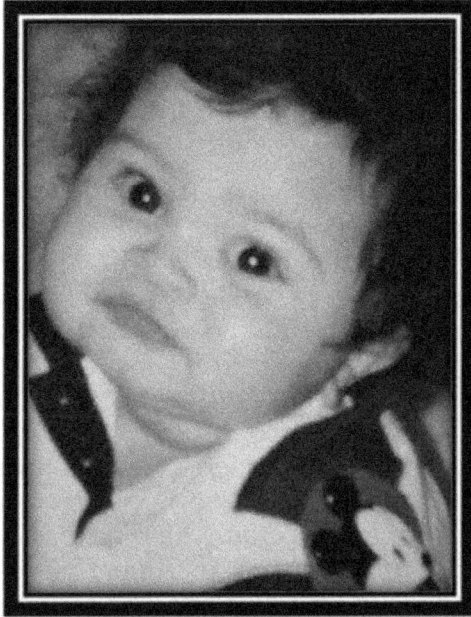

Little Max

Little Max, *my beautiful Grandson, is the personification of the word* **love***. He, unfortunately, had a terrifyingly rare disorder when he was born. He had an allergic medical condition called FPIES disorder, where food protein is poisonous. Thus, if he ate food, he could die. His condition was extremely rare in that it included odd and unknown elements in his body's biological system. In essence, our body's antibodies are a protein defense mechanism, which is the first-lines-of-defense that fights off bacteria, infections, and any unwanted organisms. His antibodies considered the intake of food an unwanted organism. Doctors were perplexed because his system didn't concur with the typical FPIES. By having been unknowingly exposed to AgentOrange at the base where I was stationed during the war, the new chemical substance, Dioxin poison in AgentOrange that the Americans sprayed as a defoliant, attaches itself to the DNAs of all biological life. Scientists realized the danger of this chemical later, but unfortunately, those senior ranking military officials and politicians did not inform the dangers. Many military* veterans were not told about the harmful affliction in their bodies via the poisonous transformation in their bodies, particularly to one's DNA—and many still don't know. I accidentally discovered the truth 46 years later after doing my own research.

Upon Little Max's birth, he had to remain in The Nationwide Childrens Hospital. At the same time, scientists of The Ohio State University Medical School worked together to solve this extremely perplexing situation. Thus, Max existed off an out-of-the-ordinary formula prepared by the team. His puffiness that you see comes from the formula's intake that kept him alive. His condition caused him to be lacking a lot in his physical and cognitive areas. But he was full of love. I have never seen him whine or cry. He communicated through his eyes. (Look at them.) And just when he was beginning to walk, a week before turning four, he died. I didn't know at the time that I had been exposed to AgentOrange. The military said the base where I was stationed during the Vietnam War was safe from AgentOrange's exposure. The truth, however, was revealed to me in 2014, 46 years later!!! All during that time, I didn't realize that I was the one causing all the sicknesses in my family by the contaminated genes in my body from the poison in AgentOrange.

My first marriage endowed me with two sons. The first one was born before I went to war, and five years later, my second son was born. He is the father of Max. And in retrospect, AgentOrange can be blamed for the many misinterpreted causes of my divorced. A lot happened that I now can understand in hindsight about the marriage. When I told my son, who was 41, what I just learned about my exposure to AgentOrange, he was still recovering from Little Max's demise, and now this perplexing news not only shocked him but compounded the pain. Subsequently, after Max's death, my son joined the Navy; however, he was medically discharged because his legs would periodically swell for no apparent reason. Indeed, it puzzles me as to why didn't my Government inform me about my AgentOrange exposure? Revealing perplexing issues would have been understood and maybe even solved; plus, the medical community would have appreciated the information.

240

Moreover, like his half-sister Priscilla, my son was also born with Autism, which subsequently formed into Aspergers Syndrome. However, no one in the family realized it. The term Autism and Aspergers were not in our vocabulary at the time.

I feel his pain; the heartache of losing his son is three-dimensional. All sides hurt. Three generations of pain all for what?

I currently am dealing with hypothyroidism, heart failure, high blood pressure, plus having had kidney cancer, survived two pulmonary embolisms, brain nerve damage, etc., etc., all by having been exposed to AgentOrange. Indeed, after learning that AgentOrange exposure attaches itself to one's DNA, was it my body the tool that killed my Little Max? And no, don't thank me for my service, especially since the Veterans Administration claims my medical benefits are not service-connected. Although numerous white veterans have trouble receiving VA Benefits, research records prove that Veterans-of-Color are frequently and administratively discriminated against. Indeed, many white veterans are fortunate to be guided voluntarily by the dominant culture of VA staff. This racially impacted injustice has caused me to pay the Government for my family's expensive medical care and my own. It was the cause of my having to file bankruptcy twice. I swear every time I look at **Little Max's** *picture, my eyes moist.*

****

Lastly, some very uncanny medical phenomenon has occurred in my life, which has left me wonderfully perplexed. With all the racism and injustices in my life, I seemed blessed with these unexplained spiritual experiences.

An Executive Officer (EO) of a military unit is usually the second in command. When the Commanding Officer (CO) at my first Coast Guard unit in Columbus, Ohio, was about to retire from the Coast Guard, the EO typically replaces them. This unit's EO had helped me lateral into the Coast Guard from the Air National Guard, where I had the same duties and rank, but wore a different uniform with Petty Officer 2nd Class, Hospital Corpsman rank.

The Headquarters of the Coast Guard in Washington, D.C. did an extremely abnormal thing when the CO was about to leave, they closed the Columbus, Coast Guard Reserve Unit. The troops now had to make their drills at other units as far away as Pennsylvania. Central Ohio would no longer have a Coast Guard Unit to assist with any training or emergency needs.

Insofar as why the high-ranking officials at the Coast Guard Headquarters in Washington, D.C. wanted to make such an unprecedented move, puzzled the Central Ohio community, as well as the individuals in Columbus Coast Guard Reserve Unit itself. Could it possibly be because the Executive Officer was African-American?

Recently the former EO suffered a brutal stroke leaving him partially crippled and with a severe speech impediment. He noticed my bitterness about my life's situation and told me something I consider a blessing. He said,

"Charles, don't be bitter, be better."

Mom and Willie

The Tablets on the Cover

The Tablets' phenomenon appearance on the Cover of the first edition of *The Day Howdy Doody Died,* my Memoir, happened overnight on my computer while I slept in 2000. I am neither a saint nor a Bible-banging, hyper-religious zealot. And I've never seen any flying saucers or the Big Foot Monster. I consider myself a very pragmatic person who's naturally skeptical and suspicious about anything unexplained. Subsequently, people asked if a computer virus could have caused the appearance of the images. I had a computer expert from the university where I worked to come over the next day to analyze my system. He found nothing unusual in my computer system. Then we checked all my deleted *HowdyDoodyDied Memoir* files on the computer, and boom! There they were! Same images. Finally, he suggested we checked the old discarded hard copies in my old files in my drawer and those in the trash containers. They all had the same tablets superimposed just on the covers of The *Day HowdyDoodyDied* Memoirs, to our incredible surprise. I got Goosebumps! Viruses don't leap from a computer to an outside physical entity. (Either I had walked in my sleep, or there are such things as Guardian Angels.)

Since the original Ten Commandments were said to be miraculously written in stone, why can't these Tablets be a cyberspace version of the same thing, but as a modern-day message for today's humanity? Perhaps they were manifested for us to be mindful of the brief passage of our lives and to be more loving as suggested by Christ's request: *Love one another, as I have loved you,* which sums up the whole 10 Commandments.

www.ingramcontent.com/pod-product-compliance
Lightning Source LLC
Chambersburg PA
CBHW032042080426
42733CB00006B/169